HOW TO REALLY

RECRUIT, MOTIVATE, AND LEAD YOUR TEAM:

MANAGING PEOPLE

Helen
Best wishes in your journey

HOW TO REALLY

RECRUIT, MOTIVATE, AND LEAD YOUR TEAM:

MANAGING PEOPLE

Acknowledgments

Frank Carney, one of the founders of Pizza Hut, once noted, "You buy things, but you *invest* in people." Today, businesses large and small are recognizing the truth of that proposition; moreover, they are paying more than lip service to the notion of investment in people. But where to place that investment? What strategies work, and how can you maximize your return? How do you prioritize employee needs, and what do employees actually want?

The answers are the focus of this guide, which is based on material created by a dedicated group of *Inc.* writers and outside management experts (all are listed in the appendix on p. 249). Their contributions include case histories of exceptional companies and exemplary leadership, feature articles about managing and motivating people, and "Good Forms," which are graphic examples of proven ways to make employee communication and data gathering really work.

Sharing expertise is one thing; translating it into a practical management tool is quite another. For their professionalism and considerable support in this effort, we thank the following members of the team: Susan Dahl, designer and desktop chief; Leslie Graham and Jacqueline Lapidus, copy editors and proofreaders; and Michael O'Loughlin, researcher.

Finally, we express special appreciation to Hilary Glazer, project manager, who demonstrated what it really takes to recruit, motivate, and lead a team.

Ruth G. Newman
with Bradford W. Ketchum, Jr.

Contents

Introduction

What makes good employees? At one time the answer to that question might have been, They don't make waves, or They keep their noses to the grindstone, or They keep their eyes on the ball, or some other bromide that depicts a well-behaved, cooperative, and somewhat robotic workforce.

Today, the byword is *team*: problem-solving team, self-directed team, cross-functional team. And, no surprise, the whole organization is now a team. Good employees? They're "team players." There's sufficient reference to "teamwork" to make one skeptical. Has business created another platitude? Can people with diverse personalities, talents, and needs be melded into a team working to attain shared goals? The answer from the entrepreneurs and experts who have contributed to *How to* Really *Recruit, Motivate, and Lead Your Team: Managing People* is a resounding yes, but it isn't easy.

Building a team starts with recruitment: being clever, careful, and diligent in finding the right people. It does not necessarily follow that, once found and hired, they will all move forward happily in unison. They must first be made to feel satisfied that their individual contributions are needed and respected. They must also be helped to believe that as their organization prospers and grows, so will they. In short, good employees are those who feel good about themselves and their companies. To empower a workforce takes knowledge, attentiveness, creativity, and a high tolerance of risk. In a word, it takes *leadership*.

To create a book about managing people, we considered a profusion of excellent ideas and approaches that we had seen in action for the past few years. It was difficult to find an orderly way to classify them, because exceptional companies do so many of the right things simultaneously, or at least in no specified order. But ultimately, we did perceive a pattern — not a straight line from one point to another but a circle: recruitment — finding the right people; motivation — keeping them vital and committed; and leadership — the sustaining force that, having achieved its ends, makes the cycle begin again. That is the organizing principle of *How to* Really *Recruit, Motivate, and Lead Your Team: Managing People.*

Managing the recruitment process — identifying and hiring the best people — is clearly where human-resource management begins. Chapter II, "Recruiting Your Team," explains how to plan and carry out a successful recruitment and hiring program. It provides practical advice about screening candidates and conducting interviews, focusing on what it takes to ensure mutual satisfaction beyond the final handshake.

Businesses that manage employees well value people as their key resource. Chapters III and IV, "Motivating Your Team" and "Training Your Team," suggest ways to build strong cooperation and gain commitment to corporate goals. By inviting active employee participation and offering opportunity for growth, exemplary businesses provide abundant evidence that people really are their first priority. Closely related is the issue of appropriate compensation — the punctuation point for participation and opportunity (see Chapter V, "Compensating Your Team").

Finally, Chapters VI and VII, "Communicating With Your Team" and "Leading Your Team," examine what most experts describe as the two essential attributes of outstanding leadership: communication and taking charge. Despite varied styles, personalities, and approaches, entrepreneurs who are exceptional leaders have two things in common: 1.) They consistently stimulate honest and open communication; and 2.) They take charge by creating an environment in which a shared vision and the free exchange of ideas are propellants toward growth.

R.G.N.
B.W.K.

Views from the Top

The two viewpoints that follow summarize the management terrain. The first scans the soundest practices of the 1990s and outlines a set of criteria that is the basis for creating a powerful, virtually unstoppable workforce.

The second, written in the voices of the managers who helped to make it happen, describes how four companies found individual ways to meet those criteria. Each has an extraordinary approach to managing people. And each is sure that the payoff is well worth the effort.

The Secrets
of Success

*Once you get past the innovation, the marketing,
and the financial wizardry, once you look behind the
rapid growth, the single most striking characteristic
of high-performing companies is their extraordinary
approach to managing people.*

—

For most employees in most businesses, a paycheck buys only time and routine effort. American workers historically have been taught to do as they're told and to leave the company's problems to management. As a group, they have learned that lesson well.

But people might go the extra mile if they feel they work for a truly unusual company, one that shows in a dozen ways that employees are at the center of its concerns. People might do it for companies that offer a new kind of implicit employment agreement. Employees might say, You provide us with a great place to work — not just a pleasant environment with a few nice benefits, but a company that offers real opportunity and that we can feel is in some measure ours. In return, we'll provide you with the level of commitment and involvement you need to succeed in today's marketplace.

Here is where all those innovative people-management practices come in. The purpose of employee stock ownership plans (ESOPs), training courses, and day-care centers isn't just to make employees feel good (though they may) or even to cut down on turnover (though that may happen, too). Their purpose is to create an organization that employees at all levels care about and for which they are willing to extend themselves. Such programs help to develop a culture of mutual trust, obligation, and respect. The top-performing companies are those that have created such a culture.

Want to run that kind of organization? There are four criteria for superior management of people. In one way or another, the most successful small companies meet them all.

1. The Basics: Compensation and Culture

Here's how to define the basics of a good workplace: the level of wages, benefits, and working conditions that employees have come to expect. Underperform on any of them and employees will think you're such a piker you'll have no chance of winning trust or respect.

Some of those basics are obvious: Wages and salaries that are at least average for your industry and region. Scrupulous attention to workplace health and safety. Fair treatment — no company-sanctioned discrimination or harassment. Effective procedures for airing problems and suggestions.

Also, a benefits package that includes health insurance. To be sure, companies that are struggling financially may require employees to share the cost. But the alternative available to most is no coverage at all. Compare and contrast: According to the Employee Benefits Research Institute, only 15% of all new jobs in America offer health benefits. Among the latest *Inc.* 500 — phenomenally successful young companies that have created more than 64,000 jobs in the past five years — 95% offer health insurance. There's a lesson there.

Then there are the basics that aren't so obvious, such as providing employees with clear, consistent direction and the resources they need to do their jobs well. Such nostrums sound simple; they aren't. How many companies have delivered high-minded lectures on quality, for example, only to retreat to the get-it-out-the-door-at-all-costs mentality as the end of the month nears?

One key issue these days — for a lot of employees it's a touchstone — is how much flexibility a company allows. Besides being receptionists and accountants and machine operators, people are parents, homemakers, caregivers, patients of doctors and dentists, and citizens. Occasionally, an obligation in those spheres conflicts with an obligation at work, particularly when both partners in a couple are now likely to be employed outside the home. No company can let every employee schedule his or her job completely, nor should any company pay a full-time salary to someone who misses a day of work every week. But companies that allow no flexibility at all — no personal calls from the office, never a few hours off to renew a driver's license, no time to care for a sick child — will find that employees don't care much for the employer, either.

2. Create Opportunity for Employee Growth

Opportunities for people to grow appear in a variety of forms: Stanley Gerhart makes cowls — metal engine covers for light machinery — at Stone Construction Equipment Inc., in Honeoye, N.Y. For 16 years his job was to crank 'em out, put 'em on the shelf, punch out, and go home. Then Stone's new managers asked Gerhart to redesign his job from the ground up — and to run his one-man department as its own little business, dealing on his own with "vendors" and "customers" elsewhere in the shop. Today Gerhart can point to a dozen timesaving or quality-assuring ideas he has come up with. "It makes my job a whole lot easier because I control my own destiny," he says.

Ray Morgan started as a union laborer at Granite Rock Co., in Watsonville, Calif., 31 years ago. In the past couple of years he has attended a supervisors' training school and dozens of other classes and seminars, including a Dale Carnegie course, all at company expense. He is now shipping and production supervisor at the company's quarry.

Peggy Laun, a loan processor at Phelps County Bank, in Rolla, Mo., researched, proposed, and is now helping to implement a system of upward evaluation, or employee reviews of supervisors. Dwight Joseph, a technical-support supervisor at Intuit, a software company in Menlo Park, Calif., organized a group of experts to help answer customers' questions in one highly specialized area. Both companies encourage employees to search out ways of improving operations — meaning that no one need be limited by the boundaries of a job. Work at Intuit thus provides "an opportunity to really think," says Joseph.

Unlike, say, a raise in pay, opportunity means different things to different people. Some seek advancement to the next rung on the occupational ladder. (Does your company offer tuition reimbursement? Does it promote from within?) Others crave more autonomy and responsibility where they are now. (How closely are seasoned workers supervised and controlled? How rigidly is the work prescribed?) Still others want to learn new skills and explore new horizons without necessarily moving up. (Do employees have access to in-house training courses and cross-functional groups and committees? Do you permit or even encourage lateral transfers?) The best companies — like those just cited — offer a wide variety of avenues to a wide variety of people.

Make no mistake: there will always be individuals who want only to do the job they know best, without any additional responsibility. Just don't assume that everyone in the company falls into that category. Besides, there's reason these days to encourage even the most unassuming employees to broaden their purview. In the past some companies could offer employees job security: steady work and a modest pension on retirement. In today's chaotic marketplace not even the giants can offer such assurances, and small companies have even less of a chance.

People's best security lies in the skills and abilities they have developed, both in school and on the job. The more your company allows employees to develop their talents — and the more it encourages employees to do so — the more you are helping to secure employees' futures.

3. Share the Risk — and the Wealth

From a financial perspective, working for a small enterprise is a risky matter. Usually, on average, small companies have not paid as well as large corporations. Benefits are fewer. Worst, small businesses have a nasty propensity to fail, merge, be bought out, or otherwise undergo metamorphosis. In effect, employees are always shouldering part of the

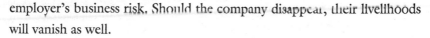

employer's business risk. Should the company disappear, their livelihoods will vanish as well.

Therefore, offering employees a chance to share in the business's success seems only simple justice, and plenty of people perceive it in just that way. "It's really unfair for other companies not to share the profits," says Javier Castro, a machine-setup worker at the Los Angeles plant of Connor Formed Metal Products, whose employees own 42% of the stock. "Once you work for an employee-ownership company, you'll never go back to non-ownership."

There's no one best method for providing employees with a financial stake in corporate achievement. FourGen Software, in Seattle, offers stock options to most of its staff; once a worker is vested, the options are redeemable in cash at the employee's discretion. Jamestown Advanced Products Inc., a metal-fabricating company in Jamestown, N.Y., rewards employees with bonuses if they beat certain labor-cost targets. One pair of entrepreneurs, before they even started their company, signed an agreement to sell it to the employees 10 years later. Another CEO created some 20 different spot-bonus programs, handing out anywhere from $40 to $400 at a time for helping the company reach certain objectives. Broad-based profit sharing can take any number of forms, from annual checks to deposits in tax-sheltered retirement plans.

The most far-reaching method of sharing the wealth is the employee stock ownership plan (ESOP). Properly executed — which means investing the ESOP with sizable amounts of stock and taking pains to ensure that employees understand their new rights and responsibilities as owners — the plan can be a powerful way to mold individuals into a group with a common purpose. Unlike bonuses, ESOPs distribute the rewards of long-term growth, thus directing people's attention toward company objectives and performance rather than toward short-term individual or departmental goals. And unlike most conventional profit-sharing plans, ESOPs don't limit an employee's share to a certain percentage of total compensation. If the company grows, the stock rises in value, and even lower-rank employees can do well.

A logical corollary of stock ownership is open-book management.

Teaching employees to understand and track the company's financials not only allows them to keep score of their collective progress but also makes them feel like the owners they are.

4. Build on a Sense of Community

Ultimately what matters is how people feel — about the company and themselves in their capacity as employees. And the feelings of most human beings are affected by more than how much they make or even how much they are learning. The best companies to work for have an intuitive understanding of less tangible factors, and operate accordingly. A corporate sense of community has at least three dimensions:

1. Pride. Walk into a company that's a recognized leader in product quality or that's known throughout its industry as a great organization. The offices and shops hum; employees are quick to greet a visitor. On the job, people offer suggestions and volunteer to solve problems because they believe the company cares and will therefore pay attention. Pride in a company has diverse sources. Some companies sell products or services that are critical to life or health, and they make a point of stressing that mission. Others exhibit a companywide commitment to preserving the environment or getting involved with community agencies and charities. Mostly, pride boils down to a feeling among employees that the company stands for certain values — and puts its money where its mouth is.

2. Belonging. At most companies, critical information and plans are the province of a few top managers. They're the ones who know the hot prospects the salespeople are courting, how the computer system will be revamped, and what last month's numbers showed about the spring marketing campaign. Knowing all that may make those managers feel great; not knowing it makes everybody else feel out of the loop. Compare that all-too-typical situation with what happens at a company such as Manco Inc., a Westlake, Ohio, distributor of duct tape, home office and crafts supplies, and other materials. Charts on Manco's cafeteria walls track numbers such as revenue growth, productivity changes, and up-to-the-minute sales figures. Weekly gatherings — open to everyone — air salespeople's reports on their territories and allow people to toss ideas around. Monthly meetings for all employees review the company's profit-and-loss statements.

Such extensive communication — invariably regarded as a bothersome chore by managers of traditional companies — may help people do their jobs better. It is guaranteed to help them feel a part of the company. So, incidentally, will any other gesture that communicates a we're-all-in-this-together message, such as top managers taking turns doing frontline jobs, celebrations, awards, and recognition in the company newsletter.

3. Privilege. Pro Fasteners and Components, a hardware and electronics parts distributor in San Jose, Calif., buys a set of top-quality San Francisco 49ers tickets every year, along with tickets to concerts and performances at Shoreline Amphitheatre, in Mountain View, Calif. Employees put in preferences for dates, and everyone's assured of attending at least one event. Cost to the company: a few thousand dollars a year. Value to employees in terms of bragging rights: high.

Such perks can come in any number of forms: An apartment in the nearest big city that employees can sign up to stay in. Special trips or unusual events. Holiday gifts. Company gyms. Free lunches. Discounts on computers. Awards in such categories as the top-performing salesperson don't count. Neither do perks reserved for managers. How much an item costs isn't important. The key criterion is whether the perk is something employees can boast about, something that will make them feel privileged because they work for your company.

What this describes is not company-as-Santa-Claus; it's a system of mutual obligation, a two-way street. If you provide the kind of workplace the best employers offer, you have a right to expect employees to work smart, to commit themselves to the company's goals, to involve themselves in their jobs. That doesn't mean everyone automatically puts in 60 hours a week. It does mean no one in your organization — no one — should be content with doing as little as possible. Live up to your side of the bargain, and you can reasonably ask your employees to help in producing the innovations, the cost-cutting ideas, the levels of quality and service that today's marketplace demands. From a business perspective, that's the rationale for trying to create a great workplace in the first place.

Most of us find work most rewarding when it ties in with some larger objective. The larger objective may be individual, such as a chance to practice a skill or meet new people or earn enough extra money for a down payment on a house. The larger objective may also be collective: people who feel their company is growing, making money, and accomplishing great things — and that they are an essential part of the process — get the same kind of satisfaction as athletes on a winning team or partisans with a winning candidate or volunteers at a soup kitchen. They experience a sense of purpose and the exhilarating sense of community that comes from pursuing that purpose together.

The policies and programs that characterize great workplaces do not by themselves create either purpose or community. A few organizations (big insurance companies come to mind) would score high on the policies-and-programs scale just because they're so rich, yet their employees can be as apathetic and alienated as any Department of Motor Vehicles bureaucrat. And many organizations, from enthusiastic start-ups to the U.S. Marine Corps, generate an enormous sense of common purpose without providing much in the way of goodies.

Creating a great place to work is thus not a matter of following a laundry list; it's a matter of building an organization that is itself challenging and involving and that people enjoy working for because together they are accomplishing more than they could on their own. ■

What It Takes to Build a Team

Insights from four companies that have invested heavily in highly individualistic people-management programs

—

Bread Loaf Construction
Middlebury, Vt.

At Bread Loaf, a $30-million, 88-employee full-service construction company, the focus on providing a good workplace grows out of a natural concern for employee hopes and needs. But there's a strategic payoff, too, says Executive Vice President John Leehman: Its reputation for having a happy and creative workforce positions Bread Loaf as the creative leader in its market — and it attracts customers. Explains Leehman:

We do a lot to build a sense of teamwork among our employees — things that really open up communication. When there's a complaint of any kind we address it right away. We want the negative information because only then can we do something with it.

Our employees know managers have open doors; that's just our culture. So we're always looking for ways to break the barriers to communication, like having a consultant come in and spend a half-hour with each person, or doing a ropes program — a kind of personal-adventure center, in which our employees, wearing harnesses, climb 30-foot trees, then dive into a net.

Our practice has been to take about 12 people at a time, for three

> "We have an image in the marketplace that's much different from everyone else's. We're considered to be employee focused."
> — John Leehman

days, on that kind of trip. It's designed for team building and to make us stretch beyond our personal limits. In the evenings we teach people how to build their personal visions, and we talk about how to build the company so people can use it to reach their goals.

We also practice a lot of teamwork on a smaller scale around here. People are grouped into teams so they get used to working with the same people, and communication shortcuts are developed. That teamwork even carries over into our rotating-layoff policy: our employees agree to work 33% fewer hours during off-peak seasons so we don't have to lay anyone off totally.

There are two reasons we try to differentiate our workplace — why we do all this stuff to build a sense of teamwork among our employees. One, we like it. We really like working in a place where there's creative energy, where people are able to feel pride. Two, it brings work to us. A lot of the more creative designing-and-building work comes to us first. And generally speaking, we negotiate a tremendous amount of our work directly, without having to go to the bid market. It just comes in the door.

We have an image in the marketplace that's very different from anyone else's. We're considered to be employee focused, honest, of high integrity, and always giving the customer what we promise. Several years ago we came up with the slogan "Promises Made Are Promises Kept." So we're seen first as trustworthy, and second as a very innovative company, not only in terms of our employees but also in terms of actual product ideas — and we get a lot of those from our employees.

Customers perceive us as being different because of our employees. A couple of years ago we enlisted a marketing consultant to pinpoint for us what the marketplace perception of us was and what made us different from other companies and to help us determine what we should be focusing on. The main message we got was that people outside the company had the perception that everybody who works at Bread Loaf has high integrity and that our people are innovative and creative. That's the stuff that's made us different from competitors. — *John Leehman*

White Storage & Retrieval Systems
Kenilworth, N.J.

When Donald Weiss became CEO of White Storage, in 1975, the company, an offshoot of a now 48-year-old family business, posted $4 million in sales. Nineteen years and thousands of training hours later, Weiss's company, which manufactures automated retrieval systems, employs 400 people and generates more than $60 million in annual revenues.

"Training programs literally changed our company culture."
— Donald Weiss

I remember attending a seminar on quality in 1988 and being completely inspired by it. I went back to the office inflamed with the idea of bringing quality to life in the company. But I took one look around at our workforce and realized it would be impossible to instill the concept of quality in people who didn't even have basic language or math skills. So many had never been properly trained or educated. More than a hundred barely understood the language. We were going to have to start at the beginning — with basic English.

I began by paying a couple of teachers to come in two hours a week. Employees volunteered their time and came in after-hours. We had about 40 in the beginning. For about two years, the first classes were held two hours a day, two days a week. We started to get some attention in the media and in government circles, and we obtained state and federal grants to underwrite a full-blown workplace-literacy program. We got teacher salaries covered and started offering the classes during working hours. Soon we had 100 students in five levels of English classes. And training started to take hold of the entire company.

We started teaching other skills — mathematics, blueprint reading, Japanese manufacturing techniques. We started preparing people for their high school equivalency diplomas. We taught team building so we could implement team management in parts of the company. We began inviting other companies in to train our people (AT&T taught a class on quality). In 1991, 1992, and 1993, we offered 7,000 hours of training each year, everything from English as a second language to how to use small tools.

We did it all in-house, bringing together people from all departments. Running this kind of program in-house gives you more control over the curriculum. You know where the money you invest is going. We can use our own materials — manuals, job specs, company newsletters — so while people's basic reading and English skills are improved, so is their understanding of their jobs and of the company. We can teach employees the specific skills they need to be effective on the job.

The benefits of such programs accrue in a number of ways. The most significant benefit is the sense of dignity people acquire. The training programs have literally changed the company culture. People appreciate the opportunity to educate themselves and improve their skills, and they feel more confident and secure in their jobs. We used to hear countless grievances through our two unions. Today we don't. We actually settle contracts early now. The old walls of distrust between management and union have fallen because of the way we treat our people.

Turnover used to be above 25%; now it's below 10%. We've seen tremendous improvement in safety. In 1988 we had 180 reported accidents; now we're down to just over 30. The number of workers' compensation claims has plummeted; we now pay one-tenth of what we paid four years ago. And productivity is up. In one year alone we saw the turnaround time on orders drop from seven days to one.

As for costs, the program has been surprisingly inexpensive. We've spent a couple hundred thousand in payroll by taking people off the floor or away from their desks to train them, but we get a return on everything we spend. We get more productive people, people coming in who are not checking their brains at the door. We get better ideas out of them, better performance. A 5% improvement in productivity or quality of ideas negates the cost. Plus, we get better relationships with people. The power of the people who work for you is incredible if you choose to use it. But you have to unlock it by educating them, by giving them the opportunity to develop their skills. It's at the top of my list of concerns. Satisfying your employees is not something you decide you'll budget 20% of your time for. You have to do it all the time; you've got to live it. It's got to be part of your style of doing business.

This is not some kind of heroic effort. It's a necessity. Most of our competition comes from foreign companies. They don't have the education or language problems we have. In Japan and Germany, workers tend to be better educated. So for us to invest so heavily in training is sort of playing catch-up. Many enlightened companies are doing what we're doing. There is a growing realization that if you don't empower workers, if you don't educate them, teach them to pay attention to quality, you will lose out in the long run. You've got to turn to training to compete and survive in a global economy. Maybe in some industries that haven't yet been touched by foreign competitors, managers can afford to sit back like fat cats and not worry about improving or satisfying their people. But their day will come. This is the direction all companies will have to take. — *Donald Weiss*

MacTemps
Cambridge, Mass.

While John Chuang has been in business only seven years, he has already grown his temp agency, MacTemps, into a company that made the 1992 and 1993 Inc. *500 and generated revenues of more than $40 million in 1994. With 70 full-time employees coordinating 1,500 temporary workers each week, the agency is a national player. Getting and keeping good employees when you have only limited resources isn't that difficult, says Chuang, if you attend to the "core" issues of job satisfaction and don't try to compete on the "peripheral" ones. There is, he says, a clear difference.*

Since we are vying for full-time employees against much bigger temp agencies — billion-dollar companies — we can't really compete on perks and health plans. So we've thought a lot about what people really want from an employment situation and how we could satisfy them by differentiating — what is core from what is really peripheral.

There are four issues we think are core in making a company good to work for. The first is a *voice* — that people know they have a say in a job design or in their work environment. We don't, for instance, give people procedures to follow when they open a new office — and we've got 22 offices nationwide, as well as one in London. We'll tell them how

> *"'Empowering employees' can sound touchy-feely. Our experience is that all this stuff translates to the bottom line really well."*
> *— John Chuang*

something was done in the past and give them a model, but they're encouraged to improve upon it.

The things you tell employees early on in a job are the most important; such things leave indelible impressions on their minds. So it's very important that they have good first experiences, which means you have to give them a fair amount of autonomy. We've never had a disaster with that, giving people so much trust. We've occasionally had people who weren't a good fit with our company, but on the whole, it has worked out very, very well.

With a voice comes *responsibility*. We try to make clear to every employee that even the most mundane task is extremely important for the company. And people are happier when they're totally responsible for the task and when they know how it fits into the success of the company.

If you asked someone to just stuff envelopes to get our invoices out, no one would want to do it — it's a drag of a job. But if you explain that getting invoices out two days earlier can increase the cash flow to the company by $100,000, well, that's a big number, and it becomes clear why it's important. The idea of empowering employees can sound touchy-feely when you read about it in books, but my experience is that such practices translate to the bottom line really well. We've found that if you give an employee an open-ended challenge to, say, make collections more efficient, that employee will go for it and thus like his or her job more.

The third issue is *learning:* If you're giving people responsibility and trusting them to take action on the company's behalf, to make a frontline decision and act the way *you* would normally act, you've got to have people learning all the time. If your company's culture doesn't stress learning as well as sharing good decisions and learning from bad ones, the responsibility part really won't work. We have a program called Back to School, in which we fly all our staff employees to the main office to discuss the processes they're using in their local offices. We'll teach people business school topics such as cash-flow analysis; we'll clip articles to pass around to everyone. Business isn't rocket science; it's a matter of talking about ways of improving.

The fourth issue is *compensation*. I consider us small now, but we were really, really small when we first began, and we had to be able to retain employees and keep them happy without just bombarding them with money, because we didn't have any. Good pay, though, is one of the very important things that a job should provide, and now that we're bigger, we're shooting to get our compensation to be twice the industry average. We're going to do that by keeping out layers and getting rid of hierarchy. All these issues are interrelated; you can't de-layer and save for the frontline people all the money you'd give to middle managers if you don't have the learning. What we're really trying to do is trade a lot of control for a lot of trust, because otherwise it's hard for a company to grow quickly. — *John Chuang*

Rhino Foods
Burlington, Vt.

Rhino Foods has fared well from its association with Ben & Jerry's ice cream. In addition to making cakes and ice cream sandwiches, Rhino supplies the cookie dough that's smooshed into a hit Ben & Jerry's flavor, and as that flavor's popularity has fattened, so has Rhino, growing in two years from 13 people to 70, with more than $5 million in annual sales. Mark Koenigsberg, Rhino's director of sales and marketing, says the company also has grown its programs to help promote a healthy life outside the workplace for its staff.

We're kind of a work in progress as a company, and we're working really hard to be a good place for people. We have a company list of purposes, which declares among other things that "Rhino Foods is a vehicle for people to get what they want." That's a pretty ambiguous statement, and it's unusual for a company to use the term *want*, but that's the way it's always been with Ted Castle, the founder and president, and his wife; he was determined that the business wouldn't run him, that he'd still have time for sailing, golf, climbing mountains. And he figured that if the business served him, he wanted it to serve the other employees, too, even though they hadn't started the company. Maybe that's radical, but that's the kind of company he wanted.

**"We see people coming to the company now with incredibly great attitudes, people who are working hard."
— Mark Koenigsberg**

One of our projects is called Focus on Families. A group meets every Thursday to oversee programs for employees and for community groups like the Boys and Girls Clubs and the Special Olympics. The meetings last about a half hour, on company time, with anywhere from 7 to 25 people attending. We're about to start the Nurturing Program, a 15-weekend program that works with parents and kids to develop better parenting skills. It's run from the Vermont Center for the Prevention of Child Abuse, to which we've contributed money. The center normally offers that program to a community, but we wanted to offer it to our employees.

Many people in our workforce come from tough backgrounds — broken homes or lousy childhood experiences. Many of the mothers here are single mothers or have a mate who's not the father of their kids. Six people from our company went to an educators' conference on children recently, and ours was the only company represented there. Those who went were the only laypeople there — people who make cheesecakes for a living. They reported back to the Focus on Families group on what they'd heard, but they also got a huge shot of self-esteem: they had gone as representatives of their business. That sort of stuff works. We see people coming to the company now with incredibly great attitudes, people who are working hard, who feel they're getting something back for it. And people here work very hard; production work is not easy stuff. It's physical; you're on your feet; it's fast.

We've also hired a woman who used to work in the human resources department at W. L. Gore & Associates, a major company known for its creative personnel policies. Her job is to help us create our future and be good at what we say we want to do with workers. Right now we have a staff meeting once a week, and new people sit there and say, "What, are these guys crazy? I thought I was coming here to make cookie dough, and now these people are talking about families and work environment."

On the other hand, this is still an amazingly levelheaded organization. We don't think this way out of charity; there are some very left-brain reasons. We view the things we're doing as good business. We have lower turnover; we have fewer sick days; we have people who are psyched about coming to work. It makes sense that people will be more productive if they're happier at home. It's the idea of thinking globally but acting locally: for us, "locally" is right inside this company.

— *Mark Koenigsberg*

* * * *

These four managers demonstrate what every experienced company builder knows: Even if you're successfully satisfying the needs of your employees, you'll have to work to maintain that level of success in the future. Things will change, and swiftly. Competitors will come and go; the economy will boom or bust; fortune will smile on you, or frown. Your employees — experiencing it all — will change their minds about what they need, want, or think they deserve.

There are a lot of balls to juggle: team building, job satisfaction, self-esteem, opportunity, growth, responsibility, rewards. And you're the one engaged in the balancing act. Getting it right will require judgment, creativity, effort, good timing, and good sense. But to be among the best, that's what it takes. ■

Notes

_____

_____

_____

_____

_____

_____

_____

_____

_____

_____

_____

_____

_____

_____

_____

_____

_____

_____

_____

_____

_____

_____

_____

Recruiting Your Team

The Key Word:
Commitment

Entrepreneurs have high expectations for their employees. Typically, you have brought more than time, money, and effort to your business venture. You have given it your utmost in talent, creativity, and enthusiasm. You want to find and hire employees who are willing to do the same.

The overriding principle presented here is to manage your recruitment process — to get directly involved in every stage, from the initial planning through the final selection. The following chapter focuses on the specifics. It tells you how to read between the lines of résumés, how to locate the most promising candidates, and how to recognize them when you've found them. It tells you what questions to ask (and not to ask) when you're screening references and interviewing prospects. And it provides suggestions on how to evaluate your job offer realistically, so that you can predict the caliber of candidates you might attract.

This chapter also covers some of the newer, more exotic screening methods such as drug tests and psychological exams. They can either offer you protection or make you vulnerable to a lawsuit. Given today's litigious climate, if you choose to use them, you'll need to be well-informed. And if, even after doing everything right, you believe you've hired the wrong person, you have options to consider before you fire the employee. You'll find expert advice here on how to fix the situation or, at the very least, cushion the blow and take actions that prevent future mistakes. ■

How to Recruit High-Quality Candidates

*Finding and hiring the best employees
takes more than time and money.*

■

by Susan Cejka

The difference between a diamond and a lump of coal comes from generous applications of time, pressure, and money. That adage applies to recruiting a qualified candidate as well as to mining. But many entrepreneurs skimp on those three essential elements. They provide only meager amounts of time, pressure, and money; they settle for coal instead of prospecting for diamonds. And as part of that omission, they fail to manage the recruitment process, from conducting telephone screening interviews and checking references through evaluating the on-site interview and moving to a final offer.

Invest Your Time Wisely

Organizations frequently invest the time of the owner, principal, or CEO in recruiting. Although you may be able to delegate the hiring of lower-level clerical or service workers, a significant percentage of recruiting is too important to be minimized or assigned to the human resources department. This is especially true if you're hiring a high-profile manager or executive to oversee a turnaround or launch a new product line. In fact, many

*Susan Cejka is
president and CEO
of Cejka & Co., in
St. Louis.*

savvy executives even interview candidates for such pivotal or highly visible positions as receptionist, telemarketer, or customer service rep. Why? Because such employees safeguard an organization's image and reputation.

All too often, entrepreneurs delegate to subordinates such seemingly routine tasks as developing job descriptions, screening résumés, and conducting on-site interviews. As a principal or owner, you'll want to get involved in the recruitment process without becoming overwhelmed by it. Although you can't participate in every interview, you should take time to analyze your organization's short- and long-term personnel needs, determine how a position fits those needs, and develop — or at least critique — position specifications, job descriptions, and candidate profiles.

Getting involved in recruitment gives you the chance to assess such "sales features" as your geographic location, your industry's status and growth potential, and the financial and promotional opportunities of the position. And you can reflect on the attitudes, beliefs, values, and personality characteristics needed for success in your organization.

Realistically, you can't screen or interview every candidate at every level. You can, however, develop and orchestrate a recruitment process that gets you the candidates you need.

Put on the Pressure

Pressure doesn't mean coercion or strong-arm tactics. It means keeping the process moving by developing deadlines for each stage of the recruitment process — specifically, for the following schedule of activities:

- Development of position specifications, job descriptions, and candidate profiles
- Writing and placing ads and position listings
- Completion of networking by telephone and by mail
- Solicition résumés from networked sources
- Screening résumés according to criteria in each candidate profile
- Telephone screening interviews with candidates
- Appointments for and conducting on-site interviews
- Telephone reference-checking
- Making the offer

All too often, executives flounder for months with no timetable. Or they invest too much time in just one phase of the recruitment process — soliciting résumés, for example. When reality finally sets in and they realize they're just two weeks away from their need-to-hire deadline, they run seven candidates through a marathon of interviews that exhausts both the candidates and the staff. Evaluation and comparison of candidates are rushed and haphazard, and the result is a faulty, shoot-from-the-hip decision. If more time had been built into the process and the deadlines adhered to, there would have been more time to reflect on each candidate's qualifications or to interview additional candidates if needed.

Ante Up the Cash

Quality usually commands a premium. Even in today's highly competitive job market, it's rare to find highly qualified candidates at bargain-basement prices. In many industries, the most qualified candidates already make above-average salaries and operate with such high professional commitment that they scarcely have time to engage in a traditional job search. In the business world, pay has become a relatively accurate indicator of professional or career worth. A barely adequate salary attracts a barely adequate candidate; predictably, it won't buy you an outstanding performer for your team.

Evaluate the Job

If you apply broad guidelines or easy generalizations to your recruitment effort, you'll come up short. Instead of assuming, "In this market, we ought to be able to get someone really good for $65,000," or "Lots of people have been laid off and they're desperate for work," take a realistic look at the job offer. By evaluating the job according to three criteria — location, position, and salary — you can predict the caliber of person you'll be able to hire and the length of the recruitment process.

Some elements of a position are fixed. Much like height and shoe size, location is something you cannot control. Assume your plant is in Charlotte, N.C. You're in the high-growth field of medical research. Because the company is profitable, you can afford to hire a vice president of sales at a base salary of $175,000, with total compensation of $250,000. Given the desirable location, the high-profile position in a growth industry, and the generous compensation, you are likely to have your pick of candidates.

But here's a different scenario. Your organization is situated in muggy, industrial Tidebone, and does most of its business in that region. Enticing a candidate to leave a job in scenic Colorado Springs is going to be difficult. Similarly, if you need a manager to run your turkey processing plant, there's little you can do to glamorize the position. You can, however, enhance the salary so that strong candidates view Tidebone and turkey processing in another light. Thus, your organization may have to "buy" a qualified candidate. Unfortunately, many organizations settle for an acceptable candidate when, for a few thousand dollars more, they could have attracted an exceptional one.

If an opportunity ranks relatively low, lacking desirable location, position, and money, you have two options: You can hire a lightweight — someone on the way up, with an adequate technical background but short on experience. Or you can hire a retread — someone on the way down, with years of experience, lacking the drive and enthusiasm you had hoped for, but who could be nurtured and rejuvenated.

In defining the money component of the deal, consider a base salary plus a bonus plan. Just about everyone in an organization — even the chief financial officer — will benefit from a compensation plan made up of, say, 80% salary and 20% bonus. Even so, invest time in crafting the compensation package. Attend to the specifics. If you offer a potential bonus but provide no details on how it will be calculated, you are not likely to motivate the candidate to decide in your favor. The bonus must be clear, specific, measurable, and evaluated periodically.

Pick the Right Recruitment Channels

Once you've evaluated your position in terms of location, position, and money and made appropriate adjustments, you can begin the recruitment process. Many organizations have learned there's no single effective recruitment channel. For some, advertising in regional versions of major publications such as the *Wall Street Journal* works well. Others succeed by using the listing services of local chambers of commerce. Still others network with graduate school programs, professional associations, civic organizations, and job-search groups.

Still, every recruitment channel carries a price tag. Networking over the telephone with five to ten professional associations is time-consuming, but placing advertising in five major trade publications may break the budget. You'll need to evaluate each recruitment tool continually in terms of costs and benefits. For example, if you invested $1,000 in an ad, how many qualified leads did the ad deliver? Ultimately, you may want to experiment with diverse recruitment channels: advertising, networking, industry exhibits, and postings in newsletters or bulletins. If you try several of them simultaneously, you'll be able to evaluate the impact of each.

All too often, organizations ignore the most logical and valuable source of qualified candidates: their employees. By giving employees recruitment bonuses of as little as $100, you can turn them into a front-line sales force for your company. They'll keep their eyes open for qualified candidates and pay attention to job vacancies. And, since they understand the organization's culture, they'll be more likely to recommend candidates who are a good fit.

Another tactic is simply to engage employees in the process by asking, "Whom would you most like to have as a colleague?" When members of one department at a physician group practice were asked that question, they were quick to respond. The person they recommended was called immediately and ultimately accepted the position. You can implement a similar strategy by asking, for example, members of your purchasing department to recommend potential sales representatives.

Don't forget that the greatest repository of talent may lie within your own four walls. Qualified internal candidates know your organization and may have invested years preparing to fill the right vacancy. If you suspect you may have qualified internal candidates, handle the situation delicately but honestly. Tell candidates where you stand in the recruitment process and how many people you intend to interview. Then let them know whether they will have to participate on an equal footing, that is, move through the same battery of interviews and reference checks as external candidates.

Conduct the Screening Interviews

Use the telephone to get to know the candidates. An adequate telephone screening interview usually takes at least one hour. The goal is to learn about the candidate's current status, objectives, complaints, and timetable.

Ask open-ended but explicit questions: What do you want in a job? What do you need in a job? What's lacking in your present situation? In most cases, candidates accept new positions because of a hurt, gap, or problem in their current position or organization. Unless you can show how your organization can address that need or pain, you may never make it to the face-to-face interview.

Among the comments you may hear from disgruntled potential candidates are the following: "There's a lack of opportunity in my current organization," "I'm bored," "I'm not making the income I think I should," "I'm on the wrong side of a political battle and I'm getting squeezed," "My family doesn't like living in the area."

These grievances may or may not be legitimate. For example, "lack of opportunity" may mean lack of career development programs or opportunities for promotion. Or it could be that the organization doesn't envision the candidate as senior-executive material because of chronic conflicts with colleagues and subordinates.

Continue to probe for more information. For example, in the case of the candidate who perceives limited opportunity, you might ask, "How long have you felt this way?" or "How do you compare with other executives at your level?" or "What promises about promotions were made to you when you were hired?" or "How do others in the organization view your work?" or "What do you think is standing in your way?"

Be alert for knock-out factors. Money, for instance, can be a knock-out factor. What is the candidate currently earning? If he or she is already making $145,000 year and your position pays a maximum of $80,000, you may decide not to move forward to the on-site interview.

But if you sense the candidate is looking for a career shift, a slower-paced lifestyle, or a more desirable geographic location, a personal interview might still be appropriate.

Some knock-out factors are personal. Although some candidates like to boast, "My spouse and kids will follow me anywhere," the reality today is that both partners may have professional objectives and long-standing careers. The decision to change jobs and relocate is usually made not by the candidate acting alone but by the candidate, spouse, and children. Say your organization is located in Fargo, N.D., and your leading candidate's spouse is a successful San Francisco fashion designer; you may want to interview the spouse by phone to explore his or her personal, professional, and family needs.

Finally, the telephone screening interview should pin down the candidate's time frame. Many candidates want to change jobs or relocate but feel no real sense of urgency. You'll want to ask: "Would you be prepared to move if the right opportunity came up within the next 90 days?" If the candidate hesitates, chokes up on mention of leaving a region, or expresses concern over the mental health of a preteen child, you may be dealing with someone who's not primed to move.

Control the Interview

Once you've scanned résumés and completed telephone screening interviews, you're ready to conduct the face-to-face interview. In most cases, you'll want to invite the candidate and spouse — and sometimes even other members of the family — to visit your company and the community. Although some organizations invite the spouse on the first interview, others choose to make him or her an integral part of the second, follow-up visit.

Never go into an interview — whether by telephone or face-to-face — unprepared. In an all-too-common scenario, an executive stumbles like a sleepwalker through a few minutes of awkward small talk. Next comes a 15-minute monologue — a lecture on the organization's assets and liabilities. And then, for the finale, a vague question: "So, what brings you here?" In conducting an interview, there are four objectives:

(1) to develop a better understanding of the candidate; (2) to impart knowledge about the organization, department, and community to the candidate; (3) to determine whether the candidate fits your needs; and (4) to determine if you and/or your company fit the candidate's needs. In sum, your overriding goal is to exchange enough information so that both of you can make intelligent decisions. Accomplishing these objectives rests on advance preparation.

You'll need to brief each interviewer in the company on the candidate's background. Give everyone plenty of time to review the résumé and supplemental notes from the telephone screening interviews. Also, to ensure some consistency, you may want to provide each interviewer with a set of questions. Or you might suggest that each interviewer concentrate on a specific subject. For example, you could assign your chief financial officer the task of exploring how well the candidate handles budget planning and monitoring.

Most organizations have problems — both real and rumored. Problems need to be addressed in the interview. But if you allow everyone on the interview schedule to dwell on negatives, the candidate may conclude that your organization is overwhelmed with problems. A smart tactic is to assign the discussion of problems to one person. For example, if you have a high turnover rate, ask one interviewer to cover that issue and to describe how you are coming to grips with it.

A sound formula that each interviewer can use is to dedicate the first three-quarters or so of the interview time to listening, and the last quarter to talking or commentary. After greeting the candidate, one of the best ways to launch an interview — and begin to listen — is with an open-ended query: "Tell me about yourself," or "What are you really good at?" Such questions not only provide data but also uncover significant character traits: Does the candidate demonstrate self-knowledge? How honest is the candidate?

A delicate point: There may be questions you would like to ask, but you worry about the legal implications of asking them. The quiz on page 35 will help you test your knowledge of what you can and cannot ask. Also see "Screening: What You Can and Can't Do" (p. 54), which explores this issue in greater depth. To encourage an honest and open response, you might tell the candidate who *you* are. For example, "I'm an entrepreneur. I was not such a good employee. I just don't fit well into a corporation. I'm a great executor, but a poor planner. I do love a crisis, though... Now, I'd like to know who you are. What drives you? What makes you want to come to work in the morning?"

Try to place your best interviewer in the wrap-up position on the interview schedule. If you receive feedback from interviewers during the candidate's visit and sense the candidate is a strong fit, you may want to go for the close. But first ask the candidate, "Do you have any unanswered questions?" or "Are there any issues that came up today that we need to deal with?"

The best feedback to the candidate is personal, direct, and meaningful. "We really like you and feel the interview went very well. We believe you'd be an excellent fit for our company." Then, say to the candidate, "What do you think?" If the candidate seems to like the organization, community, position, and salary and seems prepared to make the decision, you may want to cut and close. In that case, if you've already done your reference checks, you're home free.

One more suggestion: In the process of paying attention to the candidate, don't forget the spouse or partner. Even though you're under no obligation to find a spouse a position or assist in a relocation, you may want to set up courtesy interviews anyway with some potential employers, churches, schools, and real estate offices. Let the interests of the spouse, working or nonworking, dictate the agenda.

Check References

Letters of reference provide valuable insights, but they are no substitute for an in-depth telephone conference with a reference. In fact, most reputable executive search firms refuse to present candidates until they have verified at least three references by phone. You should do the same. Don't hesitate to call.

Although many organizations still choose to leave their reference checks until the very end, it makes more sense to talk to references before inviting the candidate for a face-to-face visit. Why? Because references let you know if you're wasting your time. They alert you to potential red flags, idiosyncrasies, and trouble spots. And, most important, they spotlight issues you'll want to cover in the face-to-face interview. After that initial interview, it may get too late to explore potential conflicts or problems — unless, of course, you want to invest time and money in conducting a second interview.

Not all references are alike. Whenever possible, go beyond the references recommended by the candidate. Make sure those references you choose to interview conform to the following criteria: They should have known the candidate for at least a year in a professional capacity. (Friends and family don't count!) Also, references should have recent experience with the candidate.

Once you've introduced yourself to the reference, open-ended questions generally get things off to a good start. Try something like, "Give me your professional evaluation of this candidate" or "What kind of person is this candidate?" The touchy subject of weaknesses might be approached with the following comment: "Everyone has strengths and weaknesses. Can you give me an idea of this candidate's strengths and weaknesses so I can get a balanced view?" You can get good insights into a candidate's style and personality by inquiring, "What is it like to work with this person every day?" Finally, if for any reason you feel a need to check the reference's credibility, you might ask a "validator" question such as, "If you were in business for yourself, would you hire this person?" In most cases, if you hear anything but the word yes, you can discard the reference.

It's not easy for today's busy entrepreneur to invest time in networking, screening, and orchestrating the interview process. But consider the cost of hiring a person who's just plain wrong for your organization or the economic and human-resources costs of leaving a pivotal position vacant.

People are your organization's greatest asset. The time and effort you invest now in preparing job specifications, networking, screening candidates, and conducting face-to-face interviews could pay huge dividends down the road. ■

QUIZ: WHAT QUESTIONS CAN YOU ASK A CANDIDATE?

Test your knowledge of legal restrictions on interviewers

Answer each question with true *or* false:

1. You may ask about age if you don't
   care about the answer. T F

2. You can ask about substance abuse. T F

3. You can ask about physical
   impairments or diseases. T F

4. You can ask a candidate about
   sexual orientation. T F

5. You can check any reference you
   want—whether or not the candidate
   has authorized it. T F

6. You can use any information in forming
   an opinion about a candidate as long
   as you don't share it with anyone. T F

7. You can ask about disciplinary actions
   such as loss of license and penalties for
   driving while intoxicated. T F

8. As long as you don't write it down,
   you can ask anything. T F

Answers are on the following page.

Answers to Quiz

1. *False.* You may not ask age-related questions. Nor may you ask questions that would lead to age-related answers. Examples of such questions are, "When did you graduate from high school?" or "How old is your mother?"

2. *True.*

3. *True.* You can ask about health issues, but only if they are job related and only if they would affect the person's ability to perform the job.

4. *True.* You can ask a candidate about sexual orientation. However, you cannot ask a candidate, "Are you gay, homosexual, bisexual, or lesbian?"

5. *True.* However, if, in the process of checking references, you cost the candidate a job, he or she may sue you. If the candidate is in a competitive situation in which contacting references could jeopardize current employment, you can ask for the names of colleagues within the organization. Or you can proceed with the interview, making it clear that an offer will be contingent on reference checks.

6. *True.* In some cases, search firms learn something negative about a candidate in reference checking but refuse to tell the client. One organization learned that a candidate had been a naked skydiver in college. Although the company had every right to eliminate the candidate from further consideration, it erred by sharing the information with other, similar organizations. The candidate sued and won. Lesson: If you learn something negative about a candidate, keep it to yourself.

7. *True.* It's within your rights to ask about this history. It's also within your rights to check on such actions with appropriate authorities. However, you must secure the candidate's written permission before you do so.

8. *False.* Don't ask what you shouldn't ask even if you can't write it down. Rule of thumb: If it's not a job-related question, don't ask it. ■

How to Read
Between the Lines

*Astutely analyzing the résumés that cross
your desk can simplify the task of selecting promising
candidates. Moreover, if you know what to look
for, a résumé can pinpoint issues you need to explore
either before or during an on-site interview. Here's
advice from a team of savvy executives.*

In many ways, today's brutally competitive job market is a minefield for both employers and potential employees. The pressure to hire right the first time is greater than ever, but so is the pressure for employees to sell themselves to an employer.

At the center of the stormy process is the résumé, a highly variable, enigmatic, and often misleading document. Although CEOs of successful, growing companies aren't an easily fooled bunch, even the smartest can get into trouble when it comes to reading people. And nowhere are the stakes higher than in hiring for a key management position. "I don't look at the résumé as anything more than a snapshot of what the seller wants me to know about the product," says one executive. "Résumés are dangerous when taken at face value."

Mastering the art of reading between the lines of a résumé can take years of experience. To accelerate your trip along the learning curve, here are insights from six executives of small to midsize companies who share their secrets for hiring right the first time. The executives include:

Cyndie Bender, CEO of Meridian Travel, a corporate travel agency based in Cleveland with more than 60 employees. When hiring travel agents, Bender typically seeks people with nine or more years of experience, and she prefers to cherry-pick the best agents from among her competitors

Mary Black, co-founder and vice president of Super Wash Inc., in Morrison, Ill., which sells, builds, equips, and services car-wash stations. At its corporate headquarters the company employs 65 people, who oversee about 400 stations. A former schoolteacher, Black rarely hires from the outside, preferring to train promising employees and promote from within. The company has a turnover rate close to zero.

Harry Featherstone, CEO of Will-Burt Co., in Orrville, Ohio, a machine-tool shop that employs more than 300 people. Featherstone, who has several graduate degrees and more than 40 years of hiring experience, emphasizes the importance of education, and the Will-Burt employee-education program is legendary. Featherstone's primary concern is to hire managers and employees who are in step with employee-empowerment principles and can be good team players.

Howard Hansen, vice president of human resources for Great Plains Software, in Fargo, N.D., a maker of accounting software for small and midsize businesses. The company has 427 full-time employees, and Hansen has interviewed more than 2,000 job applicants. He believes it's important to have multiple perspectives on a candidate; thus the company conducts three rounds of interviewing by a team of people who will work closely with the person to be hired. Then the group convenes and builds consensus, so the manager can make an informed decision.

Jim Koch, CEO of the Boston Beer Co., a microbrewery in Boston with 115 employees. Koch has sometimes hired people for positions that don't necessarily jibe with their experience: He hired an accountant who is now a successful sales representative, and a woman who began as his secretary is now vice president and a partner.

Sidney Rubin, CEO of Mr. Bulky's Treats & Gifts, in Troy, Mich., a chain of 225 candy stores that employs 70 in its headquarters and 1,400 in the field part-time. Rubin promotes from within as much as possible. That means giving employees of Mr. Bulky's outlets first crack at job openings at headquarters. For store openings, Rubin insists on retail experience and an elaborate training program to minimize turnover.

For this excercise, the "hiring team" reviewed an acutal résumé, p. 44, that represents a mosaic of banking, consulting, sales, and microcomputer experience by an attractive candidate who could be useful to a company in many different ways. Still, each potential employer managed to spot a few red flags — indicating reasons to question whether the candidate would be suitable to his or her company's needs — or at least issues to explore with the candidate during the interview process.

The group's attention was directed to seven key areas. Compare the following observations and conclusions with your own.

1. What to Make of a Mixed Bag of Skills

KOCH: "Microcomputer expertise" tells me nothing. I need to know what programs she knows.

BLACK: The description of "financial professional" doesn't tell me what she wants. It should read, "I would like to continue being a financial professional." People reach different levels of maturity at different times, and it's difficult to gauge her maturity from this.

FEATHERSTONE: Her skill set is impressive, but where is it leading? I need a clue.

BENDER: I need to see more experience in one department.

RUBIN: Her brief jump into sales and then back out into an analytical job tells me she'd rather analyze various accounts than sell them.

2. Job-Hopping: A Plus or a Minus?

KOCH: Such short time horizons make me nervous. You'd get the person in and — poof! She'd be gone.

BLACK: When I saw her professional skills, I thought, this is really nice. Then I read the work record, and it doesn't show any commitment or dedication.

HANSEN: I wonder how proficient this person got at any of these jobs. I'd be inclined to ask harder-than-average questions to find out if her emphasis was on what she was moving away from or on what she was moving toward with each move. One could interview her and find out she has an insatiable capacity for learning. That could be a real plus for a company that learns to keep opportunities in front of her to keep her satisfied and interested.

RUBIN: I've already gotten over the fact that there's tremendous job jumping in people's résumés today. She's probably 35 years old and has reached an age at which stability is more important than improving skills on an annual basis. There are more positives that outweigh this negative.

3. Is Entrepreneurial Spirit a Problem?

KOCH: I like to see people strike out on their own. It shows they've got good self-confidence and an adventurous spirit.

HANSEN: I want to know more about her managerial side and about her skills beyond the financial ones.

RUBIN: She jumped to start her own consulting company. That's fine with me. But I want to know why she didn't stick with it.

FEATHERSTONE: I want to know some specific deals she made and problems she solved. What were the results?

4. Is Sales Experience Helpful?

KOCH: Selling teaches you how to get along with people and build consensus.

HANSEN: I'd want to know about customer profiles. What kind of businesses did she sell to, and how high was their demand? Was it a team approach to sales? What kinds of applications did she sell?

RUBIN: There are so many factors that can come into play. It would be very easy to increase sales of a brand-new product, but what can you do on a comparative basis, year to year?

BLACK: I want to know why she got into sales and why she got out. I would also ask her what were some of the problems she solved for customers.

5. How Important Is Education?

KOCH: The natural-sciences degree, coupled with her financial skills, indicates that she's a formal thinker.

FEATHERSTONE: The fact that she's taken courses since graduating shows she has a keen sense of learning, which is great. After perusing a person's educational background, I look at how that's translated into experience and what types of choices the person has made.

BLACK: It tells me how much a person is willing to invest in his or her own future. Hers is impressive and shows a healthy work ethic.

6. What Do Personal Interests Tell You?

KOCH: This is obviously a high-energy person. Five varsity letters, my goodness! She's probably very competitive and aggressive.

HANSEN: I suppose she has other, nonathletic interests as well, but she doesn't mention them. A wider range of interests is important.

FEATHERSTONE: Most of these are individual sports. Does she like playing on teams, or is it all just the "I" factor?

BLACK: Her squash-captain title shows that she likes to be a leader, but it doesn't tell me if she's good at it. What kinds of conflict does she encounter?

7. Is What You See What You Get?

HANSEN: I'd want to get a look at one of these report packages, see what she actually does, how she communicates with clients. Then I'd ask about why she made specific decisions in the package itself.

BLACK: When inquiring about her software experience, I'd ask how she set up a particular system. The most-organized people with developed planning skills can rattle off the five steps they took to achieve their goal and why those steps were so efficient. I noticed in her banking experience that she increased a loan portfolio. I would like to know what she did to achieve profitability. If a person can explain his or her plan clearly, it helps me tell whether that person did it unaided or just assisted someone. She can obviously work with a budget and understand the importance of structure. That comes through in this résumé.

KOCH: She may have sound financial analysis skills, but how much daily accounting experience does she have? If I were looking at her for a position in my company, I'd want her to beef up her accounting experience some more.

BENDER: She was promoted but then moved to another company in the same position. Why would someone leave a company right after being promoted? It doesn't look good.

Would You Hire Her?

HANSEN: We push some of our products through the types of places to which she has sold. She might be able to go out in the field and tell us where the channel is working and where it isn't.

KOCH: I think this person would be a good assistant controller for someone who needs banking expertise to handle debt or to work with a bank.

BLACK: She could step in with very little training and lend us some good ideas about what we could be doing with our software packages. That, combined with her financial skills, makes her very attractive

FEATHERSTONE: She'd probably be good in an information systems type of job.

* * *

The Candidate Replies

On the lack of a job objective: If I said I wanted a job in accounting, an employer wouldn't think of taking advantage of my marketing skills. I want potential employers to see the opportunities my skills present for them. There's so much cross-training of professionals today that I didn't want to limit the possibilities prematurely.

On job-hopping: I took another job only when it presented better opportunities to grow, learn, and make money. I'm still learning and growing at the company I work for now, so I'll keep working there and taking M.B.A. classes at night.

On why she quit her own company: Cash flow. I would do it again with a partner.

On where she's headed: Toward a position as an information systems manager for a financial services company, where I would be in charge of microcomputers, local area networks, software applications, and custom applications. ■

Jane Doe
Address
State, City, Zip
(000) 555-4444

Financial professional with over ten years' experience in financial, credit, and investment analysis; client account responsibility; and new business development in the communications and computer industries.

PROFESSIONAL SKILLS

Financial/Credit Analysis

Enabled rapid evaluation of loan requests and company data by creating a comprehensive computer model to project multiple financial scenarios; performed financial and credit analyses of lending institutions, communications companies, and general corporate credit; prepared cash flow analysis using various software programs on different computers to monitor loan covenants and compliance requirements.

Loan Negotiation, Structuring, and Syndication

Successful negotiation of deals with customers and senior bank management, preparation of loan packages for syndication to other lending institutions, ability to structure and understand complex financial transactions, successful negotiation on pricing to generate higher profitability for loan portfolios.

Microcomputer Expertise

Extensive training on many microcomputers and PC-based local area networks; working knowledge of numerous word processing, spreadsheet, database, communications, and network operating systems.

New Business Development

Started own consulting business, which was profitable within three months; increased new loan business and exceeded annual goals; maintained and expanded existing customer base.

PROFESSIONAL EXPERIENCE

May 1990 to present   *Investment Systems Analyst*
Perform duties of portfolio accountant with complete responsibility for specific-client securities portfolios; produce report package for distribution to clients; support all computer hardware and software systems, including a Novell network, portfolio accounting software, and all traditional word processing, spreadsheet, and database software

Oct. 1988–April 1990 *Senior Sales Representative*
Sold microcomputer-based local area networks that included both hardware and network operating software

June 1987–Oct. 1988 *Senior Sales Representative*
Sold over $750,000 of microcomputers in first year to small companies

Nov. 1985–June 1987 *Communications Consultant*
Started own consulting company

EDUCATION   **Boston University,** Boston, MA
Currently working towards M.B.A

Johns Hopkins University, Baltimore, MD
B.A., Natural Sciences–May, 1978; completed within 3 1/2 years
Five Varsity Letters: Squash, Tennis, Lacrosse, Basketball, Field Hockey

Wharton Evening School, Philadelphia, PA
Banking Administration; Fundamentals of Accounting

University of Virginia, Colgate Darden Graduate Business School, Virginia
Commercial Lending Decisions

INTERESTS   Captain of the Squash Club B Team; golf; biking; swimming
Current Massachusetts State B Squash Champion

The Foolproof Interviewer's Guide

Pat Kelly's company, PSS Inc. (formerly Physician's Sales & Service), in Jacksonville, Fla., is driven by door-to-door sales of medical supplies to physicians' offices. To conquer such a highly competitive market, Kelly needs a large, reliable, and effective sales force.

In 1985, when the company had only three branch offices but big plans to go national, he introduced in his company's hiring process a comprehensive sales-training program that enabled PSS to tackle new territory as quickly as the sales representatives graduated from it. Kelly's strategy was rewarded with low, 5% sales-force turnover, annual sales of $20 million, and a spot on the 1989 *Inc.* 500 list.

By 1989, however, PSS was losing its competitive edge: The steady stream of highly trained sales representatives was drying up, and 30% of the trainees were dropping out of the program. Overworked branch managers were hiring candidates too quickly and letting the training program take care of separating the best from the rest. At a cost of up to $20,000 per recruit, it was a luxurious hiring method the company could scarcely afford.

"I figured if we could identify on the front end who would make it through the program, we'd lose a lot less later on," Kelly says. He called a meeting with some sales managers to ascertain the behavior traits that distinguish PSSers — the company nickname for its sales representatives — from the dropouts. "I also needed to develop a tool to help my managers stop talking and start listening." The group sketched out the *PSS Sales Interview Guide* to help managers identify the qualities they wanted in employees. By its third printing, the guide had 32 questions.

Very little of the guide is about sales-related experience per se, so it can easily be adapted to any recruiting effort. As Kelly is fond of stating, "PSS hires behavior, not experience."

In 1990, armed with that secret hiring weapon, PSS managers interviewed more than 800 candidates. Only about one in five answered well enough to warrant being sent to a neighboring branch for a second interview. Of those, the regional manager interviewed 100 and made offers to 70. That works out to a one-in-10 chance of being hired, rewarding PSS with sales trainees of a much higher caliber. To keep branch managers focused on finding the best, they were given a $2,000 bonus for each candidate they hired who made it through the program. PSS sales climbed to $90 million in 1990, with 220 sales representatives on the road making door-to-door office calls.

On the following pages, Kelly uses the guide to walk us through the evaluation of a recent candidate, noting what PSS looks for and reading between the lines. "Remember," he cautions, "this is only a tool to help you get to know a recruit. There is no minimum or maximum score needed to get hired. This form functions as a gut-instinct check."

As Pat Kelly learned, finding good people takes time and effort, and hiring mistakes are costly. A systematic interview process is essential.

2 GOOD FORMS

Psyching Out the Test
"People always try to answer questions the way they think you want them to. We are 'listening for' answers that someone trying to trick the interviewer wouldn't usually predict. We also want to hear specifics, examples, details. It lets the interviewer know right off the bat if there's anything worth pursuing."

Icebreaker
The first four questions loosen up the candidate and set the tone for the entire interview: the interviewer asks questions, and the candidate talks — a lot. "We're looking for a lot of things here: values, attitudes, ability to communicate," says Kelly.

Target Behaviors
"Each of these questions is designed to reveal the behavioral trait or attitude indicated below it. There are five we focus on more than the others because we have found them to be particularly good gauges of success in our organization." Here are those personality traits or types and the questions used to gauge them:
(1) Assertor: Is the person a doer?
(2) Persuader: Can the person persuade a customer? (3) Values: Is the person honest and trustworthy? (4) Relator: Does the person get along with others, and can he or she build long-term relationships? (5) Ego: Does the person have self-regard and a high confidence level? This particular candidate was good enough to be passed on to a follow-up interview with the regional manager (Jim Boyd). Note that the questions Boyd focused on (indicated by his second set of comments) concentrate almost exclusively on the above five qualities.

Measuring Integrity
PSS likes candidates who have already had their ethics put to the test. Only two questions on the form address values directly, but all questions are designed to reveal whether a candidate is trustworthy. This candidate tells a story about enforcing a college drinking rule in his own fraternity. "He probably had to take a lot of heat for that. Now here's a person of integrity, if the story is true," says Kelly. And if it isn't true? "It's hard to keep lying about your integrity through three interviews. Plus, other questions will bring out contradictions."

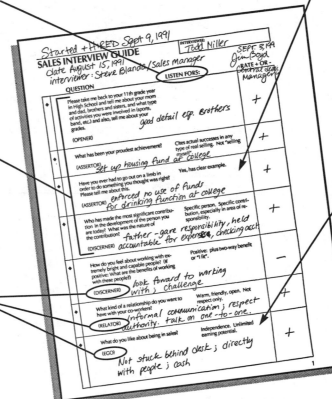

Winning Isn't the Only Thing — But Wanting to Win Is
"We look for people who want to win every situation they approach," says Kelly. "Remember, in a sales environment there can be six other sales representatives in the lobby, selling products identical to yours. As CEO, I know there's a competitor in Oklahoma City trying to figure out how to take away my business. Sales is a gladiator business, and we must win more battles than we lose. I can't explain the euphoria of beating someone out of the sale when you don't have the lowest price. Professional salespeople love the hunt and the thrill of winning a sale."

Measuring Motivation

You don't need a degree in sales to get this answer right. "We like to hear the word `money,'" Kelly says, "but I can't tell you how many candidates say `talking to people.' PSS steers clear of big talkers in favor of careful listeners."

Powers of Persuasion

"This is a classic sales-interview question, but the answers still tell us a lot about how developed a person's persuasive powers are," says Kelly. "To a seasoned businessperson, the desired answer, `By asking questions and finding a need,' may be obvious, but to a green kid out of college, it's not. Many times a person will say, `I'll cut the prospect a deal.' If a candidate gets this answer right, we know he or she is way ahead in the game."

Looking for a Relationship-based Salesperson

For many companies, generosity in a salesperson would set off the alarm that this is someone who will give away the farm on every sale. But not for Kelly: "At PSS, it tells us the person can probably develop long-term customer relationships and work with others easily."

Form 3 (upper right)

QUESTION	LISTEN FORS:	RATE + OR -
Let's say that you and your spouse or date are dining at a fine restaurant. A friend who is with you creates quite a stir when the steak he ordered is very much overdone. How would you feel? (ASSERTOR) *AGREE W/ FRIEND TAKE CONTROL & SIT. AND SOLVE PROBLEM*	Agrees with friend, supports his strong reaction. *Quiet friend down but remedy the situation in calm fashion.*	+
How do you feel when someone questions the truth of what you have to say? (ASSERTOR) *GET UPSET AND THEN SUPPORT HIS POSITION*	Reacts. Displays emotion. More than restate or convince. *emotionally insulted*	+ +
Some people seem able to see a total situation very quickly and visualize it as clearly as though it were on a television screen. Do you frequently find yourself able to do this? (DISCERNER) *the big picture, I think a college example of planning a function*	Struggles with answer; wants to be in sales. *sales only, but a sales manager; great* An unqualified enthusiastic yes. If asked, gives clear example.	+
Would you say that you are a generous person? (RELATOR) *yes, not a very strong answer.*	Very much so. Emphatic "yes".	+
What kind of boss do you work most effectively with? (EGO) *open communication lines; intelligent; helps as needed*	Allow independence; give parameters and helps as needed.	+
What are your favorite leisure time activities? (INTENSITY) *athletics, strenuous sports*	Active sports, action-type hobbies.	+
	Respect you and talk of being demoted what would you (?) *talk to in quiet fashion.*	Consoles, offers support, comforts.	+
your very best of one of the best? *Has*	Has a real need for my product and services. *need quickly - service important*	+

3

Form 2 (lower left)

QUESTION	LISTEN FORS:	RATE + OR -
What number of hours do you think it takes to be a good sales person?	55 to 60 *close to 60*	
How would you feel if a co-worker wanted to share a family concern with you? (EMPATHY) *thinks its great, communication helps us to...*	More than just listens. Wants to help; really cares. *better, helpful; friendship*	+
Your sales manager is convinced that the best way to generate sales is by blanketing the market place with promotional materials. How do you feel about such an approach? (PROSPECTOR) *materials will be thrown away; service to customer.*	Rejects in favor of qualifying according to needs.	+
How do you persuade reluctant prospects to buy? (PERSUADER) *ASK QUESTIONS FIND OUT PROBLEMS SOLVE PROBLEMS AND BECOME A CONSULTANT*	Finding and satisfying customer need. *Create and find need first*	X +
You're working under a manager who has great ideas but is very poor with detail planning. How could you best work with this kind of person? (STRATEGIST) *try present a plan myself along informal lines of communication*	Do the detail work myself.	+
How do you feel about being asked to address a large audience? (COMMUNICATOR) *no problem if subject is known*	Enjoys, no qualifications.	+
Why do you want to come to work for this company? (BELIEVER) *1. enthusiasm 2. money*	Can aid the growth of the company or serve needs of the customer.	+
Some people feel it's more important to do their best rather than win or lose. How do you feel about this? (COMPETITOR) *DRIVEN COMPETITION MUST WIN CANNOT STAND TO LOSE*	Does not agree. Must win. *Hates to lose disagrees to a certain extent.*	- X +
If you had only three adjectives to use to describe yourself, what would they be? (VALUES) *X INTEGRITY, HONESTY HARD WORKER RESPONSIBLE PROBLEM SOLVER*	Includes: Honest, man of word, ethical, etc. *Responsible, hard working, enthusiastic; honest PROBLEM SOLVER*	X +

2

Doers' Profiles

According to traditional sales-psychology books, there are four types of people: Doers, Talkers, Pacers, and Controllers. Not surprisingly, Doers make the best salespeople. "Doers will respond to this question aggressively," says Kelly. "They have no doubt that if their integrity was questioned, they would be upset, and they would be emphatic about it. A strong value system forces a strong response to the question. It indicates that the candidate is the take-charge type of individual we are looking for."

2 | GOOD FORMS

The Essence of Selling

"It's very hard to change someone's mind," says Kelly. "But that's what a salesperson must do on almost every call. Selling comes down to providing people not with something they *don't* need, but with something they *didn't know* they needed."

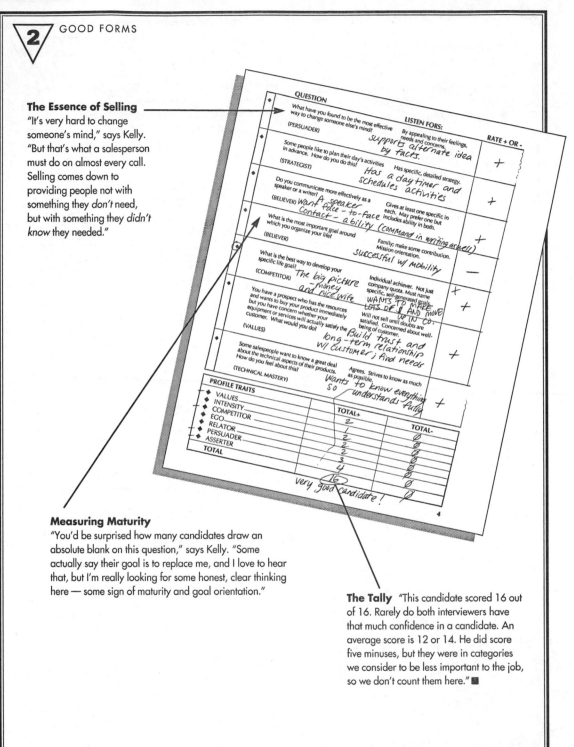

QUESTION	LISTEN FORS:	RATE + OR -
What have you found to be the most effective way to change someone else's mind? (PERSUADER)	By appealing to their feelings, needs and concerns. *supports alternate idea by facts.*	+
Some people like to plan their day's activities in advance. How do you do this? (STRATEGIST)	Has specific, detailed strategy. *Has a day timer and schedules activities*	+
Do you communicate more effectively as a speaker or a writer? (BELIEVER) *Want face-to-face Contact - ability (command in writing as well)*	Gives at least one specific in each. May prefer one but includes ability in both.	+
What is the most important goal around which you organize your life? (BELIEVER) *successful w/ mobility*	Family; make some contribution. Mission orientation.	−
What is the best way to develop your specific life goal? (COMPETITOR) *The big picture - money and nice wife*	Individual achiever. Not just company quota. Must name specific, self-generated goals. *WANTS TO MAKE LOTS OF $ AND MOVE UP IN CO.*	+
You have a prospect who has the resources and wants to buy your product immediately but you have concern whether your equipment or services will actually satisfy the customer. What would you do? (VALUES) *Build trust and long-term relationship w/ customer; find needs*	Will not sell until doubts are satisfied. Concerned about well-being of customer.	+
Some salespeople want to know a great deal about the technical aspects of their products. How do you feel about this? (TECHNICAL MASTERY) *Wants to know everything so understands fully*	Agrees. Strives to know as much as possible.	+

PROFILE TRAITS	TOTAL+	TOTAL-
◆ VALUES		
◆ INTENSITY		
◆ COMPETITOR	2	Ø
◆ EGO	1	Ø
◆ RELATOR	2	Ø
◆ PERSUADER	3	Ø
◆ ASSERTER	4	Ø
TOTAL	16	Ø

very good candidate!

4

Measuring Maturity

"You'd be surprised how many candidates draw an absolute blank on this question," says Kelly. "Some actually say their goal is to replace me, and I love to hear that, but I'm really looking for some honest, clear thinking here — some sign of maturity and goal orientation."

The Tally "This candidate scored 16 out of 16. Rarely do both interviewers have that much confidence in a candidate. An average score is 12 or 14. He did score five minuses, but they were in categories we consider to be less important to the job, so we don't count them here." ◼

Guerrilla Interviewing

*Sometimes traditional interview techniques
simply aren't enough. If you're recruiting raw
talent — and are less interested in experience —
you may need to use some exceptional tactics
to separate the wheat from the chaff.*

by Richard C. Rose

There are four characteristics a prospective salesperson must possess to have even a chance at becoming a star producer—and experience isn't one of them. Successful Dataflex salespeople outperform the industry average by unheard-of margins, yet none of our million-dollar-a-month sellers was a heavy-hitting sales pro when I brought him or her on board.

What *does* make a salesperson successful?

- Confidence in one's own abilities.
- A willingness to take calculated risks.
- A great sense of humor.
- Nimble thinking—by which I don't mean a genius IQ. I mean the ability, when put on the spot, to take available information and formulate the best possible response instantaneously. To do that, you have to be a conceptual thinker, somebody who can answer any question on a given topic, because that topic is completely understood. Many companies train their people off a script, but to be a true professional, you can't afford to depend on rote responses.

*Richard C. Rose is
chairman and CEO
of Dataflex Corp., in
Edison, N.J.*

To spot great potential in inexperienced salespeople, we make them run the gauntlet during the interview process. It starts when they answer the Dataflex ad. My assistant, Liz Massimo, has been instructed to give any callers the brush-off. Alan Fendrick, now one of our top salespeople, tells a story about how Liz tried three times to tell him why he wasn't what we were looking for. But he was persistent. He stood his ground and said, "Look, I really think I have what it takes. It's at least worth a few minutes of Mr. Rose's time." He cleared the first hurdle.

I am deliberately adversarial in the first interview. It gives me a clear idea of what candidates would be like with a customer. I try to give them criticism and a challenge. I put them on the spot, try to see if they have convictions, embarrass them. If they're too sensitive, they aren't going to do well around here.

My first words to Alan were, "Why in the world do you have 'performing stupid human tricks on the Letterman show' on your résumé?" Then I asked him, "Aren't you supposed to look nice for an interview?"

Alan came back with a zinger. He looked me dead in the eye and said, "Are you talking about me or you?"

I tell people, "Forget about what you think I want to hear. Forget that this is an interview." I try to shake them out of the standard interview mode. If they persist in giving rote answers, even after I've told them point-blank that that's not what I want, I know they aren't right for the job.

Throwing the Candidate Off Guard

After the job candidates have been in my office for about five minutes, I will tell them bluntly that I'm not very impressed—even when I think they're terrific. I'm looking for their response. I want the applicants to try to persuade me that I'm wrong about them. In sales either you believe in what you're doing or you don't. Good salespeople must believe in themselves.

When I interviewed for a sales job at Applied Digital Data Systems, in 1971, I had forgotten to pack a tie and was wearing black-and-white wing-tip shoes, which were in vogue in Florida at the time but raised eyebrows in New York City. The secretary put my résumé upside down on the desk of the vice president of sales. He was eating a tuna sandwich when I came in. Failing to find a napkin, he wiped his hands on what he thought was a blank sheet of paper but was actually my résumé. He asked me several questions and insinuated I was not packing the goods to do the job. I remember feeling an almost violent reaction to that challenge. I was thinking, someday you'll not only eat my résumé but eat those words as well. I ended up selling more equipment than the rest of the sales force combined, which comprised eight people. To this day I don't know whether his goal was to challenge me or whether he really thought I couldn't do the job. But I learned from that man the value of being challenging in an interview.

Next, in an interview, I ask for a definition of sales. Then I ask, "Have you unquestionably, without a doubt, 120% decided on sales as a career?" If they answer no, the interview is over. If they answer yes, I ask why they've chosen sales. A common response? "I want to help people." My comeback to that: "You want to help people? Go be a nurse." Another line people toss out: "People tell me I'd be good at selling." When that one comes up, I point outside my office window and say, "See that lawn out there? If people told you you'd be good at mowing lawns, would you be interviewing for that job right now?"

Zeroing in on Motivation

Then comes the real test. I'll say, "If I told you I'd give you $1 million to mow that lawn over there, would you do it?" I am looking for people who are honest enough to admit they are motivated by money, because that is the motivation for a salesperson. You'd be amazed at how many candidates try to dance around that fact. About half of the potential salespeople are eliminated at this juncture because they won't shoot straight with me. Instead they persist in saying what they predetermined would win them the job.

Why is being direct a critical trait? Customers smell it when you aren't giving them a straight answer. We have built our reputation on being honest with people to the point that if we make a mistake, every manager who had a chance to catch that error and didn't calls the client and apologizes. If somebody isn't straightforward in this company, that person has a real problem.

I'll often ask a question to test a person's honesty. I asked Alan, "Do you have some deep, burning desire to accomplish some goal?"

"You may think this is stupid," he replied, "but I'd like to make more money than my father makes."

I didn't think his answer was stupid at all. Most sons are competitive with their fathers, but it takes guts to be honest about it

Next I give applicants for sales jobs a little test to see if they are able to grasp concepts. I tell them they can ask me as many questions as they need to once I've explained a subject to them.

I told Alan I would teach him about something called a statistical multiplexer and that I wanted him to explain it back to me. I talked for about 15 minutes, providing lots of technical detail. Alan, when it was his turn, garbled the explanation something awful, and I told him so. I also told him he should have asked more questions. He said, "You're absolutely right." Conceptual selling — the ability to help customers visualize how your product or service will fit into their life — is key to becoming a professional salesperson. It's applicable whether you are selling computer peripherals or topsoil. Many people are good at memorizing or following a deductive-reasoning pattern, but if you understand something conceptually, it doesn't matter where you came in: you can figure out what's going on. You've got to understand your product conceptually to be able to sell it. Sensing a winner, I gave Alan a second chance, and he passed the test with flying colors.

The Final Test: Follow-up

I conclude interviews by telling candidates to go home and call me after they've thought it over. I tell them I'll do the same. About half never work up the nerve to call back or, I suppose, just aren't interested. Alan, however, wouldn't leave the room until he had the promise of a second interview. I knew tenacity like that would help him close tough sales. He is the only person, either before or since, who has ever done that.

Nobody is hired before getting the nod from the people in the department where he or she will be working. Why would anybody want to come to work at a place before meeting those people? All our sales-people spend 15 minutes or so with any potential salesperson who comes back for a second interview. I want all my employees to enjoy the people they work with.

The time the candidate spends with our sales staff isn't a cakewalk. For example, Alan will ask, "Does it intimidate you that during the past five years we have seen 30 people come and go?"

Some potentials will walk away right then. That doesn't bother me in the slightest. Our salespeople are an elite group. Those who have been with the company a year or more routinely generate 10 times the sales volume the average salesperson in the industry does. We sold more than $100 million worth of products and services last year, and yet we have fewer salespeople now than we had when I joined the company 10 years ago (1984) at the $5-million sales level. The interviewing process is structured to rule out the squeamish and the uncommitted. Anybody who is willing to go through it is a decent prospect.

Finally, the interviewee is invited to participate in a week's worth of sales meetings—we run two-hour sales meetings, which start at 7 a.m., four times a week. The emphasis is on the word *participate*. The same rules that apply to our regular sales staff apply to the prospects. They'll get kicked out if they don't participate. We want to see how they handle pressure, because that's what sales is. Those who survive our interview process have the extreme confidence it takes to thrive in sales. It all boils down to something simple: People who take more risks sell more. ■

Screening: What You Can and Can't Do

Thoroughness is an asset in screening job candidates. But today's screening methods run the gamut, from team interviewing to gene testing. Unless they're used with care, some less traditional screening methods can land you in court.

—

You mean you don't know the genetic makeup of your workforce?

Believe it or not, some big companies are using gene testing to screen out job applicants vulnerable to expensive and debilitating diseases. Although the practice is unusual, extreme, and legally dubious, it indicates both the lengths to which some employers will go before hiring a new employee and the range of screening methods available. It's now possible to know almost everything about job applicants. Consultants peddling background checks, drug tests, psychological profiles, medical exams, and more insist you should know everything.

None of those tests can take the place of good screening interviews. But some, used carefully, can supplement interviews and give you more complete information. In some instances, you may have strong legal justification — even the duty — to use a particular type of screening method. In others, to do so could set you up for a lawsuit.

Before you buy a test or hire a firm to conduct background checks, you should know about these common screening options and the questions — legal, practical, and ethical — that surround them.

Reference Checks

Everyone understands the importance of checking identity, education, employment history, and references against information the job applicant provides. But some companies, pressured for time, drop their guard. Witness Hatteras Hammocks.

In October 1991, the $10-million Greenville, N.C., company abruptly lost its controller. Executive vice-president Jay Branch interviewed several candidates for the position, but one man distinguished himself from the others. Recommended by someone Branch knew, the candidate came with an impressive résumé: B.A. in accounting, M.B.A. from Indiana University, CPA, and several years as controller at a large local corporation. The following March, Branch hired him after a quick call to the previous employer. After a few months, however, it became obvious that the new controller couldn't do the job, and by October 1992, Branch had fired him.

His replacement quickly saw something wrong with the company's books. The man with the fancy résumé had embezzled $60,000 from Hatteras Hammocks. A quick background check turned up no record of either of his degrees or his CPA credentials. The police arrested him and he confessed. Branch, who saw his own name forged on several checks, says, "The whole episode taught me the necessity of checking thoroughly, no matter how good a recommendation is."

The threat of lawsuits, however, has changed what is appropriate as a *response* to reference checks. Take the manager who, uncomfortable confronting an employee with a job poorly done, indicates satisfaction with the employee's work in reviews and in raises but later gives a negative reference to prospective employers. A court may first consider those reviews and pay hikes proof that the manager was happy with the employee's work and then conclude that the bad reference was false and damaging. Some prospective employers try to wheedle information by promising to keep it off the record. That may work, but only with the foolhardy or misinformed. "Off the record" won't protect a respondent against a defamation claim.

Voca Corp., a $70-million company based in Columbus, Ohio, with 2,500 employees in six states, has wide experience in screening job applicants. Hilary Franklin, director of human resources, says Voca asks references to suggest further references and then asks those for still others. "As you get two or three times removed," Franklin explains, "you get more detailed, honest information."

Background Checks

What if a repairer you hired were to burglarize a customer's home? If you hadn't checked the repairer's background to be sure no criminal record existed, you could be guilty of negligent hiring. If you hire a receptionist, however, you probably don't need to run such a check — and probably shouldn't. You should always measure what's appropriate to know about the candidate for the job.

Many of Voca's employees, for example, work closely with vulnerable clients: the company furnishes care to people with mental retardation and developmental disabilities. To ensure the safety of its residents, the company wants to know about any incident of abuse in an applicant's history. Because Voca's caregivers drive clients to appointments, they must have a clean driving record as well. The company informs all applicants that any job offer it makes is contingent upon a satisfactory background check.

Before Voca staff members run the check, they ask applicants if there is anything they would like the company to know about, and they give applicants an opportunity to explain. Then they fingerprint the applicants. Voca does not use those fingerprints in the background check. Rather, "it's our way of announcing the check, of demonstrating we're serious," Franklin says. "And it's pretty darn effective."

By running the check only after making a job offer, Voca protects itself from charges of discrimination. The company has set unambiguous standards for the information that background checks turn up, and it sticks to those standards. For instance, no one convicted of a felony and no one guilty of abuse, neglect, or mistreatment will be hired to work with clients. Finally, Voca keeps specific findings confidential to protect against defamation. If, at your company, one person handles both the background checks and the hiring, that individual must be careful to consider only job-related information when hiring. To facilitate background checks, you should get complete information from applicants — full name, address, Social Security number, driver's license number, employment history with no unexplained gaps — and ask them to sign a release giving you permission to confirm it all.

If you're too shorthanded to do extensive background checks internally, you can hire outside investigation firms, which can pry into every imaginable area of an applicant's past. Companies usually order extensive checks only for sensitive, high-level positions such as top managers or people who will handle large amounts of money. More common checks include those of the applicant's worker's compensation, credit, and criminal records. But even those checks raise legal questions.

Some companies want to know an applicant's history of worker's comp claims in order to detect malingerers. And although worker's comp records are not public, there may be legal ways for a private investigator to obtain the information. Under the Americans with Disabilities Act (ADA), however, you may not initiate a worker's comp check before offering someone a job.

As for credit and criminal checks, remember that the government protects certain classes of citizens — racial minorities and women, for instance — against discrimination. If you consistently base hiring decisions on those criteria, you open yourself up to discrimination lawsuits. You would have to demonstrate that certain information was related to the job, and in many cases that would be hard to prove. If you're hiring a driver, a drunken-driving arrest is relevant. If you're hiring a security guard, criminal history is relevant. If you're hiring a telemarketer, both may be irrelevant.

Look into state laws, too, before conducting such checks. Many states don't allow you to check records of arrests, but most — though not all — allow you to check convictions. Some states require you to get the applicant's approval before running checks, and some protect certain information. Speak to a labor lawyer before you do anything. And if you hire an outside firm to do your digging, demand a degree of legal savvy from it. Many display a cavalier attitude that could land you in court.

Drug Tests

Preplacement tests are administered after a company makes a job offer contingent on a clean result. That may be the safest time, legally, to test for drugs, but some employers wonder whether it's the least effective, since many applicants expect a test at that point.

Voca, for one, prefers to give preplacement drug tests. Its caregivers must respond quickly in an emergency, so the company has good reason for ensuring they're clean. (After seven years of testing, it consistently finds that 4% of applicants test positive.)

Voca explains up front to all applicants that any job offer is conditional upon a clean drug test, and applicants sign a form indicating they've read and understood the policy. The company offers applicants who test positive an opportunity to retest at the company's expense. And Voca is consistent in its testing: it tests all candidates for caregiver positions. For accurate readings and to protect itself further, the company sends its tests to a certified laboratory. Although that costs more, certification will help you if anyone challenges a test result in court.

Medical Exams

The Americans with Disabilities Act (ADA), which applies to companies with 15 or more employees, prohibits any pre-job-offer questions about medical conditions. You may ask only whether the applicant can perform the functions of the job. The Equal Employment Opportunity Commission has permitted certain agility tests, such as those used by police and fire departments, but the distinction between those and medical exams remains unclear. Would it be legal to ask applicants to read an eye chart? To perform a strength test? We won't know for certain until the ADA is fully tested.

After you make an offer, you can, under federal law, require a complete head-to-toe physical and access to all medical records. However, you cannot legally use any information that is not job related, says Mark Rothstein, director of the Health Law and Policy Institute at the University of Houston. Eleven states explicitly limit exams to job-related information.

If you do test for job-related fitness, don't set blanket policies —

for instance, that anyone with a back problem is automatically considered unfit. Rather, check whether each candidate can lift the weight the job requires. Try to make that distinction, too, when you talk about the applicant. Inform managers only about ability, not about condition. "You can say, 'Joe Smith has a 25-pound lifting limit,'" Rothstein explains, "not, 'Joe Smith has a 25-pound lifting limit because he's got a slipped disk.'" Otherwise, overcautious managers might restrict Joe from jobs he's capable of performing and thus leave themselves open to a lawsuit. For the same reason, keep medical records confidential and separate from the rest of your personnel files.

Psychological Exams

Employers have used psychological tests since the 1950s. The oldest of those tests, developed for clinics and adapted for employers, screen for emotional disorders. Some tests contain prying questions about religious beliefs and sexual habits. In California (a state with unusually broad privacy rights), a job applicant sued a company after being given such a test. (He won, but the case is under appeal.) Tests for emotional disorders should be used only for security positions — so you don't give a gun to someone dangerous, for example.

The psychological-testing industry blossomed after 1988, when the federal government banned the use of lie-detector tests in most employment situations. Publishers filled that void with so-called integrity tests. The simplest "core" integrity tests analyze security issues only — theft, drug abuse, and violence — and cost as little as $8 to $16 a test, depending on volume. Others may test for security plus productivity or customer-service attitudes. Some even claim to measure the likelihood that a new hire will have accidents on the job or will quit.

The tests try to predict job applicants' propensity to steal, for instance, by asking obvious questions such as, How often do you tell the truth? and less obvious ones such as, How often do you make your bed? and then matching their test results with those of known thieves.

Do the tests work? Perhaps. Just because a person's responses match those given by thieves does not mean the person will steal; rather, it means the person may be more likely to steal. You play the odds and, in the long run, may improve your chances of reducing theft.

Some integrity-test publishers scare employers by estimating that as many as 30% of all employees steal. But they may be including employees who take home pens or make personal calls from the office. Other experts say the rate of serious theft is as low as 5%. Whatever the situation in your company, be warned: even the best integrity test will produce many false positives, meaning people unjustly suspected and rejected.

Beyond integrity tests, publishers have developed all sorts of so-called personality-assessment tools to predict how an applicant will do the job and fit into your organization. Such tests may judge a prospective salesperson's aggressiveness, for instance, or an accountant's attention to detail.

Few tests work in all situations. If you are considering using psychological tests, how should you choose? Get references from others in your industry, a state psychologists' association, or a local university's professor of industrial psychology. Then contact publishers and ask to see their validation studies, which are trial runs under controlled conditions. The trial group should resemble your workforce in duties and demographics.

Also ask the publisher if the test has ever been challenged in court and how it fared, and ask what the publisher will do to help if someone challenges your use of the test. Conscientious publishers will provide you with technical assistance and may send a staff psychologist to testify, if necessary, at no charge. Remember: Tests are often wrong about an individual. For effective hiring, make testing only one part of an overall assessment that includes interviews and reference checks.

Interviews

Publishers of personality tests talk persuasively about how much more accurate than interviews their tests are. And a good test probably does work better — more accurately for you, more fairly for the applicant — than a bad interview. But a good interviewer can get richer and more relevant information, especially if you yourself participate in the interview process. It takes time to develop interviewing skills, and even more to perform interviews. Too many entrepreneurs prefer to invest their money in a quick solution.

Some also like the reassuring formula a personality test provides. A bad interview seems like purposeless small talk, but a test imposes structure on the process. Set benchmarks for each job in the same way that some personality-assessment tests do. If you're hiring a receptionist ask yourself who's the best receptionist you've ever come across. What made that receptionist so good? Categorize those qualities into certain overall behavioral traits such as sense of responsibility, attention to detail, and skill in relating to people.

Then conduct "pattern" interviews to identify those traits in applicants, using such questions as, How do you feel when someone questions your statements? and, How important is what other people think of you? These are similar to the questions personality tests ask, but they work better in interviews.

Testing forces the subject to choose between true and false or among multiple choices. If you ask the same questions in an interview, you can get subjective responses that tell you much more. And you will also get actual examples of behavior.

The Registry, based in Newton, Mass., an information technology consulting firm for Fortune 1000 companies, uses pattern interviewing. The company combines its interviews with other techniques designed to test qualities it looks for in salespeople and recruiters. An applicant for a job at the Registry meets with the hiring manager, who describes the position and reviews the applicant's background. If the applicant is promising, the manager calls in a recruiter or salesperson to describe the job firsthand. Next, the candidate interviews with the team he or she hopes to join, to determine personal fit. Each interviewer makes notes on an interview guide, which spells out questions to ask (for instance, "Why are you successful?") and the types of responses to listen for — ones that reveal a process or methodology; i.e., logical, repeatable steps.

Candidates at junior levels also interview over the phone with the directors of training and development in the Registry's Washington, D.C., office and with one or two training managers in other branches.

Those phone interviews test applicants' persistence — a trait particularly valued by the company. The managers are hard to reach and often won't return calls. "We'll tell candidates, 'Now interview with Meredith Cohen in our corporate office,'" CEO Drew Conway says. "It may take five calls to reach Meredith, who's our trainer. Do they just leave a message? We want them to find her and get her on the phone. The ability to identify and track down the right person is a part of our day-to-day job."

Before making a final decision, the Registry administers a personality test which was designed by an industry insider, so Conway believes it accurately identifies the qualities that make success more likely. He doesn't believe the profile will tell him which candidates will be successful; indeed, one of his best salespeople performed badly on the test. Rather, he thinks it indicates how naturally the qualities needed for sales and recruitment come to a candidate.

As valuable as that information is, it can't make Conway's decision for him. "Lots of companies use the profiles as an excuse not to go through the interview process. But to do good work, you have to invest the time and energy." ■

Firing: When It's Time to Wave the White Flag

*You thought you did everything right — screening,
interviewing, even testing. But it's all gone wrong.
If you're like most managers, you fire people too seldom
and too late — and as a result hurt your company,
yourself, and even the employees you take too
long to terminate. Try this seven-point plan.*

—

Firing is one of the crucibles that turn entrepreneurs into managers, because it brings you face-to-face with failure. Nothing will make firing any easier. It *shouldn't* get easier. What it should become is less frequent.

Lionhearted in the world's marketplace, small-business owners are all too often wimps in their own companies. They don't fire bad employees often enough or soon enough. For one thing, owners usually don't bring professional detachment to their relationships with employees. Nor do they lay down any clear job guidelines for them. And as their companies begins to grow, entrepreneurs feel enormous gratitude to longtime workers — often placing them in jobs for which they're not equipped. All of which adds up to a festering problem when a person who should have been fired isn't. Precious cash flow is squandered on someone who isn't producing. And productive co-workers feel cheated.

Mark Landis still winces when he thinks about his worst firing experience. He had labored mightily to persuade a key executive from a giant company to join his small information-services company in Princeton, N.J. The executive moved his family hundreds of miles, dived into Landis's Health Information Technologies Inc., and promptly fell on his face.

"Every senior person came to me and said, 'Please deal with this situation. It's hurting us all,'" recalls Landis. He couldn't. He was paralyzed by guilt. Finally, he gave the employee three months to improve. He didn't. So Landis let him have three more months to find another job. "The environment got so bad that people didn't want to come to work," says Landis, sighing. The lesson, he says, is "Make up your mind. Don't sit and agonize."

If you think of firing as a symptom, a by-product of your company's activities, then you can take responsibility for those failed employees. When you do that, you'll understand why a company that hires the right people and manages them properly does almost no firing. That should be your ultimate goal: to hire and manage so well you'll never have to fire again. Here's how.

1. Look closely at your hiring process. Are you hiring the right people? Think about the people you've fired. What behavior ultimately made those people unsuccessful? Consider three broad categories: an employee's job aptitude, work attitude, and fit with colleagues. Be specific.

With your list of terminal problems in hand, think about how you could have unearthed that problem behavior — or a predictor of it — during the hiring process. The range of possibilities is broad. You can manage recruitment and screening carefully and wisely, participate actively in interviews, and scrupulously check references (see "How to Recruit High Quality Candidates," p. 25). You can even require candidates to take psychological tests. The key is to do whatever you can to get the information your current recruitment process doesn't deliver.

Being exhaustive in hiring can also help you correct problems much faster if they occur. Donn Rappaport, chairman of American List

Counsel Inc., a direct-mail services company in Princeton, N.J., was perplexed when one of his star media buyers began having difficulty negotiating deals. He went to her hiring records. Her aptitude test showed she hated confrontation. "It was like a dash of cold water to see this glaring warning," says Rappaport. After he counseled the employee on her mental framework and her negotiating skills, her performance improved.

2. Make your expectations clear. Hiring right isn't everything. The other single biggest terminator of careers is failing to tell employees what you expect of them. The key is to give regular feedback to a new employee right from the start. Communicate your standards repeatedly, and help employees understand what they need to change if they are to succeed. Small companies can't usually afford the luxury of a discrete orientation program, but they can, and often do, rely on a two-week or three-week job rotation to teach new employees about the company and how it works, offer on-the-job training, or at least strive to open up communication channels.

Carolyn B. Thompson, president of CBT Training Systems, a Frankfort, Ill., specialist in employee retention, suggests also using continual job coaching. "Have people who are teaching the new employee fill out a performance checklist every week, indicating strengths and clarifying objectives."

At many small companies fledgling workers are assigned mentors, who provide a kind of cultural feedback that helps them assimilate. At Datatec Industries, a Fairfield, N.J., company that specializes in management information systems, mentors are charged with coaching new hires on how to achieve quality. Quality mentoring doesn't provide new employees with job-specific benchmarks. Datatec takes care of that separately. But quality mentoring does convey a kind of conceptual benchmark: that quality permeates every job.

3. Install early-alarm systems. Let's be honest, by the time most of us admit something's amiss, it's late in the game. The nonperformer knows something's wrong, and co-workers do too. So do you, but you've ignored the problem. It's likely you're finally paying attention because the wayward worker has made a sickeningly bad mistake. You greet this "personnel problem" with fury — you want the reprobate out now! But hold on. You did your hiring homework well, and you really believed you hired the right person for the job. But what did you do to strengthen your commitment by nurturing that valuable employee?

DeAnne Rosenberg, president of DeAnne Rosenberg Inc., Lexington, Mass., stresses that coaching and performance appraisal have a natural affinity for each other (see "The ABCs of Performance Management," p. 101). A manager who's actively coaching every day is appraising every day. And that's the best and earliest alarm system you can have.

Modern Business Systems, in Jefferson City, Mo., uses such performance appraisals as coaching opportunities. Once or twice a year, manager and employee meet to discuss the employee's job progress. The manager asks the employee to rate his or her success in all aspects of the job. Then they review the self-appraisal together. The appraisals cue managers on how to counsel workers on a day-to-day basis. Workers who perceive they're not working fast enough or who are fast but careless can be reinforced on their speed and taught to recognize the cost of being careless.

Benchmarking prevails at Datatec, which measures everything — defects in receivables, late orders, length of service calls, you name it. It also requires all employees to rate everyone else's performance, including supervisors', either monthly or quarterly. Leadership and morale surveys are conducted annually to check on the company as a whole and on the executive team. In addition, Datatec's quality department surveys customers for their opinions. And the results are published monthly for everyone in the company to see.

So imagine this: After a week of training, you, the new recruit at Datatec, start being graded at the end of your first month. You see immediately how you rank on every aspect of your job. It's obvious where you need to improve. Because the surveys are so frequent, problems are caught early, and better performance shows up immediately. And because managers are using the same survey results as workers to evaluate performance, differences in perception are minimized. The strength of Datatec's system is that it allows employees to correct themselves.

4. Fix the problems. Evaluating what's wrong and changing it require far more skill than anything else you'll do as a manager, because no one can fix the problem but its owner, the weak performer. You're the facilitator, the person who makes that problem so crystal clear that underperforming employees can't resist fixing it themselves.

At Modern Business, the manager sets up a special session with the employee. The manager states the performance failure, produces evidence that it's an issue, and gets the employee to agree there's a problem. "We never say, 'Do you sometimes come in late?' We say, 'Our team is having a problem because you're arriving after 8 a.m.,' " explains Rick Jordan, head of field services. Evidence might be attendance records.

Next the manager and the employee list all the possible causes, perhaps 20 or 30 of them. Then the two list as many options as they can for solving the problem. They select one option that will help most in the short term and one that will be most effective over the long term. Finally, they create an action plan for implementing the solutions. "The power of this approach is that when employees get up and walk out the door, they're committed to it because they're part of it," says Jordan.

Other companies find other forms of remedial action effective. American List's Rappaport believes in probation. Not probation as an on-your-way-out-the-door technicality, the way too many companies use it, but as a kind of shock therapy administered along with other steps. For example, an employee with a pivotal role in American List's research department wasn't getting his work done. After repeated coaching sessions between the researcher and his supervisor, Rappaport told him the company would have to let him go if his project wasn't done in the next 30 days. He met the deadline.

At Adnet, a third-party telecommunications-services company in La Mirada, Calif., president Dave Wiegand uses what he discovered during the hiring phase. He asks all job candidates, "How should an employee who fails to get to work on time be disciplined?" Wiegand can use the employee's own suggestion, and a reminder of where it came from, to cure problems.

5. Fire when it's time. If nothing has worked, take the advice of every experienced businessperson we consulted for this book: Don't sit on the decision. You will have to make sure the termination follows your company's policy guidelines, but by all means, act. Try to appreciate the employee's strengths and understand why your company couldn't harness them. Make your delivery of the bad news genuine. Scripting yourself is a good idea. By writing out your comments beforehand, you can individualize your treatment. Jordan uses this approach: "When you came in the door, the last thing I wanted to do was put you in a position where you couldn't be successful. But I seem to have done that. Here are some of the problems we worked on…"

Rappaport suggests having two people in the room in addition to the employee — the immediate supervisor and someone with whom the employee does not have a day-to-day relationship. The manager delivers the bad news, answers questions without engaging in an argument, and then leaves. The neutral person's major role is to listen, but he or she should also be prepared to answer questions or offer specific information on how the relationship is being severed. Will the worker receive severance pay, assistance in job hunting, good references? How long will the company health-insurance benefits last, and what will they cost? Is the terminated person eligible for unemployment benefits?

Before the meeting make a checklist of things to do, from collecting keys to finding a replacement for the employee. Two items that should be on the list: addressing other workers' concerns and helping the fired employee find another job. No matter how isolated the firing incident or how good the reason for it, other employees may figure they're next. Sit them down, briefly explain what happened, and assure them you have no plans to fire anyone else.

Finally, make a serious effort to help the fired employee find another job. Remember, if you really did do your best in hiring the right person, you do believe in his or her basic qualities. You needn't hire a costly outplacement firm. You could alert vendors, customers, and people in your industry, providing a formal introduction in some cases. For a limited time you could also make available some of your office's resources.

6. Conduct an exit interview. What you hear in an exit interview could be the most candid, insightful criticism you'll get. But hardly anyone does one after firing an employee. And yet, it's worth it. The best approach: keep it simple. Chris Carey, CEO of Datatec and his human resources manager conduct exit interviews over the telephone a week or two after the terminated worker has left. "I ask them what it was like to work here and if they could give me some advice on what I could do to make it a better place to work," says Carey. Assure the ex-employee that what he or she says won't cause you to withhold a good reference or other benefits you've already agreed upon.

7. Do a postmortem. Each time you fire someone, review your firing process. What was unacceptable about the fired person? How could you have predicted it in the hiring process? How could it have been corrected in the managing process? If you don't change anything after firing someone, then you're doomed to repeat the mistake.

Your firing experience could be the best instructor you ever have, not just because firing is something every business owner has to learn and not only because you'll learn to hire better. What happens is simple: a thorough analysis of your firing requires you to change your focus from your product or your market alone to managing human beings. What you'll be able to achieve with a high-quality, well-managed workforce, coupled with that terrific product or unique marketing approach, will lift you an order of magnitude above what you'll get from products or marketing alone. Getting there is not quick or painless. But it's the right journey to be making. ■

THE MANAGER'S BARE MINIMUM

The Five Basic Steps of the Firing Process

Employment-related/work-related lawsuits filed during the past 20 years have skyrocketed by more than 2,000% (compared with the 125% that overall civil cases have increased in the same time period), according to the American Bar Association.

We're not recommending you install a purely defensive firing strategy designed to prevent lawsuits by disgruntled former employees. But you should know what legal experts advise clients about firing an employee over performance problems. Here are the five steps to a bare-minimum firing process.

1. Act on problems immediately.

Employees most likely to sue you are those who feel their firing was unjust, indefensible, or discriminatory. So you must communicate with them about weak performance immediately. A minor problem can be handled in an annual performance review and follow-up meetings. Major shortcomings should be conveyed right away and tracked through weekly or monthly sessions.

2. Document carefully.

Write memos about your talks with employees. Be extremely specific in both talks and memos. Don't simply say that the employee doesn't have the proper attitude, enough initiative, or the ability to get along with people. Substantiate your characterization by describing instances. Give to the employee a copy of any memo that goes into his or her personnel file—and there should be one for every session with an employee.

3. Include the employee.

Have employees evaluate themselves. If the employee acknowledges the problem, then you'll be much closer to solving it. If the employee denies the problems, the employer has the additional ammunition — if the case ever goes to court — of being able to show that the employee did not respond to constructive criticism.

4. Act quickly.

If the employee's performance does not improve, don't delay the decision. That could look as though your company wasn't seriously affected by the worker's unsatisfactory job, thus weakening your grounds for dismissal. There is no legal requirement that you issue a warning or put a worker on probation. But you must follow your company's policy as laid out in your employee handbook if you have one. If you're firing your only female or minority worker, that employee could argue the termination was discriminatory. Your comprehensive record (steps 2 and 3 above) should reflect that poor performance is the reason for dismissal.

5. Be candid.

Candidly and clearly, tell the employee the reasons for the termination. Be prepared to make your severance-pay and benefits proposal. Have someone else from the company present to witness and record the termination and the employee's response to it. ■

RESOURCES

For Managers on the Firing Line

Every year more than three million Americans are fired or laid off, many by employers seemingly ill-equipped to deal with claims of wrongful discharge. To avoid potential courtroom appearances, you should master the art of preventive employee relations. Thinking about firing an employee? You can do it humanely and legally while staying out of court — and safeguarding precious cash — by taking a few tips from the experts.

E. Kenneth Snyder's *Employee Matters: A Legal Guide to Hiring, Firing and Setting Employee Policies* (Chicago: Probus Publishing Co., 1991, 225 pages, $24.95 plus $4 shipping and handling; 800-776-2871), written for the legally untrained executive, clearly and thoroughly lays out tried-and-true methods for creating effective personnel policies and resolving employee complaints. The guide offers strategies for minimizing damages and maximizing the chances of a favorable ruling when litigation is likely.

BNA Plus (800-452-7773, 202-452-4323 in Washington, D.C.), the Bureau of National Affairs research arm, publishes model procedures for discharging employees and conducting exit interviews and audits and will send them to you for $35 plus $7 shipping and handling.

The Friedman Group, a retail training and consulting firm in Culver City, Calif., produces a no-nonsense video, "How to Legally Fire" (about 60 minutes, $95; 800-351-8040). [Note: Friedman also offers "How to Legally Hire" and sells the two videos for $149. They are not specifically focused on the retail market.] The concise program lists the dos and don'ts of firing, shows how to test for just cause, and demonstrates negotiating skills. It also shows employers how to avoid firing altogether by taking corrective action to enhance employee productivity. The video comes with a helpful workbook full of diagnostic checklists.

If all is lost and you're ready to fire, contact Margaret Bryant of the White Plains, N.Y. office of Jackson, Lewis, Schnitzler & Krupman, labor and employment-law specialists (914-328-0404). Ask for the firm's free soup-to-nuts "Termination Checklist," a four-page quiz on discharge basics and firing techniques. It's appropriate for all levels of an organization. ■

Notes

Motivating Your Team

The Key Word:
Participation

Whenever a group of people share responsibility for the decisions that affect all of them, they are a team. Teamwork means contribution and collaboration — it requires both the freedom and the ability to participate fully.

Initially, the founder's vision and energy may serve as a catalyst to forge a small business's employees into a team. But as the organization grows and the chain of command lengthens, individuals lose sight of shared goals and of each other. With the loss of full participation comes a loss in group morale and individual feelings of self-worth. At this point, whether the need is at the top, on the shop floor, or companywide, team building requires attention and effort.

Employee job satisfaction, high morale, and worker productivity are not the accidental by-products of a successful venture. Rather, they are the assets that create success. And they are not easily obtained. You earn them by paying close attention to what motivates your employees and by responding with wisdom, creativity, and energy.

By enabling your employees to participate in goal-setting and believe in opportunity, you empower your organization to become a strong, virtually unbeatable team. ■

The Realities of Team-Based Management

*Lauded by business gurus as a time-tested model
of team management, XEL Communications,
in Aurora, Colo., swears by the now trendy concept
but still struggles with its complexities
every hour of every day.*

—

I n the mid-1980s, not long after Bill Sanko and his partners had engineered the buyout, they could see that their fledgling telecommunications equipment company was struggling.

Granted, the numbers weren't so bad. XEL Communications Inc., as they had christened the new business, was selling a lot of custom circuit boards to GTE Corp., its former parent. It was making money. But Sanko, a longtime GTE executive who took the entrepreneurial plunge at age 44, knew he'd be foolish to depend too heavily on his ex-employer. He needed to sell more to the Baby Bells and to big industrial customers that operated their own phone systems.

Talk about David and his slingshot! In most such forays, the 180-employee company would be up against the likes of Northern Telecom and AT&T. XEL's only hope was agility: lightning turnaround of orders, quicker than any big company could manage, speedy response to customer needs — all done with close attention to cost. The low bidder in a competitive situation didn't necessarily get the job, Sanko knew. The high bidder didn't have a prayer.

Fleetness of foot, unhappily, was just what XEL lacked. Costs weren't exactly rock-bottom either.

On the shop floor, for example, cycle time — the period from start of production to finished goods — was about eight weeks. That left customers disgruntled, and it tied up money in inventory. Moreover, the company's chain of command had scarcely changed since the GTE days. Line workers reported to supervisors, who reported to unit or department managers, who reported on up the ladder to Sanko and a crew of top executives. Every rung added time and expense. "A hardware engineer who needed software help would go to the manager," Sanko says. "The manager would say, 'Go write it up.' Then the hardware manager would take the software manager to lunch and talk about it."

Sanko fretted, talked with his partners, fretted some more. "We needed contributions from everybody in the building. We needed them to think about how we could better satisfy our customers, how we could improve quality, how we could reduce costs."

Soon XEL began the kind of top-to-bottom transformation that numerous U.S. companies have attempted in the past decade.

First came the vision statement, crafted by Sanko and colleagues with the help of a consultant. That turned out to include a pregnant thought: "We will be an organization where each of us is a self-manager." Next, manufacturing vice president John Puckett redesigned the plant for cellular production, with groups of workers building whole families of circuit boards. Finally, Sanko and Puckett set up self-managing teams (then a hot new concept), and they brought back their consultant to help. By 1988 the teams had been established — and the supervisory and support staff reduced by 30%.

Five years later, XEL had rebuilt itself around those teams so thoroughly that the Association for Manufacturing Excellence chose the company as one of four to be featured in a video on team-based management. Since then, dozens of visitors, from companies such as Hewlett-Packard, have trooped through XEL's Aurora factory.

What visitors see today is striking. Snappily colored banners hang from the plant's high ceiling to mark each team's work area. Charts on the wall track attendance, on-time deliveries, and the other variables by which the teams gauge their performance. Diagrams indicate who on a team is responsible for tasks such as scheduling.

Every week, the schedulers meet with Puckett to review what needs to be built. The teams meet daily, nearly always without a boss, to plan their part in that agenda. Longer meetings, called as necessary, take up topics such as vacation planning or recurring production problems. Once a quarter each team makes a formal presentation to management on what it has and hasn't accomplished. Overhead projections, with fancy charts, are *de rigueur.*

And the numbers are right where Sanko had hoped they would be. Since the advent of teams, XEL's cost of assembly has dropped 30%. Inventory has been cut by half; quality levels have risen 30%. The company's all-important cycle time has plummeted from 50 days to 3.85 days and is still falling. Sales in 1993 swelled to $24 million, up from $17 million in 1992; 1994 sales are estimated to hit $50 million.

A success story? Sure. The consultant did a fine job, years ago. But this story is as complex as it is enlightening. As XEL endured and confronted the effects of change, it learned lessons about teams — lessons you are not likely to find in a training video or a how-to text.

The following conclusions were built on the hard bedrock of XEL's experience. If you're thinking about taking the plunge into teams, they will help you to see the whole panorama — the realities as well as the rewards.

Adding New People Gets Harder, Not Easier.

Face it: though CEOs sometimes love to complain, bringing on new hourly employees just isn't that tough in traditional companies. A manager or human resources professional usually chooses candidates. A supervisor tells them what to do and helps them get started. Add teams, however, and the process gets messy. "Staffing up is probably five times harder with self-directed work teams," sighs Julie Rich, XEL's human resources vice-president and one of Sanko's original partners.

Part of the problem is hiring itself: If you want people to work together well, you'd better involve the team in choosing candidates. In slack periods, that's no problem. But when a company is growing, who has time? Then too, traditional companies need look only for the requisite technical expertise and work habits, whereas teams need skills such as the ability to handle confrontations. "We ask applicants, 'If you had a problem with someone, how would you deal with it?'" reports Ernie Gauna, an electromechanical assembler with a process team called Catch the Wave. Some candidates handle such questions poorly. Others decide they don't really want to work for a company that poses them.

But getting people in the door is a picnic compared with bringing them up to speed.

It isn't that teams don't want new members. It's that they have more immediate things on their minds — like output, for which they, not some supervisor, are held accountable. And since a production line is only as fast as its slowest member, they know output will suffer during a training period. "I feel sorry for new people," says Teri Mantooth, who operates the wave-solder machine. "Your first instinct is, Oh, no, we've got a new person and we're going to get throttled; we're not going to make our numbers."

The payoff, of course, is that once new people "bond" with the team, they're part of an intense social group. Turnover at XEL is low and loyalty strong, particularly among veterans like Gauna and Mantooth. But getting there hasn't been half the fun. XEL tried staffing up with temporaries, hoping to avoid or at least postpone the difficulties of bonding. That backfired: the full-timers treated temps worse than they did regular newcomers and showed them the door at the first sign of a foul-up. The company also tried a training team designed especially for new hires. But trainees "freaked out" — Mantooth's words — when they graduated to a regular, faster team.

More recently, Julie Rich introduced another experiment: a formal buddy system, which pairs new hires with veterans. She's optimistic, but the final verdict isn't in yet.

Supervisors Are Missed — But Not for Reasons You'd Expect.

Ultimately, a traditional supervisor's explicit tasks — even hiring — will be taken on by teams. Once that happens, the frontline manager's input won't be missed. But supervisors have an implicit job as well, namely, keeping a lid on the messy underside of human relations.

Think about it. Everyday spats and skirmishes, the kind that arise in every group, don't fester long in conventional plants because a boss steps in to discipline or separate the warring parties. At XEL there's rarely a boss in sight, so disputes can snowball. "If one team is fighting, other teams will eat on it," says Mantooth. "You know, like, Guess what so-and-so said?"

XEL has evolved an informal way of dealing with such problems: get them off the floor and get them resolved, face-to-face. A team's scheduler (who often acts as a de facto leader) or a seasoned worker will jump in, ask the disputants into the conference room, and try to mediate. Not that it's easy. For example, Mantooth cites the time two women on her team harbored grudges toward each other for weeks, and nothing she did seemed to help. When disputes rumble on, it's painful. Most important, production suffers.

Because of that vulnerability, every team member at XEL seems acutely aware of the importance of individual personalities, of people's ability to work smoothly as a team. If traditional management is like football — with everyone in a position, doing exactly what the playbook specifies — then team-based management is like basketball. One or two uncooperative teammates can lose the game for the whole group.

Team Building Doesn't Go Neatly from One Stage to the Next.

To Puckett, that was the most surprising realization. "The books all say you start in this state of chaos and march through these various stages, and end up in this state of ultimate self-direction, where everything is going just great," he smiles, a little wanly. "They never tell you it can go back in the other direction, sometimes as quickly."

At XEL the fastest backslider in recent memory was the stockroom team. To all appearances, it was working well enough. Then cracks began appearing in its facade.

One day, for example, Scott Tirone, a team facilitator, was working in a nearby area when he heard a dispute break out in the stockroom. An employee had come in 20 minutes late, unexcused, and was arguing vehemently with the team's attendance-taker that she shouldn't be given an "occurrence" on the board, as company policy required. "She had a pen in her hand and was actually going to go change it," Tirone remembers. He intervened. Puckett then began hearing complaints about the stockroom. Arguments were frequent. The stockroom's customers (the other teams) felt they weren't being well served. Soon Puckett discovered something worse: a few people in the group were cheating on their time cards and covering up for one another.

The result: Team-based management in the stockroom came to an abrupt halt. Puckett fired the abusers. He installed Tirone as stockroom supervisor, with full disciplinary authority. "My main purpose in going over to the stockroom was to do some housecleaning," says Tirone.

But his purpose now, he adds, is to work himself out of a job by retraining people in how to collaborate as a team. His model? The Red Team, which a couple of years ago was mired in discontent almost as deeply as the stockroom's and was given a facilitator to oversee its operation. That move annoyed the group — which, however, decided that the way to get rid of its facilitator was to return to efficient functioning.

"I think we just stepped up and started doing more of what we were supposed to be doing, instead of having one person controlling what was going on," says Fred Arent, a Red Team member. Today the team is one of XEL's most productive.

Managers Need Skills No M.B.A. Program Will Ever Teach Them.

One is assessing each team's "maturity," as everyone at XEL calls it, and establishing the boundaries of self-management accordingly. Teams doing well get less managerial oversight; teams doing poorly get more. "We may have to say, You guys don't have the authority to determine your own overtime, because you're misusing it, and here are the indicators," says Puckett.

But there are at least three other skills, all delicate, that Puckett has had to learn — and which he's now teaching his two lieutenants, each of whom oversees the operation of several teams. Call them diplomacy, monkey managing, and innovation triage.

Diplomacy refers to the job of managing relations among teams. It can be as simple as encouraging one team to lend a few workers to another or as difficult as untangling an interteam dispute.

Untangling is ticklish because managers seldom have firsthand knowledge of what happened. Not long ago, for example, Mantooth in the wave-solder room accused the Silver Team of trying to bypass the company's strict *kanban* production-control system. Silver appealed to lieutenant number one and got an answer favoring the team in the wave-solder room. Silver then appealed to Puckett, who overruled his lieutenant. The team in the wave-solder room retaliated by complaining to lieutenant number two, who — Puckett notwithstanding — took its side against the Silver team. The dispute wasn't resolved until all three managers, like United Nations negotiators, sat down with people from both teams.

Monkey managing, as Puckett puts it, is the fine art of not allowing someone else's monkey, or problem, to jump onto your back.

One team can't find anybody to be its scheduler. Another team can't get enough volunteers to work nights. A manager's problem? Not at XEL. "You need to make them responsible for solving the problem," says Puckett, "because as soon as you say, OK, I'll do something about that, they no longer have any responsibility at all." That, of course, turns the conventional managerial mind-set upside down: bosses usually figure it's their job to take on other people's monkeys. But so long as a problem stays within a team — and so long as the team has the resources it needs to solve it — an XEL manager learns to stay away.

Innovation triage may be the trickiest of all, because it ties directly into a key strength — and a key weakness — of team-based management.

The strength is just what CEO Sanko was seeking when he instituted teams: a lot of people thinking actively about matters such as quality and cost. The Red Team's Arent, for example, noticed that one model of board didn't need certain pieces called for in the engineering diagram. Rather than hollering for Puckett, he went directly to the engineer involved and got the specification changed.

And the weakness? Not to put too fine a point on it, but teams may assume they know more than they do. One team, says Puckett, identified a parts problem on a particular board and worked with engineering to get the part replaced. So far so good. Then the team noticed a similar problem on another board and made the same change without consulting anybody. Soon those boards were coming back to the factory: they had failed in the field.

A manager's job: Encourage and reward good ideas and innovations, but make sure teams don't take too much into their own hands.

Employees, Too, Need Skills They Never Had Before.

Some of those new skills are obvious. You can't chart defect trend levels unless you know some basic mathematics and statistical process control. You can't take an active part in meetings unless you speak conversational English.

Recognizing an acute need for training in such subjects, XEL set up in-house classes taught by its own employees and designed an extensive adult education program in conjunction with nearby Community College of Aurora. Some 60 of the 80 employees then in the shop took at least one class, in subjects ranging from English and math to stress management and cost accounting. The program attracted national attention. "America's best hope for maintaining its status as an economic powerhouse may reside in quiet efforts like those under way at XEL," the *Denver Post* editorialized.

The other skill employees need is less obvious but no less important. Call it assertiveness or ambition or simply an expansive attitude toward work life. Whatever the term, it's the opposite of the conventional employees' mentality. Traditional workers specialize; XEL's must learn a variety of skills and be willing to perform many tasks. Traditional workers do as they're told; XEL's have to set their own priorities.

Some employees, says Puckett, just want to hole up in a corner and do one task quietly. "The interesting thing is, that's no longer a possibility. You can't give people that option anymore in this environment."

Standard Systems for Managing People Go Out the Window.

Compensation and performance reviews, in particular, have challenged XEL's creativity.

Most companies have plenty of leeway in treating pay issues. Not companies with teams. "I don't think you can have effective team-based management with a traditional compensation system focused on individual performance," says Puckett. Workers can't be looking to shine on their own, he says. They have to be thinking of the good of the team. And the compensation system must encourage them to do so.

XEL's system is still evolving, but right now it walks on three legs.

Leg one: skill-based pay, an hourly wage determined by the number of skills a worker has mastered. Take a course in advanced soldering, say, and do some on-the-job training — then demonstrate to your team that you're now an accomplished advanced solderer. That will ratchet your hourly wage up a dollar. The logic: successful teams require members who can perform a variety of tasks.

Leg two: merit increases, based on a combination of team performance and peer reviews. What better measure of effectiveness than your team's numbers? And who can judge your contribution better than the other members?

Leg three: profit sharing, paid in cash every quarter, varying with the company's performance and each worker's quarterly earnings. Teams can be only as successful as the company is successful.

The system has its detractors. Gauna, for one, argues that merit increases aren't fair, because they depend too much on which team an employee is assigned to, and the employee has no control over it. And profit sharing (like all profit sharing) is disillusioning when the company has a weak quarter. The answer? Human resources vice president Rich isn't sure; she wants to experiment with a gain-sharing plan.

The performance review system has evolved over time as well. "We didn't figure this one out until it was time to do reviews," says Puckett. "Julie walked out and put a stack of them on my desk, and I had no supervisors to give them to." Puckett himself couldn't do them, because he wasn't close enough to individual workers. The reviews had to be done by team members themselves.

At first the company asked for narratives on each person, much like those they'd get from a supervisor. No go: workers had neither the time nor the skills to provide so much information. But an employee task force designed a check-box style of review, in which people rate one another on matters such as efficiency, meeting team goals, and punctuality.

Personality conflicts sometimes intrude. But they intrude on conventional supervisor-employee reviews too.

A Leader Doesn't Need to be a Supervisor.

Every team needs some kind of leader — someone to run meetings, make sure everyone's on track, and maintain liaison with management. Trouble is, employees who are appointed leaders may suddenly turn into straw bosses, issuing orders and solving problems. XEL has grappled hard with that issue and now uses three designations:

Supervisors have the same authority as at any company: to tell workers what to do and to discipline them as required. XEL assigns a supervisor to a team only when the team has somehow violated a trust or failed in its most basic endeavors. The supervisors' fundamental task is to work themselves out of a job.

Facilitators are responsible for ensuring a team's smooth functioning. They have low-level disciplinary authority. Teams may be assigned a facilitator — who earns more than production workers — if they're having trouble making their numbers. Having a facilitator has helped XEL's Blue Team, says team member Richard Zwetzig: "When there's a problem like a parts shortage, you've got somebody who can attend to it right there, and the rest of the team members can keep going. They don't have to come to a screeching halt."

Schedulers are no more than first among equals, responsible for running meetings and attending weekly production sessions. Unlike supervisors, they're expected to work regular jobs on the production line, and until recently they got no extra pay. (Now scheduling is considered a skill in XEL's skill-based-pay program.) Most teams at XEL have no facilitator, only a scheduler, which makes them truly self-managing. And who picks the various leaders? XEL's managers choose supervisors and facilitators when needed; teams choose their own schedulers. But because scheduling is a difficult task, the teams often have trouble finding volunteers.

Teams Alter Everyone's Awareness of What's Going On.

Think back to the vision statement crafted by Sanko and the others: "We will be an organization where each of us is a self-manager." Teams help turn that brave declaration into reality.

Eventually, the new reality seeps into the farthest reaches of people's consciousness. "People learn more and more that they can rely on themselves," says Zwetzig. "Some of the new hires, it blows their minds when they come in. Most people are used to these structured deals, where you do your little piece and you send it on, and you don't care what happens to it after that. Here you're involved in the whole picture. You have the mind-set that says, OK, this is the flow, and this is what we have to do to accomplish that."

As Arent puts it, XEL's employees learn to "make some decisions that normal people can't make." To watch Arent's team at work is to see how far that learning has progressed. In the course of one hour-long meeting, the group conducts delicate vacation negotiations, discusses deployment for the rest of the week, clarifies who's responsible for each part of tomorrow's quarterly presentation to management, and explores possible reasons for a high rework number.

People who assume so much responsibility in one area can't be treated like conventional employees in another. To its credit, XEL realized that from the beginning and has bent over backward to involve employees in the company in a variety of other ways as well. Task forces, staffed by volunteers, are convened to design innovations such as the training program. Climate surveys, conducted by an independent third party, help uncover potential sources of dissatisfaction. Regular quarterly meetings, with full financials, allow Sanko to walk everyone through the company's business performance.

Even now, after so many years, one senses that Sanko and Puckett, at least, are still getting used to this culture of responsibility and to the fact that they, as managers, must give up a measure of control.

"Bill asks me a lot of questions," muses Puckett, "and the answer is often, 'I don't know.' He expects me to know. And in a traditional environment I should know. But I don't. And I have the same problem. I ask a question, and it's, 'I don't know.' That's something you have to learn to accept: your people that are in leadership roles don't have all the answers, because a lot is delegated well down into the organization."

Sanko feels the same lack of knowledge and the doubt that accompanies it. He sees a car leaving the factory at 2:30, an hour before the shift ends, and wonders who it is. He sees an employee talking on the telephone (each team has its own phone) and wonders what they're talking about. Or he sees a big overtime expense. "As an old manager, you say to yourself, Who approved this? Then you realize nobody approved it in advance. It was approved after it was done. You want to ask if that overtime expense was really necessary. But then you have to bite your tongue and say, Well, let's look at it at the end of the month. Were the deliveries made on time? What were the margins? As a manager, you have to move away from what's being done at this instant."

Puckett adds firmly, "That was one of my difficult transitions. I always had a 'book' I could manage by, and I knew everything about everything. I don't have that anymore. Giving up that control — that's one of the most difficult things people from a traditional management environment have to do." ◼

The Annual One-Page Company Game Plan

Elyria Foundry was losing $3 million a year on revenues of $4 million when Gregg Foster took a deep breath and purchased it, 11 years ago. "We were a totally reactive company. We were defensive, commercially, just begging for work and taking anything we could," Foster recalls. But once the company got back on track, he says, "it made sense to start committing ourselves to goals."

Over the past six years goal-setting has emerged as a key component in the continuing regeneration of the Elyria, Ohio, producer of large-scale metal castings. Each year, management presents the entire company with a list of goals that will shape the next 12 months for everyone there.

Foster introduced written goals after he'd initiated difficult changes, including 18 months of going eyeball-to-eyeball with the union, which eventually voted to decertify itself from Elyria. As his initiatives began paying off, Foster resolved to inform the workforce. The company was doing well, and he wanted everyone involved in its continuing success. At companywide meetings he outlined the staff's achievements: increasing revenues and profits, a new bonus pool, new customers, and improvements in attendance and scrap reduction.

"I started the goals as an excuse to measure our performance for the annual meeting," says Foster, "and that's still why we do it. I wanted to be able to put up on the overhead projector a list that would light competitive fires."

The challenge was to devise a document that was meaningful, not trite or — just

Every December, Gregg Foster of Elyria Foundry incorporates ideas from company employees and posts a list of goals to guide and motivate its workforce for the next 12 months.

as bad — naïvely wishful. "The problem with strategic plans," says Foster, "is that they're usually so ethereal that they don't make sense." Still, the first time he tried to come up with a game plan, he made a common mistake — he developed the agenda completely on his own. "This was 1987. There weren't that many goals, but we didn't hit any of them." His managers were quick to point out his mistake. "They told me, Well, you wrote these by yourself. Why don't you ask us for ideas?"

So the following year the five managers (of sales, finance, production, administration, and engineering) each submitted five to 10 goals, which Foster synthesized into a single list. That was the beginning of an annual practice that has endured. In November the managers consider the suggestions they've gathered from their departments, and at December's annual meeting of all 310 employees, Foster grades the previous year's performance, goal by goal, and explains what the company will be shooting for in the next year. Each year's targets cover a broad range of issues — from 401(k) retirement-program participation to applying for ISO 9000 certification (a quality standard required to do business with certain European customers).

In 1992, *Inc.* named Foster the Turnaround Entrepreneur of the Year. By 1993, Elyria had become a profitable $29-million venture, and 1994 sales are expected to hit $35 million. "Goals have given us something to dig our teeth into," Foster says. "They're specific, but they also create a picture of how we want to be."

3 ▽ GOOD FORMS

Gregg Foster details the rationale of effective goal setting:

Put the most critical goal up front.
We surveyed our customers, and the number one reason they did business with Elyria Foundry was delivery. As we looked at 1992, 100% on-time delivery was at the top of our list, too, and we hit 73% overall and 90% or better for our top accounts. The numbers were off target in part because customers ordered items that their computers told them they needed four weeks earlier—which makes our delivery automatically late. We almost never make mistakes, but our delivery performance is never going to be 100% as long as we measure ourselves against that standard. In 1993, we tracked delivery by two dates: the customer's request date and, for our own information, the date we delivered product given our lead time.

Include important specifics, even if they affect only a few people.
These were goals in 1992, too, and we made some changes then. We hired a new receptionist and put in a second switchboard. It had been embarrassing; people would call and ask, "Doesn't anyone work there? "Our stated goal had been to answer all calls on the first ring, but the new receptionist pointed out that if we aimed for no more than two rings, she could put one caller on hold politely and get on to the next. You wouldn't think that a set of business goals could be influenced by a newly hired receptionist, but that's what those goals are for.

Repeat goals of ongoing importance.
Attendance is such a big issue. We always need to talk about how much money it saves us, how much better the company is because we have people who are here every day. Same thing with participation in the 401(k). We have a higher participation by far than even the bank that manages our fund, and that allows us to have a very steep matching program. Those items fall under "advertising." Our company has some extraordinary traits, and we don't want to de-emphasize them by taking them off the list. To have 99% attendance and 99% participation in the 401(k) is unbelievable in our industry.

As for being debt free, we aren't debt free today. We go through periods when we need to borrow money for taxes or whatever, but we hover around zero. By keeping that on our list we give people confidence that we're not on the edge. Many people who work here have peers who have suffered missed payrolls or seen layoffs. We are assuring them that Elyria is a financially responsible company that wants to be here forever.

Let the language and presentation stay simple.
We try to make sure we never get so sophisticated or so cool that people don't know where we're going. We're not that intellectual about this business. I know I'm not. I have to work on really understandable levels, or I get all screwed up about what I should be doing. And we're all above suspicion if everyone understands what's going on.

Amplify goals that were attained last year.

We had talked for three or four years about starting an education program, and once we got it on this list, in 1991, it was hard to hide from it. We started an adult education program, and two years later there were 65 people enrolled in our own school here on-site. In 1992, we aimed to decrease illiteracy by 50%, and we did. So a year later we expanded the program and opened it up to employees' spouses.

1993 Business Goals

Customer Service
- 100% on-time delivery
- Take every customer cal
- 50 employees visit customers
- All calls answered on 2nd ring

People
- 99% attendance
- 99% participation in 401K
- Improved & expanded education program
- 4 all — company meetings
  (2nd Tuesday March, June, Sept. & annual meeting)
- Continuous reduction in personal injuries

Quality
- 50 % reduction in personal injuries
- ISO 9000 certification by June 1994

Financial
- Debt-free
- Record profits & bonus for Elyria foundry 10th year

Facility
- Build small casting capabilities
- Start 2nd cell (1/3 of #3 production in cell format)
- Sand reclamation to maximum output
- Rebuild #1 sand system & mold line & complete major flask & bolster improvement program
- Update charging system in melt shop

Elyria Foundry 1992-1993

Let the list cover a broad range of ambitions.

We do list goals that seem unrelated, because reaching them will make us a better company. Many people say it isn't a compre-hensive list, and why is "Take every customer call" on the same list as "ISO certification"? Well, those are both serious, fixable concerns for us, and we can measure our progress as we work on them. I didn't know if we should even call these business goals: they're specific, ongoing improvements at all levels of the company, and at year's end we can reconcile them. It's not brilliant, but it works.

• Use the goal-setting discipline to set fiscal priorities.

Capital projects here are done on a pay-as-you-go plan. We won't take on debt to do them. We use cash flow. When a project is next in line, and we have the resources, it gets done. So everyone's always vying for the top spot.

We continually review and analyze the potential payback of the projects on people's wish lists. This is the most intense process in our goal setting. It's like playing a rugby game. In the end we have a plan to guide us. If somebody wants us to head in a different direction, I just say if you want to call a meeting and have everyone reprioritize things, if you want to go to battle over this one little project, go ahead. The list may change, but not without our consciously thinking it through. It keeps us on track. ■

The Motivational Employee-Satisfaction Questionnaire

3

In the beginning, in 1984, Wild Oats Market founders Libby Cook, Michael Gilliland, and Randy Clapp stocked the shelves and rang up sales of their tiny grocery store. The shop was fruitful and multiplied, and by 1988 the owners had stopped managing the stores and started managing a company. But they were losing touch with the store floors.

The original shop, in Boulder, Colo., bred six more across three states by 1988. Store managers were reporting all the right numbers to the home office, but back at the cash registers, employees were getting slipshod training and late performance reviews. "In our business we need to keep our staff happy because they're the first line of defense when customers come into the store," says Cook. But it was almost impossible to gauge store morale after the owners stopped working side by side with produce clerks and shelf stockers. So three years ago the owners organized a way to get the feedback they no longer picked up informally at the cash registers.

Gilliland and his management team developed a survey that reflects the company's offbeat attitude. The questionnaire asks each employee to rate morale and job satisfaction. Ten questions call for a number grade, ranging from "awful" to "wonderful," or "remarkably bad" to "terrific." The language, says Gilliland, keeps the survey from being dry and encourages the playful atmosphere the company promotes. The numerical ratings yield the "Happiness Index," which shows whether store morale is "giddy or suicidal." Wild Oats surveys the entire staff twice each year. Until recently participation was optional, and less than half the staff responded. Last year 90% of the employees participated.

The employee survey the Wild Oats staff completes twice a year is designed to generate enthusiasm.

——

The results are computerized and compiled into lists grouped by store. All three owners read the statistical overview and the individual responses. "It can bum managers out," says Gilliland. "If there are 30 great comments and five negative ones, they'll fixate on the negative." So he acts as a screen, removing nonproductive negative comments from each store's summary. And instead of mailing the information to store managers, Gilliland sits down with them individually to discuss the results.

Every round of surveys brings a surprise, says Gilliland. Not long ago he was astonished to see the worst complaints from the store with the best working conditions and the most benefits. Frustrated employees indicated that although the manager was well liked, he was behind on their reviews and had failed to fire a particularly unproductive employee. "We'd assumed it would be the happiest store, but it wasn't," says Cook.

Employees use the surveys to tell the owners what they'd like changed: Dissatisfied with health coverage, they asked for more varied benefits. Based on requests, Gilliland and Cook now set aside $200 per employee as a yearly wellness allowance, to cover such uninsured expenses as acupuncture and health club membership. And this year, Wild Oats added stock options to the benefits. In response to complaints about training and late reviews, raises are now retroactive to the scheduled review date.

Since Wild Oats started conducting the surveys, turnover has steadily declined. Each round brings in about 20 ideas and keeps the brass in touch. A footnote to all of this is the company's steady growth; by 1995 Wild Oats expects to have 16 stores.

▽3 GOOD FORMS

MICHAEL GILLILAND EXPLAINS HOW THE SYSTEM KEEPS OWNERS IN TOUCH

1 I'm looking for an overall mood. Some employees circle a very high grade, and then rag on you on 20 different points. Maybe they haven't thought their responses through very thoroughly.

2 Even now that we've added the wellness benefit, health insurance is still an issue we hear about. Because of the response to this question, this year we're going to increase the company's contribution from 50% to 94% for employees with at least one year's service. In response to recent surveys, in June 1994, a 401(k) plan was also added.

3 We used to ask, "What do you think about your pay?" but, of course, the response was always bad. The new phrasing helps us make adjustments based on employee feedback comparing our pay with industry averages.

4 Since we started this, the number one complaint was that reviews weren't done on time, so we've made raises retroactive. And people want their managers to spend some time with them on reviews, instead of just grabbing them in the aisle and saying, "You're doing OK." So in the past six months we've hired three full-time training and review people. As the need increases, we'll be hiring more.

5 If the person is happy (#1) but reports low store morale, it could be that the store is understaffed. Some of our managers get overzealous in cutting costs for the profit-sharing program.

WILD OATS STAFF SURVEY

This survey has been created so that you can anonymously relate your experiences as a staff member of Wild Oats. We will be using the numerical portion to come up with a store "Happiness Index," which will tell us if morale is giddy or suicidal. This feedback will help us create a better working environment for everyone. Please do your best to complete this survey in an honest and open manner and with as much detail and explanation as possible.

Please rate your responses by circling the number that most closely describes your experience. Feel free to use the back of these sheets for additional comments.

1. How happy are you with your job overall?

Not happy at all ——————————————Ecstatic
1 2 3 4 5 6 7 ⑧ 9 10
Any comments or suggestions? *Allow alternative work schedules for salaried workers, like a 4 day work week with 10-hour shifts.*

2. How do you feel about your benefits at Wild Oats?

Terrible ————————————————Great
1 2 3 4 5 6 7 8 9 10
Any comments or suggestions? *Love the profit sharing–real incentive! How about more "carrots" to keep people more long term – retirement benefit?*

3. How do you feel about the pay levels at Wild Oats as compared to similar employers?

Worse than most ——————————Better than most
1 2 3 4 5 6 ⑦ 8 9 10
Any comments or suggestions? *Not having such a low ceiling for hourly workers.*

4. How do you feel about the employee-review system at Wild Oats?

Hate it ——————————————————Love it
1 2 3 ④ 5 6 7 8 9 10
Any comments or suggestions? *Need retroactive pay when managers are late getting reviews done!*

5. How is the overall morale in your store?

Awful ——————————————————Wonderful
1 2 3 4 5 6 ⑦ 8 9 10
Any comments or suggestions?

6. How do you feel about the responsibilities of your job?

Too little ——————————————————Too much
1 2 3 4 5 ⑥ 7 8 9 10
Any comments or suggestions?

8 In our large stores, responsibility is decentralized, and a department manager can have more effect on an employee than a store manager might. We can learn a lot, especially if the employee answers question #11.

9 On one survey a respondent answered, "Greed." Another wrote, "To meet women." This is a mood indicator — I want to see that I've created a fun place to come to. If everyone answers, "To get a paycheck," I'll know there's a problem.

10 This is the first section I go to, because I want to make sure we're being competitive. I want people to be happier at Wild Oats than at other places they've worked, and most have worked at other grocery stores.

12 I'm most interested in new people's impressions and their fresh look at the company. I figure the people who've been here for years are probably pretty much satisfied.

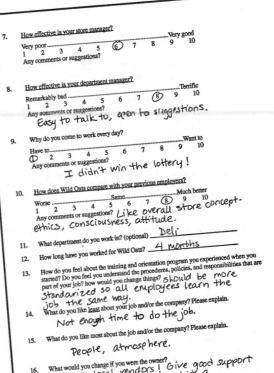

7. How effective is your store manager?
Very poor .... Very good
1 2 3 4 5 ⑥ 7 8 9 10
Any comments or suggestions?

8. How effective is your department manager?
Remarkably bad .... Terrific
1 2 3 4 5 6 7 ⑧ 9 10
Any comments or suggestions?
Easy to talk to, open to suggestions.

9. Why do you come to work every day?
Have to .... Want to
① 2 3 4 5 6 7 8 9 10
Any comments or suggestions?
I didn't win the lottery!

10. How does Wild Oats compare with your previous employers?
Worse .... Same .... Much better
1 2 3 4 5 6 7 ⑧ 9 10
Any comments or suggestions? Like overall store concept-
ethics, consciousness, attitude.

11. What department do you work in? (optional) ___Deli___

12. How long have you worked for Wild Oats? ___4 months___

13. How do you feel about the training and orientation program you experienced when you started? Do you feel you understand the procedures, policies, and responsibilities that are part of your job? how would you change things? Should be more standarized so all employees learn the job the same way.

14. What do you like least about your job and/or the company? Please explain.
Not enough time to do the job.

15. What do you like most about the job and/or the company? Please explain.
People, atmosphere.

16. What would you change if you were the owner? Use more local vendors! Give good support to general managers. maybe hire a few good people from competition who know → over

16 I like to see two pages of suggestions. I'm looking for thoughtful responses and a keen eye for retail—half a dozen suggestions says this person really has a future with Wild Oats, and this kind of person usually volunteers his or her name on the survey. I don't mind seeing criticism, either. ∎

Notes

_____

_____

_____

_____

_____

_____

_____

_____

_____

_____

_____

_____

_____

_____

_____

_____

_____

_____

_____

_____

_____

_____

_____

_____

_____

_____

Training Your Team

Accent on
Opportunity

Opportunity means a fair chance to learn, to get promoted, to receive a raise, or to earn a bonus. But most employees think of opportunity first as something less tangible: They perceive it as a force that influences their attitudes and performance on the job. They speak of a climate in which their work gets noticed, in which they will be appreciated and encouraged to grow.

Performance management and training are two halves of a whole. Together, they nurture both individual and organizational growth. But many managers approach performance appraisals and training programs with misgivings: The former are perceived as bleak occasions for negative criticism; the latter are viewed as luxuries — either expensive or superfluous.

The articles in this chapter show you how to maximize performance management, to use it as a springboard for learning and growth. They outline specific ways to focus on practical needs and real objectives. They also explain why total quality management (TQM), which emphasizes the importance of a knowledgeable, cohesive workforce, works especially well in smaller organizations. You'll learn how to produce enormous successes while avoiding enormous headaches. One company shares its system for engaging managers in setting and meeting annual goals. Another invites you to take a look at the simple but effective tool it has devised to measure job satisfaction — one that has also given employees a direct opportunity to identify problems and suggest workable solutions. ■

The ABCs of Performance Management

Investing in your employees means knowing their strengths and capacities — and helping individuals to grow in skill and understanding.

—

by DeAnne Rosenberg, C.S.P.

Ask a well-trained, treasured employee why he or she left a so-called good job, and then listen. You are very likely to hear something like this: "Nobody ever told me how I was doing. I never got any really good feedback from my boss. Who appreciated what I did? Who even noticed!"

One of the best kept secrets to employee retention is giving good performance feedback. People need to know how they are doing. And the only way they know is if someone tells them and tells them often. Performance evaluation is a measure of management's interest in their work and a measure of how they are valued. A failure to manage performance evaluation can damage more than retention; it can wound morale and inhibit productivity.

At the very least, negligence in providing such feedback might be considered unfair to employees; in a worst-case scenario, it can create serious legal problems. Consider that as today's organizations flatten

DeAnne Rosenberg is president of DeAnne Rosenberg Inc., in Lexington, Mass.

their structures, attempting to run lean and mean, employees whose value is questioned stand on a precipice. Without a record of consistent attempts at improvement — based on honest feedback — such people often become virtually unemployable. Following is an example of the legal costs of not giving such feedback.

An employee with 23 years of experience was let go by an organization that was trimming its nonproductive staff. Because he had 22 years of performance appraisals that indicated he was doing "standard" work, he did not understand why he was being terminated for "failure to perform." The references from that former employer were such that he could not land another position. So he sued his former employer. A cursory investigation proved that he had been performing below standard for a very long time. Each manager, however, had been eager to get rid of him, so to ensure his attractiveness for transfer to some other unsuspecting manager, the man had been given "standard" performance ratings. In front of the judge, he stated that by not telling him of his shortcomings, his bosses had given him no opportunity to change his behavior. The judge agreed, and the man won his case. His former employer was forced to reinstate him with full back pay and provide additional financial damages to compensate him for "hardship and mental stress."

Individual Performance Is Difficult to Compare

In most organizations today, and especially in new or rapidly growing entrepreneurial ventures, cookie-cutter assembly line procedures are rare. Individual initiatives and creative solutions count most. It is the person who shapes the work. For example, take two programmers who work on similar products for similar end users. Each approaches the assignment differently — their individual education and experience nudge them in different directions. If both of their solutions look good, there is really very little basis for comparison.

In instances like this, an employee has no formal yardstick against which to measure his or her own performance. True, there are the virtues of on-time attendance, cooperation, positive attitude, and projects completed on time, but standards for these are often entirely subjective. High-quality work, doing it right the first time, and customer satisfaction should be easier to gauge. But suppose the customer would be delighted with anything or is unimpressed with even the exceptional. A manager can make a huge motivational difference by providing the employee with a reliable yardstick through a good performance feedback system.

The fact that one person's work may not be comparable with another's represents a monumental judgment problem for those in leadership roles. Unfortunately, many entrepreneurs react by dispensing with performance evaluations altogether.

Coaching: Performance Feedback without Criticism

Performance feedback is not a synonym for criticism. It can be delivered without demoralizing the employee or breeding defensiveness. Effective, positive performance feedback is actually coaching. It can take place formally in a prearranged setting such as a sales call or a scheduled conference, or informally as a direct response to on-the-job behavior.

Many sales organizations use performance feedback as a formal part of the employee's training. Typically, the sales manager accompanies a new salesperson on a call. The customer is told that the manager is there only to observe and, indeed, the entire exchange takes place between only the customer and the new salesperson. Immediately after the visit, the sales manager and the salesperson discuss what happened.

MGR: Well, how do you think it went?

SP: I think it went great. Did you notice how I got things rolling and how I redirected their attention and pressed on for closure?

MGR: Yes, you did a fine job of presenting our product. In fact, your opening was just about the best I've heard. But, you know, they didn't buy. How do you account for that?

SP: Those guys were nervous — or maybe plain stupid.

MGR: Well, yes, they were pretty unsophisticated about our product, but what could you have done to fix that?

SP: Perhaps I might have tried to find out more about the tricky issues

they're facing. I think there were a few places where I could have
shown them how our product could help to fix things.

MGR: Great! What else did you notice about your interactions with
them?

SP: They certainly did not like our prices.

MGR: Right! How do you know that?

SP: Body language, I guess. When I mentioned costs, the head guy
crossed his arms and leaned way back in his chair. He glared at me
over his spectacles.

MGR: Right! So, what could you have done to avoid such a strong negative reaction?

SP: Benefits first, right? I should have covered benefits before price.
Maybe I could have made him see how valuable our product
would be to their business — no matter what the price.

MGR: Yes! So on our next call, what will you do differently?

SP: I'll ask a lot more questions — get at the issues the customer is facing. And when I think I have a clear picture of how our product
might help, I'll discuss the benefits before talking about price.

MGR: Super!

Not all situations, of course, enable such immediate feedback. In a
workday crisis, an employee may have to act alone and because of having
only limited information, may act incorrectly. Possibly the manager learns
about the employee's behavior days later or from a third party. If the
manager then corners the employee with an angry lecture, the employee
may think, "What do you know? You weren't there. And if you had been,
you would have done the same thing." Net result: no change in behavior; nothing has been learned.

If, however, the manager is willing to be a coach, the outcome can
be different.

MGR: I hear that Acme gave you a real hard time about our last delivery
being late. What happened?

EMP: You don't have any idea of the kind of abuse I was receiving on that telephone. You people don't pay me enough to listen to that stuff!

MGR: I'm not saying you weren't justified in telling them off. Many people are really vicious on the phone. But, look, Acme is an important customer and we were late. If the same thing were to occur again, how would you handle it?

EMP: As soon as I realize I'm losing control, I'll turn the call over to someone else.

The Right Question at the Right Time

Growth in insight and understanding results from adeptly handled performance evaluation, whether given at a scheduled meeting or in response to on-the-job circumstances. A manager must demonstrate a willingness to listen and to pay serious attention to an employee's observations and opinions. Certain questions facilitate this process, helping to steer clear of the sandtraps of negativity and rationalizing. The questions here have been categorized, but you may want to adapt the lists and the questions to match your own purposes.

Questions Relating to the Employee's Job
- What are all the things you do on your job?
- Which do you think are the most important?
- Which take most of your time?
- What are the standards by which your performance is judged?
- How well do you think you are meeting those standards?
- What would make your job easier?
- What do you like about the job (do *not* want changed)?
- What would you like to see changed? How?

Questions Relating to Performance Improvement
- What specific changes in your job would improve your effectiveness? Why?
- In what areas of your current job do you need more experience or training?
- How could that experience or training be accomplished?

- What have you done in the past year to prepare yourself for more responsibility?
- What do you think are the most important issues facing us in the coming year?
- How well prepared are you to handle those issues?
- What do you expect to be doing in five years?
- What are you doing to prepare yourself for those challenges?

Questions Relating to Deficient Performance

- What specifically was the performance agreement you made?
- How important is that agreement?
- What occurred that prevented you from doing as you had promised?
- What kinds of problems did that create for [me, the department, others]?
- Even though other issues get in the way, what can you do to ensure that you meet the agreed-on expectations for your performance?

Questions Relating to Specific Situations

- What happened?
- And then what happened?
- What do you think you should do now?
- How will that help solve the problem?
- If the same set of circumstances were to arise again, how would you handle it?
- Why would you handle it differently?
- What kinds of problems might that approach create for you?

Questions That Promote Self-Evaluation

- What are your greatest strengths on this job?
- Where do you feel you need some additional training/ development/etc.?
- Have you been taking steps to increase your ability/ knowledge/skill on the job?

- How do you evaluate your effectiveness?
- How do you think I evaluate your effectiveness?

The Power of Self-Evaluation

The kind of performance feedback that is the most motivational of all is that which allows people to appraise themselves. Consider the classic case of the lights at the Hawthorn Works of Western Electric in 1927 (Elton Mayo, *The Human Problem of an Industrial Civilization,* Viking, 1933). Originally, it was thought that remarkable increases in productivity occurred at Hawthorn because by receiving special recognition the employees were made to feel important. More recently, however, Charles CoonRadt (*The Game of Work,* Shadow Mountain Press, 1985) and other theorists revisited that study and determined that the productivity increases occurred because the employees were informed daily of their production levels. This feedback made it possible for them to measure today's successes against the yardstick of yesterday's achievement.

Similarly, the winningest coach in college football was "Bear" Bryant. When questioned about how he motivated his players, Bryant claimed that he simply said lots of supportive things ("I know you can do it; I have faith in you") and supplied some good game philosophy ("Quitters never win; winners never quit"). But the truth was that on his practice field there were video cameras every ten feet; after a practice session, every player watched a videotape of his own performance and evaluated for himself how he was doing.

Similarly, many organizations have systems that encourage employees to evaluate themselves. It works this way: Before their scheduled conference, both the employee and the supervisor complete the same performance appraisal form. Then, using the forms as a platform for discussion, the two discuss performance objectives and results. One finding from this approach is intriguing: Employees often evaluate themselves far more critically than their bosses do. Consequently, the employees often have a far better grasp of their need for additional education, training, or development in order to gain proficiency.

Turning the Tables: Employee Evaluating the Supervisor

The American Productivity & Quality Center, in Houston, Tex., reported that 78% of alleged performance problems were not the fault of the employee. They were the result of either how the job was designed or the management systems that were in place. The systems created situations that made it almost impossible to do the job right.

To get at such problems, it is productive to ask employees to evaluate their supervisors. For example, most organizations today are committed to customer service. Analogously, a manager provides a "leadership service" for employees. Therefore, logically, it is the employees who should evaluate the quality of that service, and it makes sense to have a good mechanism in place to enable them to do so.

Questions such as the following produce worthwhile information for the manager (and a good manager is willing to hear it):

- Do I do anything that makes your job harder?
- What can I do to make it easier?
- What is your understanding of my expectations for your performance?
- How can I help you achieve your full potential?
- What should I be doing to help prepare you for your next promotional opportunity?

Seven Key Purposes of Performance Appraisal

Effective performance appraisal 1) ensures that the best will rise, 2) provides your employees with feedback for development, 3) creates documentation showing that personnel actions (like termination) are legally defensible, 4) connects performance results and compensation, 5) excites enthusiasm and motivate employees to higher levels of performance, 6) solves problems that prevent optimum productivity, and 7) clarifies expectations regarding employee performance and managerial support.

No organization can afford to overlook any opportunity to accomplish these purposes. ■

WHAT COULD YOU BE DOING WRONG?

Six roadblocks to effective performance management

1. The employee is unclear regarding the manager's expectations for employee performance—and so is the manager. Both need a yardstick to evaluate performance. That yardstick must provide clear and consistent standards that answer the question, How will I know it when I see it? (See worksheet, next page.)

2. The manager is unaware of how the employee spends time. Some employees are remarkably effective. The manager assigns additional tasks knowing they'll be handled masterfully, then gives them no further thought. How can you evaluate work of which you are no longer aware? Also, technical professionals often work on technology so advanced that some managers cannot understand it. How can you give feedback on work that you do not understand? The unspoken rule in such cases seems to be: find something to criticize because, after all, isn't that the purpose of performance feedback? So the manager rates the employee satisfactory and carps a bit — the employee lacks a sense of humor, keeps a messy work area, or takes too long for lunch breaks.

3. Discussions about performance do not occur often enough to stay attuned to changes in the work environment. Performance discussions should occur about four times a year: Once to set performance objectives for the coming 12 months and discuss compensation for the past 12 months' work, three times to discuss progress on objectives and resolve any issues that may be getting in the way.

4. Although the connection between compensation and performance is clear in the employee's mind, management's systems obscure that connection. Many organizations persist in using easy-to-administer bureaucratic systems that stifle motivation; lip service is given to "pay for performance" but all employees are given identical raises on the same date no matter

what their performance level. The relationship between compensation and performance can be strengthened by setting up a game plan for each individual and sharing it with the employee at the time the performance objectives are determined (see "Game Plan," next page). That way a percentage pay increase given for performance improvement would have to be reearned every year.

New compensation systems can be designed to reinforce this idea. In some organizations, quarterly bonuses (awarded after discussion of results in the previous quarter) now take the place of salary increases. To keep pace with the marketplace, salary surveys are done every two years, and pay for "standard performance" is always at market level.

5. Many irrelevant considerations get mixed up with the performance evaluation. The result is that ratings do not honestly reflect the actual situation. A manager evaluates all staff members as marginal or unsatisfactory and worries, "Maybe I'll be judged a poor manager. Better give some a better rating than they deserve." Or a manager honestly rates every staff member superior and then worries none will feel any need to improve. And so even though all may really be superior, some get lower ratings. Similarly, sometimes conferring a superior rating on a brand-new employee doesn't feel right, so the employee is rated satisfactory.

6. Criticism is a problem for both giver and receiver. Because to many managers the word *criticism* means only negative feedback, they avoid a performance appraisal on a valued employee. When an employee is doing marginal work, some managers think, "If I criticize, it may get worse, and I might not be able to live with that." The employee then gets a satisfactory rating and is never confronted with the poor performance. ■

PERFORMANCE MANAGEMENT WORKSHEET

Key Responsibilities	Performance Objectives (quality, quantity, time, cost, conditions)	Method of Measurement (How will I know it when I see it?)	Meets Exceeds Fails

GAME PLAN: RELATING PAY TO PERFORMANCE

PAY	PERFORMANCE LEVELS	
20% Increase 15% Increase 10% Increase 5% Increase	Performance exceeds expectations	Knowing of the possibility of a large pay increase for outstanding results boosts motivation
2% Increase	Performance meets expectations	This is market level; it has nothing to do with productivity.
No Increase	Performance below expectations	Why give an increase to someone for just doing the job?

The Dual–Purpose Sales Supervisor's Checklist

Carol Gleason has seen it many times. People who are good at their job get promoted to supervisory or management positions. All too often, however, they have no idea how to do their new job, and no one tells them, and either they fail (cease to be treasured employees) or they flail. "Supervisors and managers think all the other supervisors and managers know what to do," says Gleason, director of training and development at Delstar Group, a 21-store retailer based in Phoenix.

The Delstar Group knows that problem well. The company, which has twice won awards in the Arizona Entrepreneur of the Year program, is growing rapidly and has a steady need for new supervisors. But, like any retailer, it hires lots of entry-level employees. For those employees who get promoted, managing people is often a brand-new experience.

For most of her first 20 years in business, Delstar founder Pam Del Duca or her managers trained new supervisors informally. But when the company grew substantially during the late 1980s, Del Duca hired Gleason, an experienced trainer.

Today Gleason trains all new Delstar salespeople. She also has designed a class, which meets for three months and teaches management basics to new supervisors.

Much of what Gleason has to say is about communication: listening and giving specific praise and clear direction. She likes to cite surveys, dating from the 1940s to the present, that compare what supervisors think workers want from their jobs with what workers say they want.

Year after year, managers get it wrong. They say employees are motivated by money; meanwhile, employees report that the intangibles, such as appreciation and feeling in on things, do the trick. "For 45 years workers have been saying, 'Pay attention to me, love me, give me something interesting to do, and I will produce,' " Gleason argues. "And for the past 45 years managers have been saying, 'We don't have the money.' "

So Gleason's first task is to get new supervisors to praise their employees regularly for specific achievements. To do that, she gives her students on-the-job "homework." The first assignment requires each supervisor to pick an average salesperson and think of something that person does well, even if it's only being on time or folding the T-shirts neatly. Then the supervisor calls the employee aside for a private discussion.

Instinctively, the employee expects the worst. As a result, the supervisor's formal praise, thanks, and expressions of confidence have more impact. Once supervisors see the effect praise has on employee attitudes, Gleason says, they use it regularly. "It's an eye-opener for our supervisors," she says. "We've had associates break down and start crying during the meetings because nobody has said anything nice about them for so long."

Once supervisors have gotten used to praising employees, Gleason moves on to the next step: helping employees achieve performance goals. To make inexperienced supervisors comfortable with the process, Gleason created a checklist for reviewing goals with an employee (see next page).

The Delstar Group has developed a one-page review sheet to ensure that sales personnel get the guidance they need and to help supervisors learn how to give it.

⊽**4** GOOD FORMS

Carol Gleason explains how the performance-goals checklist works:

1 I ask supervisors to write all this down because I want to remind them that they're being measured. They need to know this exercise isn't something they can put off and do at the last minute. This is homework that helps their development, and I want them to take it seriously. Asking them to write down the details reinforces that message.

2 One of the skills I'm trying to teach supervisors is how to read people. Any little thing I can do to get them to think about how the other person feels helps. That's understanding people, which is good management — and good selling, too!

3 Performance goals motivate people; they like to achieve things. All of our people sell toward sales goals; you'd be amazed how many retail stores don't do that. And when you take an associate aside formally to talk about the reasons for the sales goal, that person is both learning more about the company and feeling a lot more important.

4 One of the things I see lacking in management is follow-up. Setting up a time to review associates' performance toward the goal is crucial; without that, associates will feel as if nobody cares how they do. In the end, management is simple: all you need to do is tell people what to do and see that they do it. But what most managers do is tell people what to do — and then go away. They go eat lunch. They go eat tuna salad. They don't need more tuna salad. What they need is to give more discipline and to provide more follow-up.

5 I want the supervisor to take notes as the associate is talking. The minute you start writing down what another person is saying, you make that person feel important and more committed. If your boss started writing down the things you were saying, wouldn't you make sure you got them completed?

6 As a supervisor, you know how to achieve the goals, because you're more experienced. But I want associates to be able to think about ways to achieve goals. I tell supervisors, "Ask people what ideas they have to achieve the goals. And I don't care how far out you think the ideas they come up with are; I want you to say, 'That sounds like a great idea.' Then you can add your suggestions for other things they might try." But if I, the associate, come up with my own suggestion, I am that much more likely to make things happen. If I tell my supervisor I think I can sell more T-shirts by displaying them over here, then, by golly, I am going to make sure I sell more T-shirts. Being asked also makes associates feel important. And indeed, some of the ideas they come up with are wonderful.

ACHIEVING PERFORMANCE GOALS

NAME: _CINDY SMITH_ DATE: _MAY 1_

PREPARATION SECTION:

Associate's Name: _DENNIS JONES_

Date of Discussion: _MAY 5_

What do you expect the Associate's reaction to be? _FEARFUL_

APPLICATION RECAP:

Did you follow the suggested formula:

	YES	NO
- Give the Associate an overview of the project goal and explain the rationale behind it.	✓	
- Mutually decide on and write down the Associate's goals that will contribute to the achievement of the project goal.	✓	
- Discuss the steps to be taken to achieve the Associate's goals.	✓	
- Indicate your confidence in the Associate's ability to achieve the goals.	✓	
- Set up a review session.	✓	

Did the Associate identify any steps to achieve the goal? _YES ① PUT CACTUS PENCIL DISPLAY AT THE CHECK-OUT DESK. ② SUGGEST PENCIL OR PEN TO EVERY CUSTOMER_

What was the Associate's reaction to the discussion? _ASSOCIATE WAS CONCERNED ABOUT MAKING THE GOAL, KEEPING TRACK OF PROGRESS._

Would you do anything differently? _YES I'D TAKE MORE TIME TO IDENTIFY MORE STEPS TO ACHIEVE THE GOAL._

Were you able to use Empathic listening? _YES RECOGNIZED HIS ANXIETY AND SUGGESTED WE MEET REGULARLY TO TRACK HIS PROGRESS._

---

7 What I have to do in a lot of my classes is teach people how to listen. In retail, people are very talky, but they're not always good listeners. Empathic listening is a technique I stress in class, and I have put this question on the form as a reminder to supervisors to practice it. In empathic listening you try to sense what the other person is feeling. You don't have to agree with it, just understand it. Basically, you try to paraphrase what the person said, playing it back but adding some type of feeling word that describes how you think the person feels. It can be as simple as, "Sounds as if you're afraid you won't make the goal, Sally." Empathic listening makes other people feel important and understood. ∎

Ground-Zero Training

Who says small companies don't train employees? The hot ones always have. And in today's economic environment, even the CEOs of young and resource-scarce companies are discovering the payoffs.

—

Five or 10 years ago, with a few rare exceptions, most executives of small companies would have told you formal training was a luxury they couldn't afford. It's true that some of the small ventures that have gone on to become stars in the entrepreneurial firmament invested heavily in training. But as a rule, big companies had training programs, and small companies either hired already-trained workers or let their employees learn on the job. Times have changed.

Today, more and more, smart small companies are recognizing that investing wisely in training early on pays off in growth and financial success. Many are starting their own training programs. For example, researchers at the Southport Institute for Policy Analysis, in Washington, D.C., in 1991 studied just one type of training in small companies: basic-skills programs they dubbed "workplace education." The researchers found a dramatic increase in the number of small companies that started such programs during the previous three years. It is still a new trend: the institute reported that only 3% to 5% of all small companies have workplace education programs, but an additional 20% want to start them.

Among the factors accounting for that change in attitude is increased interest in self-directed work teams and total quality management (TQM), both of which emphasize employee decision making. (See "The Realities of Team-Based Managment," p. 77, and "TQM: Balancing People and Processes," p. 133). Even companies without such programs find that today's fast-changing, information-overloaded markets favor the company whose entire work force can solve problems and make good decisions. (Also, see "The Annual One-Page Company Game Plan," p. 89).

Most CEOs start training programs not merely because they seem like a timely, good idea, but also because training meets a real-world, concrete need. For some of those who were early starters, that need was a dramatic one — like survival. For instance, Mike Plumley realized in the early 1980s that if his family's $30-million Paris, Tenn., rubber company, which supplies the automotive industry, didn't improve the quality of its products, it couldn't stay in business. So he decided to begin a modest training program, which has since become a broad-based effort. As quality improved, Plumley prospered, and today the business reports sales of $91 million. "Training employees was not something we decided to do out of the generosity of our hearts," Plumley says. "It was something we needed to do to survive."

In other cases, the need for training is more subtle. Like most company owners, Ray Tom wants to find good employees who will grow with his business. But in Tom's case there's a big challenge: many of the jobs at his company, the Print & Copy Factory, in San Francisco, consist of operating copy machines — nobody's idea of a glamorous career. So Tom has developed a comprehensive training program for machine operators. They go through the program at their own pace and move along a career path that can lead to jobs in either management or copy-machine maintenance. Today, Tom says, about 70% of his managers are people who started in entry-level jobs at the company.

In some cases, CEOs decide training is the only way their company can gain the competitive advantage they want. At Cooperative Home Care Associates, a $5-million home-health-care company in the Bronx,

N.Y., president Rick Surpin knows his company's sole product is the service its home health aides provide. To Surpin, that means the company should invest as much in training as it can afford. Similarly, the Tattered Cover Book Store, in Denver, wants to be known for friendly customer service. So the company puts all new employees through two weeks of training that includes topics such as body language and the best phrasing to use in answering customers' typical questions.

In the end, then, all CEOs who swear by training have the same bottom line: They train because they've decided they must in order to build the companies they want.

In a world of increasingly fierce global competition, a world where many other countries have a better-trained workforce, this is a lesson more entrepreneurs will be learning. Bill Nothdurft, author of *SchoolWorks,* a book comparing the school-to-work transition in a number of countries, tells a story that sums up the attitude of overseas competitors. Nothdurft interviewed the CEO of a tiny German company ("It really was not more than just a corner garage") and was astonished to discover the substantial investment the owner had made in employee training. When Nothdurft pressed him for the reason, the German appeared confused. "He just sort of looked at me and blinked a couple of times and said, 'Well, what would the alternative be?' " It's a good question.

When big companies offer training programs, they may lavish millions on everything from interactive computer education to specially equipped training facilities. But when small-company CEOs give training, they need to know how to leverage their resources. Following are the questions most frequently asked by the leaders of small companies who want to set up training programs — and the answers smart CEOs have discovered.

1. *My business doesn't have the time or the money for a conventional in-house training program. How else can I train?*

- **Formalize the buddy system.** Everybody knows the way training gets done in most small companies: an experienced hand shows a more recent hire new skills. The only trouble is that in a busy small business, it's always tempting to put off that kind of informal training until a less harried time — which all too often never comes. The Print & Copy Factory avoids that problem by providing employees with checklists that detail specific skills that need to be promoted, and managers must check off the skills as they are learned by workers. Since many of the skills — such as operating a wide variety of copy machines — can be learned only from others, the system helps ensure that informal training occurs regularly.

- **Use books.** As a CEO, you have unique leverage. If you recommend and give a book to your employees, chances are good that many will at least try to read it. There's probably no less expensive way to get started on an employee-education program, especially on a broad theme like quality improvement. For example, at Pro Fasteners and Components, founder Steve Braccini launched the company's quality program in 1989 by giving a paperback copy of Philip Crosby's *Quality without Tears* to everyone in his workforce, which at that time numbered 30. (Today the company employs almost 100 people.) The company, a distributor of industrial hardware based in San Jose, Calif., then followed up with two months of weekly discussion groups to review the book. After all that, Braccini guesses, as many as a quarter of his employees never read *Quality without Tears*. But he doesn't mind. Through the discussion groups, even people who didn't do the reading became familiar with Crosby's basic concepts about quality. That gave everyone in the company some common language and ideas. "The reason we were able to galvanize around that book is that it was simple," Braccini says. "Everybody could understand it."

    The Print & Copy Factory also uses books and tapes to provide some of its training on an ongoing basis. The company keeps a lending library of books, tapes, and videos that cover topics ranging from selling to self-improvement. To ensure that employees really use the material they check out, the Print & Copy Factory has developed a simple form that asks employees to describe very briefly what they learned.

- **Try outside seminars and classes.** Let's face it: not everyone's a reader. Plumley spent a frustrating two years just trying to convey to his managers all the new ideas about continuous improvement of company operations that he was reading about. "I talked till I was blue in the face," he recalls. "I really wasn't getting anywhere." Plumley got much better results when he sent Larry Moore, who was director of education, to a two-day seminar on continuous improvement. Moore then designed a short class on the subject and taught all Plumley employees.

  If you send employees to external seminars, require accountability. To maximize your investment, those attending need to spread the information learned — whether through an informal presentation to other staff members or through a more structured procedure.

  In 1989 Ken Plough, CEO of Plough Electric Supply, a San Francisco electrical distributor, knew his company needed to understand total quality management because customers were demanding it. He also knew Texas A&M University had an industrial distribution program that offered a 40-hour course on quality for distribution executives. So Plough and his managers attended — a big investment for a company that at the time had 27 employees. To make the investment pay off, the managers used the material they had learned to design an informal in-house quality course for all employees. Since then, Plough says, the increase in his company's profits has far exceeded the training costs.

- **Have employees give presentations.** Sometimes you don't even have to go outside your company for seminars — especially if you have a group of professionals on staff with similar skills and interests. That's what the president and director of research, Paul Silvis, has found at Restek Corp., a regional *Inc.* Entrepreneur of the Year winner that manufactures gas-chromatography products in Bellefonte, Pa. Silvis believes that a good way to keep his scientists learning is to make staff presentations a part of many of their monthly staff meetings. It's a cheap and effective way to spread knowledge within the company, and it also helps Silvis spot chemists who have a knack for presentations. Such chemists often end up giving the company's customer-education seminars.

- **Join forces with other companies.** There are times when the need for the outside training of a whole group of employees is undeniable, but that doesn't always mean your company has to foot the bill alone. Consider the experience of Unitech Composites Inc. in Hayden Lake, Idaho, which manufactures composite components, primarily for the aircraft industry. Like most fast-growing small companies, Unitech had lots of managers and supervisors who were new at their jobs and needed training in management skills. The company was interested in a management-training curriculum produced by Zenger-Miller, but the price was steep for a small company. At a Unitech board meeting, a member who was the CEO of another local company said he, too, had some managers who needed training. Soon after, the two companies joined forces with a nearby community college and another local organization to split four ways the cost of purchasing the training program.

- **Build a career track.** Like Unitech, many small companies that become interested in training keep adding new components to their training programs. Over the long term, that approach can lead to an integrated training program that grows with the company. This has become clear at the Print & Copy Factory. Ray Tom, who founded the company in 1976, says he started training as soon as he began hiring people. Now the company reports $8.4 million in sales and has 180 employees — as well as a highly organized training program.

  In most companies, operating a copy machine is a dead-end job. But at the Print & Copy Factory, Tom has over the years organized five grade levels of machine operators, which require skills in areas like copy-machine maintenance and offer gradually increasing pay. Upon joining the company, new employees are informed of the different levels and given a checklist detailing the skills required to move up, along with a list of all the training sessions available in the company. Some training is required, but much is optional. Most classes are scheduled as needed; if even only one employee needs to learn a skill, it is taught one-on-one. The company has made videos that subsequent employees can watch to learn a number of subjects.

When employees are ready, they can take various skills tests, which include a combination of answering written questions and performing on-the-job tasks, to move up a level. The result? Since much of the training is sought by motivated employees, rather than forced on all workers, the Print & Copy Factory minimizes wasted resources. The company is so happy with its career track for machine operators that it is now creating similar programs for other areas of the company, such as administration and customer service.

2. *I want to start an in-house training program, but I'm a business person, not an educator. How do I teach? What should the classes be like?*

- **Keep it useful. If you're not sure what employees want to know, ask.** The first time the Plumley Cos. taught a short course in rubber technology, the company used a curriculum developed by a university. It bombed. Steve Cherry, Plumley's manager of technical services, remembers looking out at the blank faces of the company's production workers as he drew carbon molecules on the board. "They kind of sat there thinking, 'That's nice, and when do I get out of here?'" he recalls. "It just went over their heads." Cherry quickly found out his coworkers needed specific, practical information about the things that affected their jobs. Today he starts the rubber-technology course by asking employees to write down what they want to know about the products they make, and then he organizes his classes around the most commonly asked questions.

- **Keep it hands on, active, and lively.** Most of the entry-level employees at Cooperative Home Care have an eighth-grade reading level or lower, according to Surpin. "Most of them hated school," he says. "The worst kind of training to give the folks we work with is to sit them in classrooms and make them listen to lectures, but that's what some firms do." Cooperative Home Care tries to cover most topics in its preemployment training through hands-on demonstrations accompanied by an explanation. Employees are often asked to discuss a real-life situation, such as how to deal with a difficult patient. They then break into small groups to come up with solutions.

- **Make general ideas practical by using examples from your company.** Moore has been teaching continuous-improvement techniques to all workers at the Plumley Cos. That could be a general subject, but not in Moore's class. To emphasize how the theory of continuous improvement is related to the Plumley Cos., Moore shows a brief videotape he has made of some process in the plant. After watching the video, employees form groups. Then each group must come up with four suggestions for improving the process they watched. In general, Moore is a big fan of using homemade videos to make his points. "If you're in education and training and you don't have a camcorder, you're missing the boat," he says. Moore, like his counterparts at the Print & Copy Factory, has begun videotaping training sessions. He sends the tapes to out-of-state Plumley branches.

- **Give on-the-job assignments and tests.** At Delstar Group, a Phoenix, Ariz., specialty retailer, training director Carol Gleason spends a session in her classes for new supervisors discussing a series of management techniques for a specific situation, such as dealing with a subordinate who has a performance problem. As homework, the supervisors try out the techniques in their stores and then start the next class with a discussion of the results. That way, Gleason says, supervisors can begin learning not only from her but also from one another.

3. How do I make sure employees take the training seriously?

- **Do it yourself.** Nothing conveys the importance a company places on training more than the CEO's participation does. Be a trainer. For example, recognizing that she is the best person to present the company's history and philosophy, Joyce Meskis, owner of the Tattered Cover Book Store, which currently has 320 employees, conducts the first day of all training sessions for new employees. Or be a participant. Not only will your presence at a workshop or seminar underscore its importance, but your enthusiasm will spark everyone's interest. Moreover, the participants' interactions will tell you a great deal about your employees' ideas and attitudes.

- **Celebrate accomplishments.** Everyone wants recognition for hard work accomplished successfully. At Tabra Inc., a $4.4-million *Inc.* 500 company that makes jewelry in Novato, Calif., employees who completed the company's English as a Second Language training received a certificate, a rose, and lots of applause at a staff meeting. And when managers at the Plumley Cos. asked their employees who were taking high school equivalency classes what they wanted, besides a ceremony, to celebrate passing the exam, it turned out to be the little graduation-cap tassels that many of their high-school-graduate friends had hanging from their rearview mirrors. Ray Tom gives copy-machine operators pins for their uniforms that list their grade level. That way, employees are visibly recognized for their achievements and skills.

- **Treat training as an integral part of the job.** You can make training essential in many ways. At Delstar Group, employees in the company's stores know that as soon as they're promoted to supervisory positions, they must take a class to learn about their new job. At Unitech, which relies on more experienced employees to provide some on-the-job training, the company has a gain-sharing program that shares profits with employees as a group after productivity, quality, and safety goals have been met. Thus, its workers have strong incentive to train their new colleagues well, so their own bonuses won't be reduced.

- **Use rehearsals.** When Plough Electric was preparing its quality course, Ken Plough created a steering committee of managers. Each manager presented an outline of his or her section of the course to the committee for suggestions. Then, before teaching the class, each manager staged a dress rehearsal for the committee. That, Plough thinks, improved the experience for both the teachers and the taught.

1. Where can I find course material — or someone to design a course?

- **Big companies you work with.** If your company is a supplier to large companies, they can be an excellent source of training material, and it's usually in their interest to provide it at a reasonable cost or even for free. Unitech, for instance, borrowed an old blueprint-reading curriculum from customer Boeing, then added, deleted, and modified material to fit its own needs. Similarly, the company has found that manufacturers such as DuPont, which makes one of the materials Unitech uses extensively, are happy to send in technical staff to teach relevant sections of the company's training program.

- **For that matter, any company you work with.** Braccini has followed that approach. In addition to hiring consultants he knew to teach classes, he turned to business associates for their expertise in particular areas. Pro Fasteners' lawyer, for instance, taught a class that explained Occupational Safety and Health Act regulations to the company's employees. And when Braccini wanted his employees to learn more about the company's financial statements, his banker taught that class for free.

- **Trade associations.** Professional trade associations offer publications that are good resources for industry-specific in-house training. In a few cases, they may even have a detailed training curriculum customized for your industry. For example, the National Association of Printers and Lithographers (NAPL) in Teaneck, N.J., has developed an essential-skills program specifically for the printing industry. The employee workbooks ($20 for members, $30 for nonmembers; 800-642-6275) teach employees to solve problems that crop up in printing operations, such as converting the measurements on a job ticket from inches when using a European-made metric machine. Unfortunately, programs like NAPL's are still rare.

- **In-house expertise.** Is there anyone in the company who has received formal training in a particular area? When Silvis and his vice president decided to offer a management training course, they each culled material from their own reading as well as class notes from courses they had taken. With both their notes and their ideas, they were able to develop a curriculum they liked.

5. Is there any outside assistance available for in-house training?

- **Community colleges, local institutions, and local chapters of professional associations.** Often community colleges are the educational institutions best suited to provide affordable and practical training for small companies. In addition to regularly scheduled vocational classes, community colleges may be able to supply instructors and help develop a customized curriculum. In fact, Bill Reinhard, director of communications at the American Association of Community Colleges in Washington, D.C., claims he doesn't know of any community colleges that do *not* have training relationships with area businesses. One caveat: If your training is relatively brief or nonacademic, it may get short shrift at a community college. For example, Surpin tried using a community college to train home health aides, but found the college gave low priority to teaching a three-week hands-on class to a group without much formal education.

  Then, too, community colleges aren't the only local resources available. Expert freelance trainers, many of whom are entrepreneurs, can be found in your own backyard. Ask your customers and vendors to recommend such people. Inquire at nearby colleges and universities, as well as local chapters of training and professional associations. Many of the latter have directories listing local people who will work on-site, pay close attention to your needs, and stay within your budget.

- **State programs.** When Tabra needed to train its production employees in English as a second language, the company was able to get two grants from the state of California to cover the cost of an outside instructor for its intial training program. Human resources manager Joyce Shearer learned of the state program through the local literacy council, and she reports it was not complicated to obtain funding.

  The good news is that many states have some type of funding available for training; when the American Association for Training and Development (ASTD) last surveyed the states, in 1989, 46 were offering training funding or tax credit. The bad news is that state programs can be housed in one of many state departments, from education to economic development to labor. A good place to start looking is your state's economic development authority, because its mission is business assistance. Even if a training incentive is conducted by another department, the economic development staff may be able to direct you to it.

- **Federal programs.** You can expect increased emphasis on training under the Clinton Administration, even though a campaign proposal requiring that companies either spend 1.5% of payroll on training or pay the money into a government training fund has been dropped. According to Todd McCracken, legislative coordinator for National Small Business United in Washington, D.C., that's good news: "We won't have a worker-trainer tax. But a new worker-trainer program has been proposed. It will consolidate lots of existing programs and should be good for business." In the meantime, there is a federal program called the Job Training Partnership Act (JTPA). However, its subsidies narrowly target so-called economically disadvantaged employees, such as low-income people or displaced workers. If that description fits much of your employee population and you do a lot of training of new employees, it's worth looking into; for example, Unitech and Cooperative Home Care both use JTPA funds. You should also know that the JTPA mandates that employers say how they are going to perform the training. If your company has no formal training programs or training personnel, you will want to prepare some careful documentation, including job descriptions and training needs, before applying.

  Be warned, however: There are plenty of problems dealing with JTPA, and amendments Congress has passed may soon make it even tougher to work with. Surpin, who works directly with the program, describes the paperwork as "a bookkeeping nightmare," and the cash flow in reimbursement as "terrible." Unitech avoids that problem: It uses the Panhandle Area Council, a local economic development group that works with many of the area's unemployed, as a referral source for candidates for entry-level jobs. The council takes care of the JTPA eligibility requirements and paperwork; in addition, Unitech saves time interviewing, because the council screens out unlikely candidates.

6. Now I've got a lot of information, but where should I start?

Unfortunately, there's no one good answer to that question. The organization of training in this country is highly fragmented and the delivery highly inconsistent in quality. It could be that in your location, you have one of the best community colleges and the worst state training incentives around — or it could be the reverse. While academics and policy types are busy lamenting this confusion, as a small business you're pretty much on your own.

Many small companies make some false starts before they develop the training programs that work well for them. What matters more than where they start is that they take action — somewhere, anywhere. As they develop their training programs, the companies begin to understand their own needs better. They then switch providers or find better resources.

Tabra's training program, for example, started with private English-as-a-second-language (ESL) tutoring for two key production employees. But human resources manager Shearer wasn't satisfied with that approach, which was expensive. So she decided to take training from the local literacy council to become a tutor herself. Eventually, through the council, she found out about California's training funds, which enabled Tabra to offer full-fledged ESL classes. In the end, Shearer's experiences with private tutoring helped her design Tabra's ESL classes, for by that time she had already learned that the key to the program's effectiveness was to focus strictly on work-related English.

You don't need a lot of resources up front to launch a training program. Instead, it's more common to start small, as Tabra did, and expand gradually. What seems to happen is that as managers gain more experience with training and its results, their commitment begins to escalate.

Probably the most dramatic example of that phenomenon is the Plumley Cos. When Mike Plumley started out by hiring the local vocational school to teach his employees statistical process control, he had no idea his company would someday be offering in-house classes in everything from basic Japanese to rubber technology. But he found that the more he trained his people, the better his company did, and that was enough for him. It's a simple equation, really. As Plumley puts it: "The more we've been able to improve education, the better we've been able to manage our business." ■

The Double–Duty Sales Script

Mounting competition was threatening C. A. Short Co.'s primacy. In 1955 the company had started up as a pioneer in managing incentive award programs for employers eager to improve safety, attendance, or morale. But by 1989 CEO Charles Davis was feeling the presence of other players and pressure from the newly public company's stockholders, who clamored for growth. He figured that the fastest way to expand sales beyond states close to the Shelby, N.C., headquarters would be to bring in an army of sales reps.

But Davis worried about tracking customers as the then $1.3-million company grew. Accounts might disappear with departing reps, and few of the 130 new reps, mostly independents, had ever sold incentive programs.

Davis knew he'd have to systematize the selling process. Up to then, a sales rep called on a prospect and then tried to prepare a successful sales proposal, based on market trends, that would respond to the prospect's needs. After juggling some 2,000 stock items and incentive programs, the rep would still have to close the deal. And Davis had no mechanism to monitor sales calls.

To track performance, take the administrative burden off sales reps, and build account records, Davis developed a new selling process, with the one-page Incentive Needs Analysis (INA) as its cornerstone. The INA's questions lead reps through their initial contact with prospects, prompting them to ask about problems incentive programs might address, programs already in place, and budgetary outlines. Following their first call on potential customers, reps mail completed INAs to North Carolina where, within five days, the home office generates a sales proposal. Those proposals allow even the newest hires to steer their follow-up sales pitches in the right direction. "The INA frees the salesperson to sell," says Davis. "It cuts sales time in half." And, knowing how quickly the home office will have the proposals ready, reps can set up callback appointments during their first call.

It took some time before reps got a handle on the process. Reps were dutifully completing and forwarding INAs to headquarters, but instead of calling on their prospects to make the sale, they simply mailed them the proposals and waited. The challenge was to educate the sales force to use the INA only as a sales tool, especially for prospects unfamiliar with incentive programs. So Davis instituted frequent training sessions, "and I hammered them on their closing ratios," he says.

Once the kinks were ironed out, the INAs spurred C. A. Short to form more of a partnership with customers. As reps gathered information on companies' safety and attendance problems, they started offering solutions. That value-added approach has spawned more detailed INAs that help reps target opportunities. "The sales reps are expected to record additional comments at the end of the form, which are vital," explains Jim Barr, vice president of sales, "because without them we're just generating canned proposals. With them we can meet customer's specific objectives."

When sales grow from $1.3 million to $44 million in three years, it's crucial to have all your new salespeople moving in the right direction.

4 ▽ GOOD FORMS

Sales-Support Manager Jim Barr analyzes the INA:

1 If the rep goes in totally blank, with no idea what the customer's doing, this gives a general picture of which market segment to approach. Wellness programs are becoming more popular. When we see new trends, we certainly want to get a piece of the market. So we develop a new program.

2 Of course, if the prospect says no here, the rep should introduce what we have to offer. If the answer is yes, we find out why the program's successful. It's a classic sales approach: get potential customers to talk so we see where we fit in. Say a prospect has reduced accidents by 10%; we may think we can reduce them by 30%. But we have to be careful when we approach areas in which we feel a prospect is delinquent. We don't want to destroy the relationship we're building.

If the prospect has no sure response here, it could be we're not talking to the person with the answers. Very tactfully, the rep tries to get an appointment with the decision maker.

3 We get all kinds of responses here. If the prospect says the company doesn't have problems, we might suggest a maintenance program. But if the rep prods a little bit and continues to get that response, the best thing a salesperson can do is close the interview and leave. It's a pretty good sign that we're not going to get any cooperation out of that prospect.

4 If you ask the question just like this, you're asking for a no answer. With a prospect, you always want to have that assumed consent. You should say, "Let me show you some programs I think you'll be interested in."

5 This is a good lead-in to sell our service. For example, a lot of companies just give a cash award because it's a no-brainer, but here's the opportunity to explain the philosophy of the awards concept of ongoing recognition.

6 & 8 If we know how many are in the program and the budget per employee, we can come back with a very realistic proposal. Companies have budget limits, and our programs will meet them. We need this information in order to introduce our programs' cost-savings results.

7 More and more, we're getting into companies at which decisions are made by committee, especially in union-type situations. If that's the case, the rep ought to meet with the committee.

9 Some companies don't want the hassles of administering their incentive programs, others prefer to keep administration in-house. That information changes our approach. Some programs run more smoothly when we handle the administration.

10 This tells us how sophisticated and serious a company is about its incentive program. It changes our sales approach and helps us design the company's program. A good follow-up question to this would be, How often do you recognize your employees?

11 We ask about workers' compensation because most of our programs are safety oriented, and this helps us do an investment justification. But we don't always get the information. Lots of customers regard this number as confidential and don't even want to see it printed in a proposal. If that's the case, we wouldn't use the figure anywhere. We still regard those cases as prospects, and if we become too demanding, we're going to lose them.

C.A. SHORT COMPANY
THE AWARDS PEOPLE
incentive

Account Representative Name: Dave Stahl
Proposal For (Company Name:) Tulsa Widgets
Address: 555 Avenue A
City, State: Tulsa, Oklahoma
Contact: John Machado - President

INCENTIVE NEEDS ANALYSIS

Target Human Resources/Safety Coordinators

1. What type of Incentive Awards/Gift Programs are you currently using ?
   - ✓ SAFETY
   - ___ ATTENDANCE
   - ___ SALES INCENTIVES
   - ___ PRODUCTION
   - ___ RECRUITMENT
   - ___ BIRTHDAY
   - OTHER: Wellness
   - ___ HOLIDAY/BUSINESS GIFTS

2. Is your program successful ? If so, why ? Yes. Reduced accidents by 10% last year

3. What problem areas would you like to target ? Simplified administration. Individual Productivity

4. Would an incentive Program addressing several problem areas be of interest to you and your company ? Yes

5. What type of awards are used ? (For Example) Belt Buckles, Jackets, Merchandise: Cash. Gift Certificates

6. What is your Incentive Award/Gift budget per employee ? $130 (If not sure), what is your total Incentive Award/Gift budget for your company ? $11,000/year

7. Are your Incentive Programs designed and decided upon by plant, division or corporate ? Committee

8. How many employees are participating in the program ? 85

9. Do you currently handle the administration of your program in house or is it handled by an outside source ? In house

10. Do you recognize your employees:
    - ✓ By Individual
    - ___ Departmental
    - ✓ Team or Group
    - ___ Company Wide
    - ___ Other

11. What was your annual workers compensation premiums ? (If Human Resources does not know, check with Safety) $100,000 billed (Confidential)

The C.A. Short Company is a division of C.A. Short International

TQM: Balancing People and Processes

Total quality management can help you gain an advantage over your larger competitors and even improve company morale, but it takes wholehearted participation by everyone — especially the boss.

by Joan B. Pinck

Total Quality Management (TQM) is a concept, a strategy, and a system. It requires complete employee participation to achieve maximum business effectiveness, which TQM defines in terms of how well a business meets the needs of its customers.

Traditionally, the champions of total quality management have been large corporations. But smaller, entrepreneurial organizations are taking a close look at TQM. The passion and energy that typically mark their leaders, their organizational flexibility and informality — their very smallness — can give them a head start in implementing TQM.

Can TQM do for small and midsize companies what it has done for many of their larger competitors? Among the salutary claims made for it are that it has helped them to compete better, solve problems, energize their workforce, and increase employee self-esteem.

The good news is that many of the characteristics of small- to

Joan Pinck is vice president of the Juran Institute, in Wilton, Conn.

medium-size businesses make them especially well suited to achieve successful TQM initiatives. The less-good news is that TQM doesn't offer a quick fix; typically it takes at least two years to see results. And TQM doesn't come cheap. It requires companywide participation, a generous investment of costly time and resources, and a hefty dose of courage, patience, and determination.

TQM strategy rests on five principles:

1. It is led at the top of the company.
2. It is almost obsessively customer focused.
3. It emphasizes processes.
4. It is concerned with facts and uses measurements.
5. It utilizes workforce teams.

Leadership at the Top

TQM *must* begin at the top. The CEO must be the one who becomes educated first and best in TQM's principles and procedures. (Even with the most brilliant CEO, though, it won't happen in a day!) Then, as a mentor and team member, the CEO actively participates in educating those at the next level, who will in turn train others. As the knowledge and new approaches cascade through the organization, the CEO must continue to participate actively. The CEO's ongoing responsibility will be to set quality goals and to establish and *maintain* quality priorities. Also, undoubtedly, in the re-engineering of processes that accompany TQM, turf-protecting managers and supervisors — reluctant to accept change — will need to be won over.

Chances are good, however, that a strong leader's enthusiasm will be contagious. Entrepreneurial companies are driven by the vision of their founder and CEO, and because that driving energy is pervasive, employees are likely to share the same vision and buy into what it takes to accomplish it. TQM leaves many changes in its wake: new ways of thinking and new ways of doing. If presented by the leader as a means of attaining the company's defined mission, those changes are much more likely to gain support.

Smallness is also good because, unencumbered by a bureaucratic hierarchy through which ideas and actions, policies and processes must be cleared, the CEO is frequently in direct contact with the people who do the work. Typically, the CEO is familiar with, even knowledgeable about, the employees' work processes. If new processes are to be implemented — and as quality objectives get established, they inevitably will be — employees need to believe that the boss knows both why and how their jobs are changing. The person at the top needs to work continuously to make their belief a reality.

Customer Focus

Business history is strewn with the wreckage of companies large and small that thought they knew better than their customers what those customers wanted or needed. Successful TQM companies focus on the needs of their customers. All their customers. All the time. And they take a wide view of who their customers are.

External customers include the end user, of course, but they may also include wholesalers, retailers, and persons who buy the product for use in or with their own products. External customers may also include regulators, inspectors, and other outside parties to which a company is responsible, such as the community and the industry to which the business belongs. A long list!

Internal customers are part of the company. They are employees who, working in a process to deliver a product or service, depend on other employees in order to do their own job. All employees are customers of, for example, human resources, on which they depend for accurate paychecks and for processing the paperwork involved in their benefit plans.

TQM requires that all in an organization learn to identify the customers for the product or service they are working to produce. Each employee must understand that the first order of business is to determine the customers' needs.

A rapid or creative response to an external customer's needs takes flexibility — a nimble adaptation that many small and medium-size organizations are particularly good at. As for internal customers, the working culture of smaller companies tends to be informal and cohesive. People talk to each other. They know each other and they know what roles others play in accomplishing business objectives. It is easier for employees of a smaller company to be aware of the interdependence of supplier and customer than those of a larger organization, in which boundaries between functions and departments are harder to cross.

Focus on Processes

One of the strongest precepts of TQM is that "processes fail, *not* people." People often get trapped by the processes in which they play only one part.

Products and services are produced as a result of processes, which culminate in the delivery of those products or services to the internal or external customer. Each employee's work forms one part, or one event, in a process. Once employees perceive that they serve each other as suppliers and users, they learn what some of them already know or suspect — that the failure to deliver a high-quality product or service is more often than not caused by an inadequate system, or process, rather than by the individuals who are lockstepped in the process.

Historically, almost all quality control has relied on inspection to detect and identify errors and failures. All too often, the inspector pegs the problem to an employee — the "bad apple" in the production line or process. One or more people on the scene are blamed for errors rather than asked to use their judgment about why something has gone wrong.

TQM teaches that people closest to the problem, not an inspector or outsider, are most likely to know or be able to discover the cause of a failure — and to prescribe a remedy.

Facts and Measurements

A lot of the foregoing may sound like a simple shift in attitude, a quick fix. It's not.

When problems are embedded in a system, people often *think* they know the cause. They rely on hunches rather than facts; they go after symptoms rather than causes. TQM offers ways to avoid those common but dangerous pitfalls. It requires that employees be trained in a problem-solving methodology that relies on meticulous data collection, careful analysis, and constant measurement.

TQM's approach is both rigorous and systematic; it uses a handful of simple but reliable statistical tools to assist in the problem-solving process. For example, one TQM tool called the Pareto analysis (after Vilfredo Pareto, a 19th-century Italian economist whose work on the distribution of wealth revealed inequalities) enables priorities to be set by providing a way to quantify the size of a problem. An often-quoted example of a Pareto analysis is "20% of your problem will give you 80% of your grief."

Whether small or large, a company will think twice about the substantial investment in education and training that enables employees to understand and use TQM's tools and techniques. But one thing is certain: Employees recognize and appreciate that the boss is endorsing time off from normal work tasks so they may participate in training. Training sends two signals: One, that the leader is committed to the improvement process, and two, that he or she values the contribution workers can make in accomplishing significant improvements.

Work Teams

Work teams, even when not specifically identified as part of a TQM approach, reflect TQM's concepts and methodology. Members of the work team participate fully in all activities that enable the team to deliver the product or service for which it is responsible. Xerox Corp., Polaroid, and a host of the nation's other major corporations have instituted systems of work teams. And while no one has ever maintained the transition to work teams was easy, the concept is beginning to catch on in the small business environment. Here are two examples:

    • The *Wall Street Journal* spotlighted the success of one company — Published Image, a Boston-based publisher of shareholder newsletters for mutual fund companies. Eric Gersham, its founder and owner, started the company in 1988 with $5,000 in personal savings and watched it transform itself into a success story — generating $600,000 in sales by 1991. But, he says, the rapid growth had a high cost: diminished employee morale, reduced quality, and disintegrating customer relations. In fact, the company was losing a third of its clients each year.

Echoing a TQM principle, Gersham told the *WSJ* reporter: "We had a company whose employees believed their job was to please their boss instead of their customers. We needed to radically change the organization." In the spring and summer of 1993, he did just that, breaking his workforce of 26 into four largely autonomous, self-managed teams. Every member specializes in a skill, and all can perform any function needed to meet daily deadlines. The result? Employee turnover, which had been at 50% per year, virtually stopped. And the company is losing customers at a rate of less than 5% a year

It was not as easy as it might sound. Gersham first developed a 250-page document to guide the reorganization. He initiated the transformation with a day of celebrating "how we blew up the old company," designed a new reward system, and continues to work closely on a daily basis with the teams and their members. He notes, however, that their need for his input and oversight is rapidly decreasing

Because most processes involve people from various functions, it follows that the teams assigned to solve a problem are usually multi-functional. Thus a TQM company forms small teams of workers who have intimate knowledge of the process to be improved. Often, as was the case with Published Image's employees, team members can step in for one another. Team members train together and, significantly, are rewarded for team performance. Rewards systems, by the way, depend on performance and quality, not on numerical output. TQM forces management to buy into the concept that producing 200 perfect widgets is far better than producing 300 with a 40% defect rate. Our second example highlights these TQM concepts.

• The *Maine Times* tells the TQM saga of Moss Inc., a maker of tents with a prize-winning design and an $800 price tag. Moss, with its 55 employees, undertook its TQM transformation two years ago when a consultant told Cynthia Moss, the owner, that the company was "selling the best tents [in the world], but not making them."

Moss's quality inspectors were identifying defects in fully 25% of all tents. Production was high, but even with high production, high sales, and high prices, the costs of inspection and product defects, that is, the costs of poor quality, were eating up all the profits.

Cynthia Moss perceived that she would need a major transformation. She shelved the old production goal of 100 tents per day (assembled in the classic production line, with each employee repeating the same tasks a hundred times). Instead of a daily output of 100 tents (75 okay, 25 defective), her new target was a daily output of 40 (all perfect).

Moss also sectioned the workforce into teams, each team responsible for creating an entire tent. In addition, the workers on each team were cross-trained to perform each other's tasks. Workers were spared the mind-deadening repetition of the production line process. Coincidentally, they (and the company) were also spared work-related injuries resulting from repetitive motion.

The ability of team members to do each other's jobs also provides the company with a valuable safety net when workers are absent. Because the team is responsible for inspecting its own work at each stage of the process, employees are challenged to do what inspectors used to do; they appreciate the additional responsibility and find the work more satisfying. One employee says, "It's more challenging, but it's also more fulfilling. I feel we're more in control of what we produce."

To accomplish this, Moss and all her employees reexamined literally every part of the production process, asking themselves: Can we do this better? With less waste? With fewer steps? Every process was subjected to scrutiny from the machines to the patterns. The prevailing question was: Just because we have always done it this way, is this the best way to do it? In two years, production has increased 38%, largely as a result of cutting the costs of poor quality.

Moss doesn't say that this happened overnight, nor was it free. It took a major commitment of her time and a major commitment of her money for retooling, reorganizing, and retraining. "You have to give it your time, your money, and your energy. From senior design engineers to team leaders to stitchers, they have to be passionate about wanting this to work." She says the payback is "superb." ■

Notes

_____

_____

_____

_____

_____

_____

_____

_____

_____

_____

_____

_____

_____

_____

_____

_____

_____

_____

_____

_____

_____

Compensating Your Team

The Art and Science
of Compensation

Compensation was once a fairly simple you-get-what-you-pay-for-and-pay-for-what-you-get process. You paid more for employees with more skills or experience, offered promotions and bonuses for seniority or exceptional performance, and provided some fringe benefits for everyone.

Today, in most organizations, employee compensation typically represents one-third or more of total expenditures. The importance and complexity of managing this enormous investment have grown in tandem.

To attract and retain high-quality employees, compensation must be externally competitive; moreover, it must be perceived as internally consistent and equitable. A good compensation system also needs to be responsive to your current and long-term goals for profit and growth. Most important of all, it should motivate your employees to feel invested *and* rewarded in their jobs and their organization.

Although the worth of compensation cannot be entirely severed from the dollars invested, a large proportion of employees do not know the value of the benefits those dollars provide. By enabling your employees to participate in goal-setting for themselves and the firm, by educating them about the true cost of benefits, and by allowing them to choose those they most need and want, you can maximize your investment in compensation.

Paying People:
The Art of
Getting It Right

*By applying a few well-chosen principles
when setting base and variable pay, you can
make your compensation more effective
and make your employees more satisfied
with what they are earning.*

—

by Eddie C. Smith

Consider the following scenario: The president of XYZ says to the vice president,

> *"Barb, I've been going over next year's budget and it looks pretty good. The one big question I have is about compensation. I hadn't realized until now, but the compensation we pay our employees represents about 35% of our total expenses. That's a lot!*
>
> *A few percentage points up or down makes a big difference to our bottom line — as much as 20% to 30%. Are you sure our pay scales are set correctly? What are you using for guidelines?"*

At this point, the VP begins to duck and weave verbally, hoping to convince the president that the numbers are what they should be. But is the VP sure? No. Is the company's compensation program effective? Probably not

Eddie Smith is president of Management Compensation Services, in Scottsdale, Ariz.

Like many small and midsized companies, XYZ's compensation programs are a mishmash of concepts derived from "the way we did it where I used to work," some ideas picked up at an industry seminar, and the system a compensation consultant put in ten years ago. Even if your compensation system is not totally wrong — after all, it works to the extent that your company can hire and retain enough people to get the job done — ask yourself the following questions:

- Is the compensation system effective?
- Do the pay programs deliver internally equitable and externally competitive remuneration?
- Are employees rewarded for performance?
- Does the total labor cost fit the company's financial plan? Does it permit profit optimization while providing adequate investment capital?
- Are the employees reasonably satisfied with their pay?

When evaluating your own compensation programs, you'll certainly want to be able to supply a confident 'yes' in answer to these questions.

Setting Base Pay

Except for full-commission sales jobs, and perhaps a couple of others, most compensation in the United States is delivered via base pay: an amount of money typically established once a year and delivered to the employee at regular intervals such as weekly, biweekly, or monthly. Over time, an individual's base pay typically changes at a rate very close to inflation and is viewed by most companies as a fixed or semifixed cost. An effective base pay system provides a salary or wage that is *externally competitive* with the labor market and *internally equitable* within the organization.

Most companies want to make sure they are paying close to what other employers pay for similar jobs and skills. The easiest way to see how your company measures up is to compare jobs at your company with similar jobs at other companies in the industry (called benchmarking). Data on competitive pay in the marketplace are widely available through surveys (public or private) as well as anecdotally — although it is important to consider the source (often employees or search firms) of that anecdotal evidence.

If employees have other opportunities to boost their pay, the *total* cash compensation amount is what's important, not just base pay. For instance, when gain sharing, team base pay, incentive bonuses, and the like are in place, a company may deliberately set base pay below the market average. This is done in order to encourage workers to strive to increase their compensation level. Similarly, the absence of these plans may require an above-average base wage in order to achieve a competitive total cash package.

In addition to being market competitive, jobs must be internally equitable, that is, paid fairly when compared with other positions in the same company. When you have market data available, as with benchmark jobs, the process is very straightforward. You need only decide if your job is more or less valuable than the average and then adjust the target pay accordingly.

However, many jobs — often most of them — cannot be matched in the marketplace because different managers organize work in different ways. Still, these jobs need to be paid appropriately according to their relative value to the company. Determining relative value is usually accomplished by matching, or slotting, unique jobs against similar benchmark positions within the company to calculate an appropriate base salary. Many companies use a formal job evaluation process that measures skills on a quantitative level for this step. Others simply make a judgment call to determine which jobs are more valuable than others.

Once the estimated compensation value (commonly called the midpoint) is determined, salary ranges are developed. Traditional ranges have provided an earnings opportunity from about 80% to 120% of the midpoint. Today, however, there is growing use of much wider ranges (called broadbands), which allow greater flexibility in setting compensation. In both approaches, new or inexperienced employees on a job are paid about 80% to 90% of midpoint, or market. As they gain experience and their performance improves, their pay moves to 90% to 110% of market. The pay range beyond 110% of market is usually reserved for outstanding performers.

Introducing Variable Pay

Variable pay is a catchall term that refers to a portion of the compensation plan that varies with results. It could be based on the performance of an individual (bonuses), team (team-based pay), or group (gain sharing, group incentives). (By this definition, commissions and profit-sharing plans would also be variable pay, but they are usually treated as separate concepts.)

In the late 1980s and early '90s, managers learned a hard lesson about designing pay programs on a totally fixed-cost basis (all base pay): When business declines, cost-cutting measures force a reduction in the number of employees or in their pay — two extremely unattractive options. Variable pay — or results-sharing — as an alternative to 100% base salary, has been growing steadily ever since. Currently, 68% of companies have some form of results sharing plan in effect, up from 51% in 1991.

Successful variable pay programs have the following characteristics:

- Individual employees must be able to have a significant impact on results. Only then can you establish a true link between pay and performance. (Because cash profit-sharing also varies with results, no single individual can significantly influence the outcome.)

    Well-designed variable pay plans are very effective ways to increase employee earnings and, simultaneously, to raise productivity — a win-win situation. In addition, such plans enable compensation cost to flex with revenues (up to a point) and possibly even reduce the number of new people needed to reach the next revenue plateau by increasing output per employee.

- The employee must know what results are expected and be given continuous feedback on performance. Employees can't tell what steps are necessary for improvement if they don't know what to do and how well they are doing it (see "The ABCs of Performance Management," p. 101).

- The expected results (performance goals) must be reasonably achievable. The best way to destroy a variable-pay program is to set impossible goals. And, of course, a program that fails creates a much worse situation than a program that was never started.

PREVALENCE OF RESULTS-SHARING PROGRAMS

Overall Prevalence

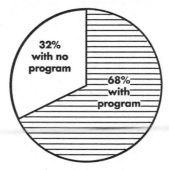

32%
with no
program

68%
with
program

Prevalence by Award

Type of Award	% of Companies		Average Earned Award (% of pay)	
Individual performance (bonuses/incentives in addition to regular merit program)	37%	(736)	9.2%	(406)
Special recognition	35%	(706)	4.3%	(304)
Team/group productivity or gain-sharing (based on local operating performance)	19%	(379)	6.4%	(193)
Cash profit-sharing (based on companywide success)	18%	(359	5.5%	(204)
Stock ownership/option/purchase	14%	(275)	12.7%	(55)
Business incentives (that combine financial and operating measures for companies or business units)	13%	(257)	10.8%	(134)

Year of study: 1993–94, Salary Increase Survey (Hewitt Associates), released September 1993.   n=2,016

- For the plan to inspire that extra mental or physical effort, employees must have the opportunity to earn significantly more through the variable pay plan: 5% to 20% is a good target for most jobs. This amount need not be earned by employees every year, but the potential to earn it must be great enough to motivate behavior change.

- Variable pay plans don't need to pay off every year, but it is essential that they produce some extra earnings the first year so as to develop credibility. This may sound like rigging the system, but it is just common sense. New compensation programs are often met with suspicion at the start, and a failure to pay out in the first year just reinforces employees' skepticism. This is particularly true if the variable pay program has been partially funded by restricting base pay increases. A first-year payout can be accomplished by thoughtful goal-setting or, perhaps a better approach, timing the implementation of the plan for an upswing in business.

Satisfaction with Pay

Perhaps you have developed what you believe to be a sound compensation program — fair to employees and aligned with company goals. Doesn't that ensure that everyone will feel well satisfied and put forth their best effort? Hold on! Even the best-designed pay plan can create dissatisfaction among employees. Internal equity, external competitiveness, and extra earnings opportunities are important, but by no means do they guarantee satisfaction.

Satisfaction is a much more complicated and emotionally charged concept than is equity or competitiveness, and its achievement requires a lot more effort. Remember the old adage: You can satisfy all the employees some of the time and some of the employees all the time, but you will never satisfy all the employees all the time. However, even though you'll never make everybody happy, there are ways to keep dissatisfaction to a minimum.

The three most important ways to satisfy employees with their pay are *communication, communication, communication.* Gone are the days when employees were content to let the boss set their pay and bonuses in a dark room and surprise them with the amount once a year. Granted, there are companies where compensation information is still kept under the boss's blotter, but in most cases this approach satisfies neither the employee nor the company. When employees cannot determine whether they are fairly paid, they are inclined to assume the worst. Even when compensation is generous, the company gets no added output for the added expense. After all, if employees don't know how their bonuses are calculated, they also don't know what actions are necessary to earn more.

To understand and appreciate the value of their compensation, employees need to be able to interpret their pay package; this means providing them with accurate market data and a good understanding of expected results.

• MARKET DATA — Some employers hesitate to share this information because of a concern that they will restrict their flexibility in setting pay (e.g., employees will know when they are paid below market). But employees will always try to find out if they are being paid fairly. If information doesn't come from the employer, it will come from newspaper employment ads, association magazines, or friends. Almost certainly that information will not be as accurate as the company's market data, and management will have no chance to assist employees in interpreting it.

Situations do arise, of course, in which base pay levels are below market. If the low pay can be reasonably justified (e.g., tough economic times or sudden market changes), most employees will understand, particularly if the company has a history of fair treatment and shared information. Some companies in this situation have found it helpful to show good faith by installing a variable-pay plan that guarantees raises when company results improve.

If a company has no good reason for paying below market managers will have a hard time justifying that to employees, and so may need to increase pay to a more competitive level. The full adjustment can be made over time, as long as the timetable is clearly communicated.

Employees are more likely to accept below-market compensation if they know the company is working to correct it within a reasonable period of time. If a variable-pay plan is used to increase earnings, the prospect of a bigger paycheck can lead to an increase in productivity, which may offset the added compensation cost.

• EXPECTED RESULTS — Employees need to know what they must do to earn more money for base pay programs as well as variable-pay programs. When employees know what it takes, motivation and productivity often increase. But note that these gains will not continue forever. Each employee will reach a personal point where the earnings opportunity and the effort required to achieve it offset each other (e.g., they are willing to do what is required for a 10% bonus, but not what is required for a 15% bonus). That balance represents the employee's performance limit and is the most that can be expected in most situations. Emergencies or large increases in earnings potential may boost performance for a short period of time, but the level is not usually sustainable.

Active employee involvement in determining performance goals is also important to building employee satisfaction with pay.

Because of their flexibility, smaller companies have a much easier time involving employees than do large companies, with their more rigid guidelines for managers. The idea is simple: If you set goals for me, I feel imposed upon and manipulated. But if I set my own goals, how can I complain and what excuse do I have for failing? A good, workable approach is to invite employees to participate in joint goal-setting; the aim is to arrive at targets that meet the company's needs while offering an attractive earning opportunity for the employee.

Another important element in pay satisfaction is the right to be heard — to ask questions about pay and get accurate, straightforward answers. Less successful employers avoid answering such questions (or make it very difficult to ask them) because they fear employees may not like the answer. But that's missing the point. If certain questions go unanswered, employees assume that management has something to hide. Sure, they may not like the answer, but the important issue is whether the company is willing to listen to them and provide explanations.

Developing and maintaining effective compensation programs is a never-ending job. As circumstances change, so must compensation plans. Even with your best intentions, no plan can be fair and effective in all situations. But if employees understand how and why they are paid what they get, they become more accepting of change in the compensation program. Your employees are likely to go that extra mile if they know what it takes to increase their earnings. And that can be good news for your bottom line. ■

The Interactive Employee Review

As a manager for several companies, John Strazzanti had lamented the lack of review systems. "They just told me not to mention raises. The goal was to make people feel as if they'd be hassled if they asked for more money." When employees did work up the nerve to ask for a raise, they came armed with all sorts of rationales; few had anything to do with performance or what other companies paid. "It became this really emotional thing."

As general manager and, since 1985, president of Com-Corp Industries, a Cleveland metal stamper that supplies $14 million worth of lightbulb shields to General Motors each year, Strazzanti was determined to do away with the keep-'em-in-the-dark approach.

He wanted his new review system to do two things: establish a fair and open standard of pay, and make people feel important and involved. If he could do that, he figured, employee motivation would take care of itself. So he asked for volunteers for a salary committee and gave the group the job of setting wages by surveying the marketplace to find out what other manufacturers were paying. He also asked all his employees what criteria they thought should be included, and he incorporated their responses into a scoring system.

Now, three times a year, each Com-Corp employee's technical proficiency and professional attitude are evaluated both quantitatively and qualitatively. All workers are measured, not only against past performance and set goals, but also against industry conditions and marketplace standards.

A fair and open salary-review system is the cornerstone of employee motivation. The system John Strazzanti created pays back much more than it pays out.

To encourage improvement, Com-Corp offers a steady stream of classes — from corporate finance to blueprint reading — to employees who have problems in a given area or want to move up in the organization.

In addition, three times a year each employee submits a detailed review of the company's performance, often questioning methods and values and offering suggestions for improvements. Strazzanti finds that this review process has shone a spotlight on just about every corner of the business, from benefits to manufacturing techniques. Today the employee-review system is part of the everyday workings of the company. "A meeting might start out with something that came out of a review and leads into a discussion of continual improvement or engineering. For most people here, the review process is just a way of life."

Strazzanti, his supervisors, and his human resources director pore over the results of workers' evaluations of the organization, looking for oddball scores and trying to read between the lines. The president schedules a companywide meeting three weeks after the reviews.

What's the return on this investment of time and energy? Turnover is low, about 3% in 1990 and 2% in 1993. Absenteeism and tardiness stand at 2.5%. The company has made money every year since Strazzanti began the program, 13 years ago. In April 1991, Com-Corp got one of the highest ratings ever awarded under GM's Targets for Excellence program.

5   GOOD FORMS

Solve Problems

"The review process," Strazzanti emphasizes, "goes hand in hand with classes."

Taking classes made [one particular] employee not only technically more proficient but more aggressive about spotting problems and suggesting solutions. "In a past review of the company, this person was one of the few employees that felt our equipment was the reason for our 1% rate for bad welds. I said, 'Gee, we thought 1% bad parts was pretty good,' but this employee thought we could do better, pointing out that we were throwing away $500 a week in bad parts. That made it a $30,000 problem. The equipment turned out not to be the problem, but bringing the whole thing up made us realize we could do better. We've got it down to 0.2% bad parts now.

"Every review, I get a handful of major improvements like that. We get all the suggestions because people know it will benefit them as well as the company."

Encourage Effort

"You can tell a lot from the scores for making the company a better place to work. This is where people gain or lose the most points," reveals manager Al Treichel. "We review people so often they do get more involved. [A particular] employee had been getting almost all zeros in this category before but, with this review, started speaking up, making suggestions. This person has been making more suggestions ever since and, in a recent review, went from 9 to 12 points.

"After a while, you don't have to get as detailed in the attitude section because people know what's expected. I'm not limited by a real tight structure. It's the involvement I'm looking for. If someone takes a class, it's the effort that counts on the attitude side. It's an investment; the employee is going in a direction that will help the company. On the technical side, I focus on how he or she actually did."

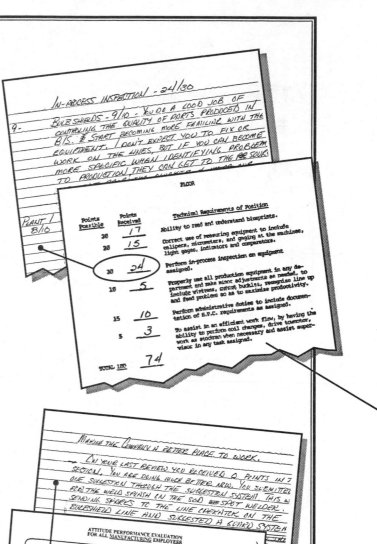

Key In to Industry Trends

"The salary committee spends about an hour a day during the last three months of the year contacting manufacturers," says former HR director Kathleen Pullella. "We describe the job and ask what they would pay someone who does it."

"If the high for a job is $9 an hour and I have someone making $7, that doesn't make me feel good," says Strazzanti. "I'd rather have someone performing at the $9 level, because the multiple of the effect on sales is much higher than with that $7 worker. The high rate for this job [floor inspector], which is based on the research we do, is a lot lower than the high rate last year. That doesn't happen too often. The marketplace is showing that floor inspection is becoming a dinosaur. That basically confirmed a trend we could already see happening here as we brought in new technology. The important thing was to encourage this person to move up, take more classes."

Once Is Not Enough

Doing a two-way review three times a year with each employee creates an ongoing dialogue about every aspect of the organization. "You get to see trends — good and bad — before they've gone on for too long," says Treichel. "If things are left for 12 months, they tend to stew. This is a way of stirring the pot."

Strazzanti adds, "You really have to be in tune with what's gone on in the past. If someone usually gives the company all 10s and I see an 8, that also concerns me."

New employees are reviewed once a month in the crucial first 90 days. "When I came to Com-Corp I thought the whole thing was a little strange," admits Treichel. "But doing a review every four months forces you to take a look at an individual and really tailor a job. I don't think I'd get the same results if we did this once a year."

Define and Redefine Jobs That Need to Be Done

In [the floor inspector's] case, the pay rate is actually above the industry high. Treichel emphasizes the employee is "earning every penny of it. Still, the marketplace is saying that the absolute best floor inspector is worth only $8.70 an hour. It wasn't the employee's fault; I realized our job description wasn't reflecting reality anymore, so we weren't getting the right numbers. That told me it was time to rewrite the job description. The new job definition is more about process improvement. The new high rate will be about $11 an hour. We're definitely getting a better return on what this employee is doing for us now. The whole point of this system is to say, Here's what you can do to make more." ■

Catering to
Cafeteria Benefits

Employee benefit plans used to be called
fringe benefits — decorative and standard
embellishments to compensation. Not so today.
Benefit packages are an integral and important
part of compensation. You know this is
true by how much they cost. Your employees also
know it, and they are increasing their
demands for variety and choice.

by Gary B. Kushner

Not too long ago, the typical employee was a man with a wife and 2.3 children at home. He was well satisfied with a basic medical plan that covered both him and his immediate family. Today, however, there is no such thing as a typical employee, for the traditional description fits less than 10% of all workers. The major change in demographics is obvious to everyone: A multitude of single and married women are now in the workforce, and their numbers are still growing.

For males and females who are single, young marrieds who serve two different employers, parents of small children, mid-careerists with aging parents, or college-bound teenagers, traditional benefit plans are often inadequate and largely irrelevant to their needs.

While changing demographics have dramatically altered employee

Gary Kushner is
president of
Kushner & Co., in
Kalamazoo, Mich.

benefit needs, spiraling costs have forced employers to rethink the cost-effectiveness of their benefit plans. In 1953 employee benefit costs averaged only 19.2% of payroll; today benefits represent approximately 45% of that expenditure. Studies show, however, that an alarming 70% or more of employees have no idea of the value of the benefits they are receiving. In fact, if asked, they wrongly estimate benefit expenditures to be approximately 10% or less of payroll costs. This is probably because benefits are invisible, intangible, or taken for granted. Many employers get little or no return on their tremendous investment in human resources simply because their employees don't know what they are getting. Just as upsetting, many employees continue to fret over other unmet needs, at the same time as they receive the expensive benefits they undervalue.

Realizing that traditional programs are no longer applicable in the majority of cases, many organizations are seeking relief. Their leaders are taking a close look at flexible benefit plans, or cafeteria plans, as they are frequently called. Flex plans have been used by very large corporations for more than a decade, but now many small and midsize firms are following suit.

Why Be Flexible? The Company's Perspective

A traditional benefit plan offers uniform coverage. Typically the only choice given to employees is whether or not to participate at all. A cafeteria plan represents what is called the defined contribution approach. The company offers employees an array of benefits to choose from and gives employees a benefit allowance to purchase only those items that match their needs and preferences. Thus, through proper pricing and credit methodologies, the employer regains control of benefit expenditures.

With flexible benefit programs, employers have both the incentive and the means to offer employees choices in their compensation. From management's perspective, cafeteria plans work well for the following reasons:

- Recruitment: The company offering them is viewed as enlightened and progressive.
- Retention: Freedom of choice gives employees feelings of satisfaction, empowerment, and worth.

- Planning. A flexible approach enables management to tie benefits to broad strategic goals — especially to human resources planning.
- Cost management: Many companies use these plans to connect benefit expenditures directly to company profitability and true benefit cost.

Cost management? Contrary to management's common misconception, flexible programs are not inherently more expensive than traditional offerings. The majority of companies report that, because flex plans allow employees to spend available benefit dollars where they wish, their cafeteria program is less costly.

A flexible benefit program introduces four key elements that enable you to control and actively manage costs:

- Benefit trade-offs: Employees give up some benefits in order to obtain others.
- Flexible credits: Management controls a portion of previously uncontrolled benefit expense.
- Cost-sharing with employees: Surveys and experience indicate that employees are willing to share in program costs in return for choices of coverage.
- Program enhancements: Employers can add new benefits such as coverage for day care, vision care, or dental health at little or no additional cost.

Other advantages that you should consider include tax efficiencies, reduced pressure for unionization, improved employee morale, and the impetus for better communication.

Joy of Choosing: The Employees' Perspective

For employees, the major advantage of cafeteria plans clearly is choice. Employees can select benefits that meet real needs, and as those needs change they can revise their package. Also, they have the option of taking taxable cash for dollars currently spent on tax-free benefits. Conversely, they can increase the level of benefit coverage by reducing the taxable cash component of their total compensation package.

To select from the array of offerings, employees need to understand and compare benefit features and costs. If management provides information and education that enable employees to appreciate the real costs of benefit options, then employees will value their plan and feel more positive about their total compensation. Such insight can boost their confidence in their job and in their earning power. (See "The Eye-Opening Benefits Worksheet," p. 165.)

When employees are allowed to buy additional benefits with tax-free dollars, the tax savings increase further: because their gross taxable income is reduced, so are their taxes (and so are the taxes of their employers).

Flexible benefits solve equity problems by fixing the total cost of the benefits package rather than, as was traditional, defining what the package will be, regardless of cost. Employees view the policy as fair and appropriate, because their diverse individual needs are met.

Finally, many employees appreciate the chance to participate in a decision that not only affects their personal welfare but also has strategic implications for their company. This may be especially true in an entrepreneurial environment, in which participation in such decisions is not only welcome but expected.

What's On the Menu

A flexible benefit plan is any plan that allows participants to choose some or all of their benefits. The choices can range between different levels of one type of benefit or between a variety of eligible benefits. There are many qualified benefits in the Internal Revenue Code that are allowed within a flexible benefit plan:

- health (including medical, dental, vision, prescriptions)
- group term life insurance
- accidental death and dismemberment insurance
- medical reimbursement accounts
- dependent care reimbursement accounts
- short-term disability coverage
- long-term disability coverage

- personal days
- 401(k), qualified cash or deferred arrangement
- cash

Any plan that offers a choice between two or more qualified benefits is considered a cafeteria plan. These qualified flexible benefit plans are regulated under Section 125 of the Internal Revenue Code. As required by that section, a flexible benefits plan must have the following features:

- The plan must be written.
- All participants must be employees (or spouses and dependents of employees).
- The participants must be able to choose between at least one taxable and one nontaxable qualified benefit.
- Except for 401(k) programs, a flexible benefit plan may not include any benefit that defers compensation in any manner.

Making It Happen: Implementation

A sound approach to implementing a flexible benefit plan usually comprises five phases: needs assessment, plan design, employee communication, systems and administration, and plan documentation.

• NEEDS ASSESSMENT — To determine whether a flexible benefit program is right for your organization, do a careful needs assessment. Initially, you or your benefits consultant collects and analyzes demographic data, classifying employees by such categories as age, gender, dual-income status, and family situation. During this phase, current benefit structure and costs, current plan information, and other general benefit information should also be collected and analyzed. Knowing the existing program's true cost provides a realistic baseline for formulating the budget for your flexible benefits program. Not only the benefit expenses but also the cost of administering the current plan should be considered.

Administrative needs vary, of course, according to each organization's capabilities and preferences. Some companies perform all administration functions in-house; others want to have a benefits consultant administer all or part of the work. Cafeteria plans, once in motion, can usually run on autopilot; even so, it's a good idea to have a qualified individual, either inside or outside your organization, who in addition to administration, can oversee legal compliance and accuracy.

Defining the goals and objectives of compensation and benefits is important to the plan study. Although most benefit plan goals are similar, priorities vary with each employer. For example, increased employee satisfaction may be your main goal, with benefit cost management assigned a lower priority; alternatively, cost containment may be your main goal. In both cases, your plan design would be influenced. Therefore, benefit goals and objectives must be determined and formalized prior to plan design.

Once the above steps are completed, you can decide if a cafeteria plan is feasible and right for your organization. You should have in hand a written analysis that addresses all of the issues and their implications; this can serve as the basis for a preliminary plan. After you have reviewed and understood all aspects of the analysis, the process of designing the final plan can begin in earnest.

•PLAN DESIGN — As a first step, contact insurance companies in order to select appropriate carriers to support the benefit options, coverage, and costs provided in the plan design. Insurance companies' pricing and credit methodologies are based on carrier costs, employer contributions, management goals, and plan design components. Carefully analyze the cost/benefit data (including enrollment projections and estimates of future costs) for the new cafeteria plan and compare them with equivalent data for the traditional benefit structure. If needed, changes in the plan design can be made accordingly. At this time, the necessary legal documents will also need to be prepared and reviewed with benefit attorneys.

• COMMUNICATING THE PLAN — A carefully designed communication program that educates your employees and prepares them to understand and maximize the new program's benefits is the key to successful implementation. To lay the groundwork, you will need literature that explains—in simple, clear language—the program's advantages and how it operates. (If you are working with an external benefits consultant, good material may be available for the asking.) Beyond this, you may want to hold open-door sessions, where you and your benefits expert can clarify points and respond directly to specific issues and concerns.

• SYSTEMS AND ADMINISTRATION — Even if you have designed your benefit plan with care and sold your employees on its advantages, you'll need to provide a good, efficient administrative system so as not to sabotage the program. This may be crucial for the small to mid-sized employer, where personnel resources are scarce.

• PLAN DOCUMENTATION — As with all qualified benefit programs, flexible plans have documentation requirements. As noted above, the employer must have the plan in writing. Appropriate written notices of any changes in the plan to your employees are not only common sense— they constitute another legal requirement.

A Case in Point: ODL

ODL Inc., in Zeeland, Mich., is a national manufacturing and distribution firm specializing in door and skylight products. It has approximately 350 employees. In the mid-1980s, ODL's management group recognized that the cost of the company's existing benefit programs was spiraling out of control, while at the same time not necessarily meeting employees' needs.

Management decided to pursue the first phase of the benefit consulting process, a *Needs Assessment,* to determine current needs and decide what, if any, changes were required in the existing plan. The study uncovered a number of warning beacons. First, although ODL had already implemented a self-funded medical program, higher-than-average claims costs were unpredictably causing large increases in the annual renewal figures. Second, though the plan design was quite rich, employees did not perceive the benefits as anything other than average. In fact, a rather large percentage (34%) of employees viewed the existing offerings as "less than average." Last, at ODL a large percentage of the married workforce (over 65%) had dual incomes and dual coverage, particularly for health care.

By following the remaining four phases of plan implementation during the next 10 months, ODL successfully designed and implemented a full flexible benefits program. Its new cafeteria plan consisted of employee choice within the areas of health, dental, and life insurance; disability coverage; and two reimbursement accounts. Further, employees could shift flexible benefit dollars to either cash or the company's existing 401(k) plan.

The new plan was carefully communicated to ODL's employees, who received it enthusiastically. As expected, many dual-covered employees opted for a less rich medical program, reducing claims exposure and risk liability by almost two-thirds. Health-care cost increases were cut by three-quarters, as measured against proposed rate hikes for the same group.

A Movable Feast

Each year, as your organization grows, you may discover that your priorities have undergone change. For example, cost may have become more or less important than variety of offerings or options. Your employee demographics may have shifted; for example, you now have more singles on board, or all of your 30-something managers have turned 40 and begun to settle into family life. Your cafeteria plan can and should reflect those changes.

To keep a firm hand, you'll want to maintain good communication with your managers and employees. Each year, the plan design and demographic data should be examined in light of plan performance, current enrollment, and benefit options. You should also keep well-informed about new and pending regulatory changes, which may present new opportunities.

Today, there's no need to sit idly by and moan about the high costs of benefits. Cafeteria plans do work well, but they require careful planning, effective administration, and a commitment to ongoing two-way communication with your employees. The results — greater control over your expenditures and well-satisfied employees — make the effort entirely worthwhile. ■

The Eye-Opening Benefits Worksheet

Your employees probably don't fully appreciate you. They see their paychecks, but they disregard all the benefits you fund. Your contributions to their well-being, whether magnanimous or mandated, are probably much more generous than they imagine. Too many small companies demonstrate coquettish modesty on the subject, as if they were afraid the details would spoil the magic.

Image National (IN) cherishes honesty in its relationship with employees, and honesty has seen that relationship through some trying times. Five years ago IN was a $4.5-million jack-of-all-trades and master of none. The Boise, Idaho, company manufactured custom signs for local accounts and produced display advertising and leased billboards for the regional market.

To succeed with the billboards, IN needed to be an ad agency, but without sufficient boards, it also needed to invest in more equipment and better craftspeople. The overhead was steep. And in the local market, IN was trying to compete with a guy working out of his garage to make a $1,500 sign down the street. In 1988, the company began to focus on more lucrative regional and national sign accounts, such as retail chains that open 20 stores a year and provide repeat projects in large numbers.

Choosing to go national meant walking away from a couple million dollars in small jobs and cutting the workforce. Such a dramatic change was bound to shake the faith of the remaining employees, who had already been tested by inconsistent management and performance incentives that inspired only cynicism. The company was asking its people to participate and contribute. That would happen only if they trust-

Image National renews its employees' commitment with this annual review of all the extras they enjoy.

ed the management that was making decisions — and they didn't.

Management decided to be entirely forthright and transformed a halfhearted attempt to share financial data with the employees, making it an educational responsibility. Employees were explicitly trained to understand the numbers on IN's income statement and were kept up to date by reviewing monthly results in companywide meetings. Because benefits costs have a huge impact on the bottom line, every employee knows just how much is spent on them.

Many companies that do see the value of detailing their contributions to employee benefits packages leave it to their insurance provider to summarize the information in "personalized" booklets. IN considered preparing such summaries but decided it was important that employees complete the exercise themselves. Their attention would be captured by doing the math; moreover, using their own calculations, they would be far more likely to become believers.

Once a year each employee gets a work sheet with the raw data needed to calculate the value of his or her individual compensation and benefits package.

Lynn Bass, a production worker at IN, fills out the form with his wife. As a dependent on his company health insurance plan, she too has an interest in the process. The two were surprised to find that Bass's benefits totaled $12,000. He had guessed about half that, maximum. "See," his wife said, "I told you you were worth more!"

Following is a sample of an hourly employee's worksheet.

▽ 5 GOOD FORMS

Description of an hourly employee's work sheet

A The contributions in the top section are all required by the federal government. IN doesn't pretend we're doing it out of the goodness of our heart. They aren't negotiable. We can't shop to get better rates.

B Our worker's comp insurance carrier assigns a factor to each job based on its riskiness. The people who install our signs are on cranes 80 feet in the air, around live wires, so their premiums cost us more than our office workers' do.

In 1988 a manufacturing worker's premium was about 13.9% of that person's salary, or a factor of .139. Now, on account of improvements in our safety record, it's down to .0882. Calculate that against a couple million dollars in payroll, and that's a real savings. This shows everyone the costs of carelessness.

C These numbers are right off the insurance schedule and represent the portion of employee health insurance the company pays. The employee's contribution varies, depending on the deductible he or she elects and the number of dependents, but on average, we pay about 75%. Without seeing these figures you can't really understand that health insurance is incredibly expensive.

D We mark with an asterisk all the costs for nonproductive time — holidays, vacation, sick days, in-house training — that are absorbed into employees' base pay. Because it's not over and above salary, it's netted out at the bottom of the form. We're more generous with these benefits than our competitors are, and this calls attention to how much.

E This number—86.6—is the total of 10-minute breaks, morning and afternoon, every day, for manufacturing workers. Breaks for administrative staff aren't nearly so formal, but there's still paid, unproductive time.

F We match 25¢ on the dollar for the first 6% of salary deferred to the 401(k), an effective rate of .015 of base annual earnings. Almost no one defers less because we really promote this benefit. We knew that as soon as we got people in, they'd see their money grow and they'd keep contributing. On the day people become eligible, we offer them a $100 bonus — paid to their 401(k) account — if they join.

G The Employee Assistance Program provides for five free visits to a counselor, per problem, for all sorts of problems — financial, family, drug. It's relatively cheap, and we figure if it helps us keep one good employee on track, we've made back the cost 20 times over. We started thinking that four employees a year would be good participation, and after three years the rate is running at about 11. It's not as hyped as other benefits are, but the worksheet reminds people that it's available.

H For a flat fee per employee, we get access to a hospital's 800 line. Doctors and nurses there answer questions about, say, how to diagnose and treat fevers. Employees also receive a monthly newsletter that encourages preventive care.

I A lot of companies don't pay all administrative costs of the 401(k).

J We pay for a lot of equipment, safety glasses, overalls for welders, laundry services.

K Although our policy says classes must be work related to be reimbursable, we pay for just about anything, short of swimming or basket weaving. We cover tuition and up to $100 for books or lab fees. This $367 could have been a couple of one-day seminars or a three-credit course at the local university, plus a book.

L We probably understate the amount we spend on education. This doesn't even account for time we spend developing our internal programs. This $174 paid for a segment of quality training and includes part of the speaker's fee and the money we reimbursed the employee for hours spent in class after work. The number below, $85, is what we pay for our quality workbook.

M Once the employee fills in the work sheet, he or she can ask the accounting department to generate a report that looks like this one, showing the relationship of each benefit to that employee's base annual earnings. The key is the bottom line. We pay this person $7.25 an hour, but we pay an additional 19%, nearly $3,000, in benefits.

N We contribute 20% of after-tax net income to a pool, which is then distributed to all employees who have been with us at least one year. This replaced the old, confusing incentive programs.

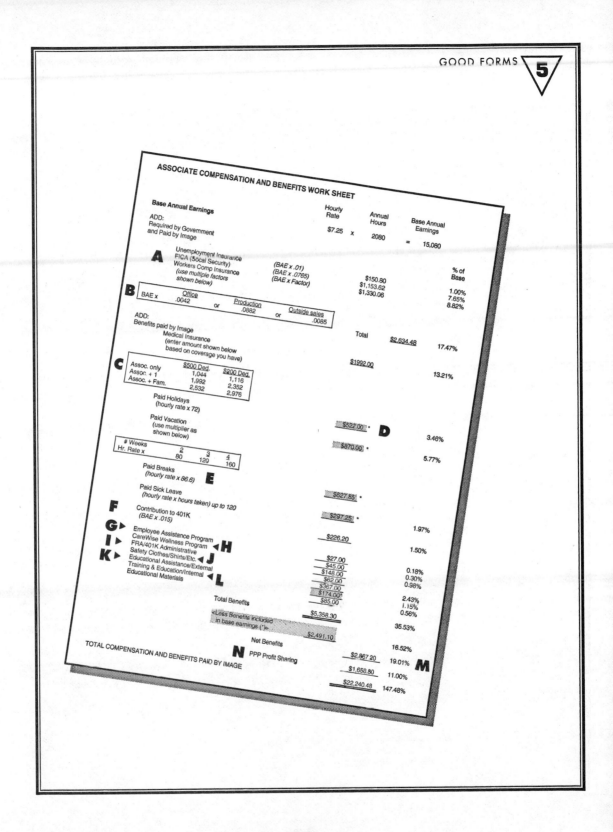

ASSOCIATE COMPENSATION AND BENEFITS WORK SHEET

Base Annual Earnings	Hourly Rate	Annual Hours	Base Annual Earnings
ADD: Required by Government and Paid by Image	$7.25 x	2080	= 15,080

			% of Base
A Unemployment Insurance FICA (Social Security) Workers Comp Insurance *(use multiple factors shown below)*	(BAE x .01) (BAE x .0765) (BAE x Factor)	$150.80 $1,153.62 $1,330.06	1.00% 7.65% 8.82%

B BAE x | Office .0042 | or | Production .0882 | or | Outside sales .0085

ADD:
Benefits paid by Image
Medical Insurance
(enter amount shown below
based on coverage you have)

Total $2,634.48 — 17.47%

$1992.00 — 13.21%

C	$500 Ded.	$200 Ded.
Assoc. only		
Assoc. + 1	1,044	1,116
Assoc. + Fam.	1,992	2,352
	2,532	2,976

Paid Holidays
(hourly rate x 72)

$522.00 * **D**

3.46%

Paid Vacation
(use multiplier as
shown below)

$870.00 *

5.77%

E # Weeks Hr. Rate x	2 80	3 120	4 160

Paid Breaks
(hourly rate x 86.6)

Paid Sick Leave
(hourly rate x hours taken) up to 120

$627.85 *

F Contribution to 401K
(BAE x .015)

$237.25 *

G ▶ Employee Assistance Program   1.97%
H CareWise Wellness Program $226.20
I ▶ FRA/401K Administrative   1.50%
J ◀ Safety Clothes/Shirts/Etc. $27.00   0.18%
K ▶ Educational Assistance/External $45.00   0.30%
         Training & Education/Internal $148.00   0.98%
L ◀ Educational Materials $62.00
                                           $367.00   2.43%
                                           $174.00*   1.15%
Total Benefits $85.00   0.56%

                                           $5,358.30   35.53%

<Less Benefits included
in base earnings (*)> $2,491.10

Net Benefits   16.52%

N PPP Profit Sharing $2,867.20   19.01%   **M**

                                           $1,658.80   11.00%

TOTAL COMPENSATION AND BENEFITS PAID BY IMAGE $22,240.48   147.48%

Starbucks Brews
a Strong
Benefits Plan

*Chairman and CEO Howard Schultz has
transformed Seattle's Starbucks from a local coffee
roaster into a profitable, $163-million national
retailer with a simple, if somewhat radical, growth
strategy: make every dollar you invest in your employees
show up — and then some — on the bottom line.*

On the far side of the glass behind Howard Schultz, multicolored boxes of coffee move like rush-hour traffic on a miniature freeway, winding their way on a conveyor belt that runs through the center of the building. The air is gently infused with the warm, fresh-brewed scent of today's blend. From where he sits, Schultz can see the tasting room, a kitchen-cum-laboratory that's located just outside his office. High-gloss snapshots of the coffee-brewing process decorate the walls, along with the current prices per pound of each of the more than 30 varietals and blends Starbucks Coffee Co. sells.

"My dad was a blue-collar worker," Schultz says, recalling his upbringing in one of New York's tougher neighborhoods. "He didn't have health insurance or benefits, and I saw firsthand the debilitating effect that had on him and on our family. I decided if I were ever in the position to make a contribution to others in that way, I would."

Schultz got the chance and seems to have made the most of it. As chairman and CEO of Seattle's Starbucks since 1987, he has overseen phenomenal growth — a compounded annual rate of 80% over the past three years — resulting, to hear him tell it, from one central strategy. "Our only sustainable competitive advantage," explains Schultz, "is the quality of our workforce. We're building a national retail company by creating pride in — and a stake in — the outcome of our labor."

The centerpiece of Schultz's vision is a generous and comprehensive employee-benefits package encompassing health care, stock options, training programs, career counseling, and product discounts for all workers, full-time and part-time. "No one can afford to not provide these kinds of benefits," says Schultz. "The desire to scrimp on such essentials helps reinforce the sense of mediocrity that seeps into many companies. Without them, people don't feel financially or spiritually tied to their jobs." Emily Ericsen, former head of Starbucks's human resources, puts it another way: "We are in the people-development business almost as much as the coffee business."

Though the connection between such an aggressive employee benefits package and the bottom line is often difficult to show conclusively, the circumstantial evidence in Starbucks's case is compelling. The company is clearly on its way to becoming the dominant specialty coffee retailer and brand in North America. Since Starbucks went public, in June 1992, its stock price has climbed 82%. Employee attrition, which typically hovers from 100% to 105% for food retailers, is less than 50%. The company is posting higher profit margins every year, beating even Schultz's own ambitious targets, and Starbucks's health care costs, despite the extensive coverage, are well within the national average.

Looking at Schultz's success so far, Corey Rosen, director of the National Center for Employee Ownership, in Oakland, Calif., notes that Starbucks is swimming against the tide. "They've clearly taken a different approach. Many retailers want a lot of turnover so they don't have to pay a lot of benefits. Starbucks doesn't want turnover; it wants loyalty." As for the stock options, Rosen adds, "It's extremely unusual to offer those. I don't know of any retailers offering them."

For his part, Schultz says he needs no further proof that employee benefits are the key to competitiveness and growth. He's convinced his employees are working harder and smarter because they have a stake in the outcome. "We can't achieve our strategic objectives without a workforce of people who are immersed in the same commitment as is management," he says.

Dressed in soft green slacks and a tieless starched shirt, fresh from selling the company stock to investors across Europe and the United States, Schultz bounds along the carpeted floor from one end of his office to the window overlooking the roasting-plant floor. Shifting from loafered foot to foot as if he had downed several gallons of his own Kona, he begins ticking off the company's milestones.

In 1971 Starbucks opened its first store in historic Pike Place Market, Seattle's landmark fish market overlooking Puget Sound. In 1982, when Schultz came aboard as head of marketing and retailing, Starbucks had 85 workers and sold whole beans. Schultz had been working in New York marketing coffeemakers to a number of retailers, including Starbucks. That introduced him to the three founding partners, Jerry Baldwin, Zev Siegl, and Gordon Bowker, who eventually recruited him to bring marketing savvy to the loosely run company.

Named for the first mate in Herman Melville's *Moby Dick*, Starbucks at the time seemed content to roast and sell beans without a lot of fuss or impressive profit margins. Then, on a trip to Italy, Schultz was awed by the amount of espresso readily available at the more than a thousand coffee bars in Milan alone. "Coffee bars are the mainstay of every Italian neighborhood," he says. "That's what I wanted to bring back to Seattle."

After halfheartedly trying to persuade the founders to open an espresso bar, Schultz left to do the same himself in 1984. Three years later he was back at Starbucks with a buyout offer of $250,000 and a plan to roll out retail shops far beyond Seattle.

He proceeded to do so with a vengeance. When Schultz first

returned to Starbucks, it had just 11 stores and fewer than 100 employees. Today the company boasts 90-plus stores in Washington State alone and almost 300 more nationwide. Some 6,000 employees are attending to two million customers per week; more than half of the sales are in high-profit liquid refreshment. Starbucks has already rung up sales of over $3 million per week; by the end 1994, the company expects that number to be $5 million per week. The target for total sales in 1994 is an anticipated $250 million.

From the beginning of his stewardship, Schultz saw a symbiotic link between Starbucks's growth curve and his ambitious benefits plan, gambling that revenues would outrun spending for Starbucks's expansion. At first, the company's losses almost doubled, to $1.2 million from fiscal 1988 to 1989, as overhead and operating expenses ballooned to $18.4 million on $19.2 million in sales. But in 1990 sales shot up 84%, dramatically outpacing expenses, and the company broke into the black.

Although Starbucks already had an adequate benefits package in place and had been covering part-timers since 1971, Schultz began to beef up offerings substantially. He added a heavy emphasis on preventive health care, for example, by providing a special deductible-exempt $300 allowance for annual physicals. There's similar encouragement for regular dental visits, with a ceiling of $2,000 in expenses and no deductible. He also kicked in vision care, and the company picks up the total tab for disability and life insurance as well.

All that, however, didn't make it easy to persuade the insurance companies to sign Starbucks up. Kibble & Prentice, Starbucks's insurance broker in Seattle, faced this daunting task. The biggest problem was explaining why Starbucks insisted on covering part-timers. A handful of retailers provide benefits for people who work 30 hours a week but not to those who work only 20. At Starbucks at least two-thirds of the workers are clocking fewer than 40 hours. "It was a philosophical battle," says Dan Guy, a vice president at Kibble. "But we made the insurers understand what the company's commitment was."

Schultz outlines his reasoning succinctly: "More than half of our retail sales force is part-time workers. That tells me that the majority of our customers are coming into contact with part-timers. How we treat our people is directly related to how we treat our customers and to the quality of our product. It's inarguable that our part-timers are key to the company's success.

"Designing the plan was rough. Our insurance premiums went up slightly when we decided to provide everyone with full coverage. But that was offset by the lower training costs associated with a lower attrition rate. We normally spend 23 hours of classroom training time on every new employee. The longer an employee stays with us, the more we save."

Starbucks's high-octane growth is now supporting its employees' benefits without skipping a beat. Despite the range of benefits, they represent just one-quarter of the company's labor costs and are holding steady at that level. Insurance makes up half the benefits expenses. At the end of the month, employees end up footing just a quarter of the total benefits costs, or $31 each, on average.

The success of Schultz's strategy has depended, in part, on the relative youth of most Starbucks employees. Schultz himself is only 41, and half his management team is younger than 50. In general, the company appeals to young people who have a more healthful lifestyle, which can justify lower insurance rates. Orin Smith, Starbucks's new president and chief operating officer, is banking on that fact. "In this business, I don't think we can expect a big increase in the age of our employees," he says. "I'd be very surprised if we had 40-year-olds behind the counter 10 years from now."

Starbucks's average monthly coverage costs $125 per employee compared with a more typical $200, according to Ericsen. "Our claims are lower, and that's reflected in the lower rates," she says. The company is hitting a claims ratio of 75%, meaning that for every dollar paid in, the insurer is spending 75¢ on claims. Medical claims were low enough, relative to Starbucks's premiums, that the company even received a $12,700 refund in 1991. An estimated $30,000 was refunded in 1992.

Nobody expects that to continue for too long. First, Starbucks is growing so fast it is paying in more than its insurers are paying out. When the growth slows, so will the rebates. Plus, common sense says that the premiums Starbucks pays will be heading upward as the stores continue to grow in number and the company expands eastward. Guy notes that health costs are higher in the eastern part of the United States than in the West. Also, the store workers are aging, having children, the sorts of things that naturally increase costs.

Already, the company is considering offering workers a cafeteria-style benefits program that lets them select different degrees of coverage. Under such a plan, monthly benefits costs could range from $200 to $240. Those are costs the company is willing to absorb.

Starbucks wants to continue attracting and keeping an effective, loyal workforce — to be "the employer of choice," as Schultz puts it — because the company continues to expand aggressively into a gourmet-coffee market ripe for the picking. Coffee drinkers in the United States each consume on average 3.4 cups per day. According to FIND/SVP, a New York consulting and research firm, the coffee market was $4.9 billion in 1992. Of that, one-quarter of the sales were specialty coffees, a category estimated to be growing at nearly 10% annually. Those brews, made with rich chestnut-brown arabica beans rather than the pale robusta found on supermarket shelves, are Starbucks's stock in trade.

Despite such vast opportunity — and a thousand franchise calls per month from willing investors — Schultz shuns franchising, which he believes would compromise quality. "We're unwilling to take the route others have taken, like franchising," he says. "The only way we're going to be successful is if we have the people who are attracted to the company and who are willing to sustain the growth as owners."

At Starbucks's Los Angeles store, manager Mark Smith, then 28 years old, pointed to the company's strong culture as a large part of the reason that he left another Seattle institution, Eddie Bauer, a few years back. Smith steered his store through a major expansion that included hiring 20 people. From that experience, he says, he can attest to the fact that Starbucks's benefits "make a big difference in attracting high-quality workers."

Schultz leaves little to chance when it comes to opening a new outlet. Stores are located in new cities with surgical precision. By tracking the addresses of mail-order customers in such a way as to find the highest concentration in a city, Starbucks ensures that its new stores have a ready audience. In San Francisco, where there are some well-entrenched rivals, Starbucks's first store was the fastest-growing Schultz had ever opened; it's now been surpassed by the New York store, which opened in 1994 and is breaking all records to date. For good reason: one-third of the store's customers were already familiar with the company through its mail-order service. Best of all, despite losing customers to newly opened stores, mail-order revenues have doubled in each of the past seven years.

Through it all, Schultz runs a tight ship. Although the company spends, by his estimate, $1,000 to train each new worker, his overhead is dropping as a percentage of sales, even as the number of stores climbs. The figure fell from 12.3% in 1989 to a scant 8% in 1992.

Schultz says, "Over the past several years, we've really focused on our infrastructure. In a series of open forums, we heard our people asking for what I call a new paradigm," an incentive not only to stay with the company but also to have a stake in its success. As the centerpiece of that new paradigm, Schultz and Smith came up with Bean Stock: Starbucks's stock options, structured to achieve both employee and corporate goals.

"Our goal here was to design a plan that would combat the attrition that is the greatest threat to a retail operation," says Schultz "We've set up a vesting period of five years; it starts one year after the option is granted, then vests the employee at 20% every year. In addition, every employee receives a new stock-option award every year, and a new vesting period begins. The percentage of the grant is tied to the profitability of the company. It took us two years to design this."

To put the plan in place, Smith had to get an exemption from the Securities and Exchange Commission, the federal regulatory agency charged with monitoring corporate governance. Any company with more than 500 shareholders has to report its financial performance publicly. That's costly and reveals information to competitors. Because Smith argued that employees would be receiving options, not shares, the rule was waived.

Before Starbucks went public, the original plan had been to let workers cash in their options based on a private valuation of the company by investment bankers. An employee stock ownership plan (ESOP) wasn't possible as long as Starbucks remained private, and stock wasn't as much of an incentive as options were. Under ESOPs workers have to buy the shares, but with options there's a lengthy period until they can be exercised, one hopes at a very low price.

Though Starbucks is now public, Schultz says the basic offering can be duplicated by almost any company, public or private. "For our plan to work in another company there has to be some type of liquidity or cash-in potential," he says. "Now we're public, but a smaller private company would have to design an alternative structure, maybe backed by buy-sell agreements when employees retire or leave the company. But these aren't the kinds of obstacles that should get in the way of anyone who is considering setting up an option plan."

In 1991, the first year that Bean Stock was offered, the company overshot its profit goal by 20%, and the board responded by nudging up the percentage of salaries for stock options to 12%, from 10%. Schultz was so enthusiastic that he went so far as to give the first wave of workers who were offered options the same 30% discount on the price as the top company officers received. But the venture capitalists and shareholders on the board weren't going to let their stake be diluted without a challenge. "Increasing the shareholders substantially dilutes our interest," says Craig Foley, former managing director of Chancellor Capital Management Inc., in New York, and the largest shareholder before the public offering. "We take that very seriously."

For months Smith and his team crunched numbers to come up with a convincing argument for continuing the plan. Smith analyzed corporate studies, including some from Rosen's group, the National Center for Employee Ownership, comparing productivity in companies whose workers owned a stake with productivity in those whose employees didn't. Most significant, Smith looked at what would be vested in four to five years and discovered that less than 3% of the entire company would be affected, based on the number of people and sales by the stores. "We could determine the number of shares offered per year, and we applied turnover scenarios through year five," says Smith.

The most convincing case was built on how few people were leaving and how much easier it was to add topflight talent to the company. After a brief discussion, the board voted to keep the plan.

As Foley puts it, "We realize that if we can reinforce the culture and reduce the turnover in part-time employees, all shareholders will be better off. The grants are tied to overachieving. If you just come to work and do your job, that isn't as attractive as if you beat the numbers."

At Bean Stock's unveiling, Schultz recounted to his employees his memories of growing up in the Brooklyn projects, where his father "went from truck driver to cabbie to factory worker and never made more than $20,000 a year." When he died, said Schultz, the children took care of their mother. "I would have felt troubled if five years from now the wealth and success of Starbucks would affect only a few."

The way Schultz describes it, the stock options and the complete benefits package act as a glue that binds workers to the company, forging loyalty and, above all, encouraging attentive service to the customer. "It has reduced attrition," says Schultz, "and we've literally changed the level of communication. You can't imagine how excited our workers were when we started unveiling our new benefits package and explaining Bean Stock. All kinds of people started coming up with ways to save money and improve productivity. Now they're invested in our future. The future of Starbucks lies in increasing shareholder value — and increasing employee value will increase shareholder value." ■

Notes

_____

_____

_____

_____

_____

_____

_____

_____

_____

_____

_____

_____

_____

_____

_____

_____

_____

_____

_____

_____

_____

_____

Communicating with Your Team

Mixing Instinct
and Information

It's often tempting to believe that communication will take care of itself: "I'll say it, and they'll hear it." But to manage your people effectively, you must likewise manage organizational communication. This means getting vital information to and from every corner of your organization with regularity and timeliness.

Some of the things you need to do are almost instinctual — *if* you pay attention to them. For instance, the tone and look of your employee handbook can be as critical to its validity and effectiveness as its contents. Similarly, if you want a second-in-command with whom you can communicate easily, choose someone with whom you have good chemistry. But also beware of the dangers inherent in too much office camaraderie.

Beyond instinctual matters, executives need to find ways that render communication systematic and fact filled. This chapter outlines methods for meeting two of top management's biggest challenges: regularly eliciting information from your senior and middle managers, and helping your employees understand why individual performance counts.

This chapter also underscores the need to provide solid documentation, starting with your company handbook. In today's litigious society, documenting your policies and procedures (in your handbook and elsewhere) in clear, unambiguous language is more than a service to your employees; it can mean survival. ■

Do It by the Book
— the Handbook,
That Is

*Good management takes good
communication. And that starts by
creating your own employee manual.*

—

Company handbooks are proliferating today. The creeping grip of regulation is forcing companies to publish them simply to cover legal requirements and avoid lawsuits. But more than that, says Wendy Rhodes, a principal with Hewitt Associates, a benefits and compensation consulting firm based in Lincolnshire, Ill., many companies are choosing to write down relevant policies and practices and package them in one document. Instead of an expensive orientation program, such a manual is a convenient and cost-effective way to orient and motivate employees as well as explain company terminology.

Too frequently, though, the company employee manual is a dusty and dry compilation of policies and procedures (some of them outdated), a loose-leaf binder that fattens with age. An example of the sorry state of the nation's employee manuals? Whole Foods Market Inc., headquartered in Austin, Tex., whose handbook *Inc.* had spotlighted in the past, asked companies that requested its booklet to send theirs in return. Whole Foods received a blizzard of handbooks but not a single idea that their staffers felt they could borrow.

Your company's handbook stands in the front line of communication with your employees. Other than perhaps your tax returns, you can't prepare a more important document. With your own handbook you can create chapter and verse on your company. You can say exactly who you are and what you do. Most important, your handbook tells employees why they should work for your company; it should detail your expectations of them and answer their queries concerning expectations of you.

Both by content and by example, you're about to get a bird's-eye view of the whys, wherefores, and how-tos of producing a workable, valuable handbook. You'll get a perspective on what it should look (and sound) like, who ought to write it, how long it should be, what it must contain, and what it can leave out. With our handbook in hand, you're on your way to producing your own manual that does its job perfectly.

Mission Statement

Because the point of this exercise is to help you write a handbook — which, ideally, contains a mission statement — let's put the mission of handbooks into just such a proclamation.

An employee handbook's mission is to
- communicate indispensable company policies and practices,
- make explicit the mutual agreements between employee and employer without being an actual contract,
- state *and* express a company's philosophy,
- excite and motivate employees about their jobs,
- convey a broader sense of the company mission.

What does an actual mission statement look like? The best ones tread the tightrope between the world of ideas and the world of reality. They do more than simply give a sense of what the company aspires to do in the world; they also say exactly how it intends to do it. There's a good example in the employee guide of the wildly successful Seattle-based Starbucks Coffee Co. (See "Starbucks Brews a Strong Benefits Plan," p. 169), which states the company's charter as follows:

To establish Starbucks as the premier purveyor of the finest coffee in the world while maintaining our uncompromising principles as we grow.

The following five principles will help us measure the appropriateness of our decisions:

- Provide a great work environment and treat each other with respect and dignity.
- Apply the highest standards of excellence to the purchasing, roasting, and fresh delivery of our coffee.
- Develop enthusiastically satisfied customers all of the time.
- Contribute positively to our communities and our environment.
- Recognize that profitability is essential to our future success.

History

When you set about writing your company's saga, go beyond reciting your Standard Industrial Classification code, company address, and founder's birthplace. Try to personalize the place by bringing the primary characters to life. Here's an excellent example: In its staff handbook, Wild Oats Markets Inc., of Boulder, Colo. (see "The Motivational Employee Satisfaction Questionnaire," p. 93), kicks off with a history titled "A Long, Strange Trip." In it, president Mike Gilliland recounts (in what sounds like a letter to a friend) the haphazard process by which he and his partners grew the company into today's multimillion-dollar natural foods retailing venture. Interestingly, Gilliland candidly includes a description of the company's greatest failure:

> In 1986, thinking we were infallible, we opened a gourmet/natural foods/convenience store called The French Market (after the New Orleans market of the same name) in the Basemar Center in Boulder. The store lacked any focus, was terribly mismanaged (by me), and was a disaster for two years. Fortunately, Stella's and Lolita's [the company's first two stores] were profitable enough to keep us afloat.

And in another display of openness, Gilliland specifies who holds Wild Oats' equity:

> Libby Cook and I each own 32.3% of the stock Randy Clapp owns 31.3%, Bennett Bertoli, the company's legal counsel, owns 3% and David Wilkinson [a private investor] owns the remaining 1%.

Gilliland has a good rationale for incorporating such frank material. "Even though we are getting larger, Wild Oats is still pretty much a mom-and-pop store. We wanted people to know it is still owned by the first three people who bought it," he explains. As for the flop story, he says the company video used to imply that everyone who worked there went straight to heaven, until the owners realized it made more sense to "be a little more realistic about how we work here. We're a good company — but our execution is not always up to par."

Philosophy

Philosophy and identity are inexorably tied together for any company. What you do defines who you are, and what you believe in should be the basis for how you act. So your handbook is the place to walk the talk. All the philosophy in the world doesn't mean a thing unless the employee manual's tenets are firmly embedded in the company's human-resources policy and evidenced by its practices.

And though your entire handbook will manifest your philosophy, the great companies take a stab at telling employees explicitly what they believe in. "You need the basics of the nitty-gritty stuff, but the place where your handbook has an opportunity to shine is in its philosophy," says Joseph Mansueto, president of Morningstar Inc., a Chicago publisher of financial information for investors whose employee handbook lives up to that credo. "The handbook helps perpetuate the culture and serves as a keeper of the flame."

Strong corporate philosophies shine out of the first few pages of the great companies' employee manuals. Take Ashton Photo Co., a 110-employee photo-image printer in Salem, Ore. The company has spent a great deal of time working out what it considers to be its operating philosophy. In addition, its handbook includes succinct charts (see opposite page) that reveal its take on the social contract between the company and its workers, because, says vice president Alan White, "we use the handbook as a common tool to communicate our values to our employees."

ASHTON PHOTO: CHARTS FROM THE HANDBOOK

Employee's Role

Typical	Ashton Photo Co.
Permission to be right	Permission to be wrong
Rote	Conceptual
Orderly	Productive
Unimaginative	Creative
Quiet	Communicative
Obedient	Assertive
Trained	Educated
Hidden	Public posted performance
Somber	Witty, humorous
A commodity	A vital problem solver

Manager's Role

Typical	Ashton Photo Co.
Hold power	Give power
Authority figure	Role model
Go on hunch	Get hard data
Avoid blame	Make no excuses, no blame
Quota set by manager	Common goal: customer
Be an obstacle to change	Remove obstacles
Turf centered	Company centered
Holder of knowledge	Teacher
Do	Delegate and follow up
Status quo	Experimental

Style

There are two "elements of style" you need to be aware of: voice and look. In terms of voice, you will be sending out a message about the company simply by the choices you make in telling its story. So, do you really want to get all wordy and formal here? Probably not. In addition to being written in language that's crystal clear, good handbooks strike a tone that is welcoming and authoritative. (Bad ones make free with intimidating discourses on policy and lists of thou-shalt-nots, typically in unintelligible and uninviting legalese.) In fact, "all the guidelines for good writing apply to handbooks," advises Hewitt Associates' Rhodes, who stresses that handbooks must be easily understood. Write short sentences. Use small words. Think clarity.

But of course, don't lose sight of the "voice" in a larger sense.

"I want the handbook to feel like the advice of somebody who has worked here for 10 years telling me what it's like to work here," says Morningstar's Mansueto. The 350-employee company's guide has a collegial, informal style consistent with the company culture. One section, for instance, sports a breezy, direct style that speaks volumes:

Chill out! It's very hard, if not impossible, to provide great service if you are stressed out, so be good to yourself. Find ways to ease the tension and stress of daily work. Bring some toys to the office, get out for a short walk, listen to some favorite music, take the time to eat a good meal or even just spend a few minutes breathing deeply.

One nice way of thinking about the tone of the book has been stated by Susan Winters, executive vice president of Bulbtronics, a distributor of specialty lightbulbs in Farmingdale, N.Y.: "You can go to a park and see the signs saying, 'No running — no food — no walking on the grass,' but you also want to know, Well, what *can* I do? By reading a handbook, employees should know what kind of company they are working for."

Now to the look of the thing. Not only should the writing be clear but good handbooks ought to be designed to be read, as well. It should be as easy as possible for a reader to know what is going on. Rhodes, who has helped write countless handbooks, advises companies to stick to a few organizing principles.

- Pay attention to the visual aspect of the handbook: include a lot of charts and tables, and use other graphic methods such as breaking out long sentences as lists rather than printing heavy blocks of text.
- Make handbooks user-friendly; that is, include a table of contents, question-and-answer sections, an index, and even cross-referencing — anything to provide direction and guidance.
- Make the handbook easy to handle. No huge notebooks, for instance, or lightweight paper. Stick with a paper stock that's substantial enough to prevent light from going through it.
- Don't let authors get carried away with "attitude." This is a consumer's guide to the policies offered, and while it should be a showpiece, you mustn't let the show get in the way.

What to Include

The section that describes the company's policies, practices, and procedures may not be the heart of the book, but that section certainly does constitute its guts. Basic principle: Think about what employees want or need to know. Rhodes calls good handbooks "event-driven," meaning that employees refer to them when events such as sickness, vacation, or other incidents stir up a question for them. The essentials include sections on the following:

Employment Policies

Basic information on issues such as equal employment opportunity, job postings, work hours, regular and overtime pay, performance reviews, training, promotion, vacations and holidays, personal and sick days, leaves of absence, jury duty, and so on.

Benefits

Fundamentals on such perks as health, dental, and life insurance; short-term and long-term disability; worker's compensation; retirement programs; tuition reimbursement; and employee-assistance programs.

Employee Conduct

Information on themes as specific as the company's dress code and as broad as personal and professional development.

Optional sections may be added on:

Glossary

"All companies have their own words and meanings for words," says Alan White of Ashton Photo, which publishes a four-page glossary in the back of its handbook "to get people up to speed on the language of the organization." There's a difference at Ashton between *late* ("not completed on time in a given department"), *delayed* ("production of a job has been suspended, awaiting information from the customer"), and *on hold* ("production of a job has been suspended for accounting reasons").

Organization Chart

Ashton also includes a chart showing how the company is organized. The chart is made up of three interlocking circles, which, according to White, depict the way duties and responsibilities overlap (see next page). He says the company's handbook also contains other charts and tables with job

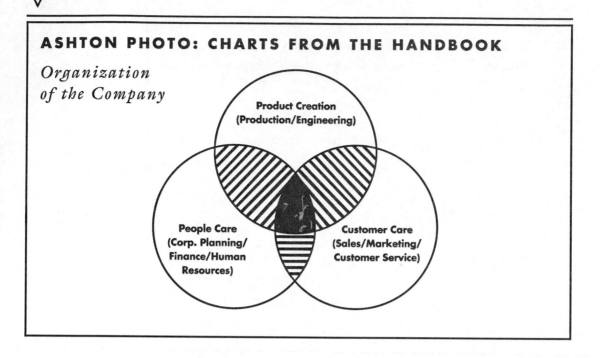

ASHTON PHOTO: CHARTS FROM THE HANDBOOK

Organization of the Company

Product Creation
(Production/Engineering)

People Care
(Corp. Planning/
Finance/Human
Resources)

Customer Care
(Sales/Marketing/
Customer Service)

descriptions and explanations of the production process that are designed to give people a sense of where they fit in the organization.

Some handbooks give the names of company officers, departments, and services; others may contain a map of the premises. Others list the office phone numbers (sometimes home numbers as well) of every employee.

What to Leave Out

When you think about what to put in, don't forget about what to keep out. The best handbooks don't spell out everything; instead, they serve as menus for action, leaving plenty of room for individual discretion.

When Ann Rhoades, vice president at Southwest Airlines Co., in Dallas, came to the company in 1989, its handbook was 380 pages and bloating toward 450 in a new draft. Horrified, she threw it out and replaced it with *Guidelines for Leaders.* The 50-page book contains plenty of material on company policy but is far more in line with Southwest's credo that employees have the right to make individual decisions. Rather than spelling out what employees should do in every situation, Rhoades says, the hand-book advises that "very few decisions are black-and-white and, as managers, it is important that we make decisions that are good business decisions and make sense, given each specific situation."

Concludes Mansueto of Morningstar: "It's important to commu-nicate the broader principles of how you want people to perform — and then let them apply those principles to everyday life."

Process

There comes a time in every company's growth when an employee manual really is essential. For Bulbtronics, that time came about six years ago, when the now 70-employee company got to the 25- to 30-person mark and policies had to be standardized, according to Winters. Until then, personnel policies had been decided on an ad hoc basis. "But at 60, 50, even 40 employees, you are better off with something that has no ambiguities," Winters says.

Winters, who runs Bulbtronics's operations, says people always had the same questions: What were the hours of operation? What was the vacation policy? When were they entitled to benefits? Finally, she realized there were too many "little things that may not have been communicated, but I didn't want people to know after the fact."

Last year, the company revised its handbook. Looking back, Winters thinks that having a handbook has its pros and cons. "While it does enable you to be fair and consistent," she says, "it leaves some of the discretion out of the employer's hands. If you put things in writing, it feels like you lose the human factor."

Although contacting an expert can help in certain key areas — such as legal assurance — there certainly is value in writing the handbook your-self. Consider the experience of Kingston Technology Corp., of Fountain Valley, Calif., which topped the *Inc.* 500 list of fastest-growing private companies in 1992. It commissioned a handbook several years ago, sometime around employee number 75. According to marketing director Ron Seide, the hired hand merely used the handbook of AST Research Inc. (a competitor of Kingston's), called up the search-and-replace function on the word-processing program, and spat out a revised version.

Kingston's employees hated it. So they did something about it: They threw out the hired hand's tome and wrote their own. Listen to Carol Ruprecht, in international sales: "The owners thought the handbook would be something they'd distribute and then file in drawers. They never expected that anybody would be offended by it. But it contained all this legal butt-covering language, which made it seem as if the company didn't trust us and we didn't trust it."

"I was hired by Kingston's president, who told me he does everything by a handshake," says Seide. "In fact, we 'shook hands' over the phone when I was hired. Right away, it was made clear to me that this was an environment of trust and loyalty.

"So some of us confronted the owners and said, 'The company handbook is one of the first exposures people have to Kingston. A new employee will think this is the kind of company they're working for.' The owners' response was to ask me and my sister [who works in marketing] to rewrite it.

"We spent a lot of time talking with John Tu and David Sun, the two founders, about their philosophies on all our policies, such as, 'What is the philosophy about sick leave?' And from that we wrote a handbook that is simple and straightforward. Now, if I had more time to do the next employee handbook, I would change one thing: make it more simple and straightforward."

The foregoing shows the value of *creating* a handbook: the mere act of writing one gathers companywide information in a central place and forces companies to make policies clear. "Whether they are explicit or not, companies already have policies in place," says lawyer Robert J. Nobile, a partner at Epstein Becker & Green, in New York. Nobile, who has written a guide to employee handbooks, says the act of making a handbook can be a step forward for a company in determining what its policies actually are.

Legal Stuff

"The handbook is the most important document a company can have," says Nobile. "I have seen companies go into court with it in hand

and have cases against them thrown out of court. But it is a double-edged sword. I have seen employees be successful in their actions against companies because of poor handbook draftsmanship."

This is where the handbook gets serious. First of all, companies can't avoid including several company statements on specific laws. The Family and Medical Leave Act policy must be in a company handbook. Also, you are strongly advised to include a written sexual harassment policy and a section on dispute resolution. In addition, in more and more states, a smoking or nonsmoking policy is now required. Since requirements vary from state to state, the wisest course of action is to consult your state employment office or your attorney.

The central legal aspect is that a handbook is not a contract, and while stressing the importance of company policies, employers should explicitly state that the handbook should not be viewed as such. Nobile adds, "From a legal standpoint it is very important to reserve the right to make changes."

As for avoiding lawsuits, Nobile warns that the most common mistakes he sees are policies that are not drafted clearly. A handbook may refer to a policy for "all employees," he says, when in fact the policy applies only to full-timers.

Nobile's guide includes an all-purpose disclaimer that many companies ask employees to read and sign:

> This Handbook is not a contract, express or implied, guaranteeing employment for any specific duration. Although we hope that your employment relationship with us will be long term, either you or the company may terminate this relationship at any time, for any reason, with or without cause or notice.

Many company handbooks also ask employees to sign a page acknowledging receipt of the handbook and recognizing its statement that everything in it is subject to change. (See also "What's the Law," p. 217.)

How Many Pages?

So how long should your handbook be? There's no one right length; it's really up to you. The goal is to make it thorough but accessible. Whole

Foods' version, which is currently undergoing major revisions, runs 104 pages; Kingston's runs 20 (and they are small pages). It's far more important to focus on whether or not the handbook is comprehensive. If it addresses the key questions employees have and conveys the company's basic operating beliefs, then you can say your piece and get it printed.

How Much Money?

Handbooks needn't cost a bundle. White of Ashton Photo estimates that if he factors in the staff time taken to write his company's handbook and type it up, several hundred dollars for a lawyer to review it, and the initial printing costs, the manual cost roughly $800. Now, when he needs extras of the typed, plain-paper document with its thicker stock cover, White takes it to a local printer. His cost: about $1.50 each. ■

RESOURCES

Encyclopedia of Employee Handbooks, by Stephen D. Bruce (Business & Legal Reports; $129.95; 800-727-5257, ext. 169).

Guide to Employee Handbooks, by Robert J. Nobile (Warren, Gorham & Lamont; $149; 800-950-1211).

The Employee Handbook Audit, by the Alexander Hamilton Institute ($65.25; book and diskette for personal computers [IBM or compatible] $96.95; 201-825-3377).

Making It Work with Your Number Two

Sharing responsibility at the top is never easy, especially when you own the company. An effective working relationship with your second-in-command depends on many intangibles: mutual trust, chemistry, style, and values. Compatibility eases the way, but not without clear, ongoing communication.

—

Leadership is a two-way street. Seconds-in-command grumble about the frustrations of working for entrepreneurs — the latter's capriciousness, closed-mindedness, and constant interference. Conversely, many business owners would sooner strain themselves to the breaking point than trust anyone to make important decisions for them.

But the reality is that you can't do it all by yourself — not if you want to grow your company and buy some personal sanity. What entrepreneurs need to learn is how to work closely and productively with a second-in-command. They need to know how to structure and maintain the relationship and how to build trust through clear communication and mutual understanding.

With those objectives in mind, *Inc.* talked to more than 150 CEOs and their number twos about how they work together. We asked them lots of questions about what works, what doesn't work, and how things could be improved. We think we've gained some insights into what number twos and bosses think of each other and how you can achieve the best possible teamwork at the top.

Be honest about what you want. Should be obvious, right? If we are to judge from what we hear from CEOs and the men and women who work for them, however, it isn't. Why? Because number twos get hired for all kinds of reasons: pressure from bankers and/or investors; weariness, even boredom, on the part of the founder; and once in a blue moon, because a CEO is truly interested in sharing some responsibility.

Before you bring someone on, commune with yourself. Stand in front of the mirror. What are you really trying to achieve and what kinds of decision making are you willing to part with? As you try to articulate your ideas, they probably will change. But that's good, because when the time comes to communicate the job structure and your aims to number two, you'll know you have clearly defined them for yourself first.

Think chemistry. Considering the hours CEOs and their deputies spend together and the close quarters in which they spend them, liking each other is an absolute must. In the course of selecting your second-in-command, you'll find plenty of individuals who look good on paper. But you need to test compatibility, too.

Ken Davidson, chairman, president, and CEO of Maxxim Medical Inc., a manufacturer of specialty medical products in Sugarland, Tex., was lucky. He persuaded a former college roommate to take the number-two job. The two play together in a rock-and-roll band on weekends, as they did in the late 1960s. If you have no longtime friends either suited for the job or available, however, do what Kent Williams did. Before making his decision, Williams, CEO of Jiffy Lube, the "quick-change" company in Greenville, S.C., went out to eat three times with the man he ultimately hired. "I'd known him in a business setting," Williams says, "but I wanted to feel comfortable with him as a private person as well."

You don't need to like everybody you hire, but your number two is different. Good rapport and compatibility facilitate communication; moreover, they make it a pleasure. If you can't imagine being stuck with the person for five hours on a layover in a remote airport, keep looking.

Contrary to what you may think, values matter. You don't have to enjoy the same music. You don't have to like the same food. But on business basics, including attitudes toward growth and how to treat people, you need to be on the same wavelength or be able to agree quickly. If you're not of one mind, you'll split the company in two. Employees will take sides. They'll pit you against each other. To hear people who have skipped this step tell it, things can get ugly.

Figure out — ideally *before* you bring a number two on board — the principles underlying what you're trying to accomplish. Be specific. Put those principles into words. If personal goals figure into the equation (one CEO, for instance, wanted to optimize the potential sale price of his business), spell them out, too. Make sure that you and your prospective deputy are in agreement. Otherwise, you'll be at loggerheads needlessly. Whatever the basics are, hold your deputy accountable to them, and be prepared to be held accountable in turn.

Carve up the territory and stand back. If you really want to build a productive relationship at the top, be specific about who'll be handling what. You and your right hand should pin down each of your areas of responsibility and levels of authority regarding spending, hiring, and so on, and clearly articulate the hoped-for results. Then get out of each other's way, and be prepared to avoid each other at certain times if necessary: most CEOs find it's painless to draw the lines but next to impossible not to cross them at some point. The name of this particular game is self-discipline. Set the ground rules and obey them religiously.

There are several good reasons to stick to your knitting. If you're constantly hovering, your number two will feel less responsible for what happens, which means that all sorts of problems will be *yours*. The people who work for the deputy will soon figure out whose opinion really matters, and they'll try to pull you back into the loop. Ultimately, the person you hired to alleviate your burden will be rendered totally ineffective, and you in turn will become less effective by taking that burden back on yourself. No matter how neatly you define your respective roles, rest assured there's always going to be some overlap between the two of you. Ideally, though, you'll think twice before gumming up the works.

Loyalty. Inexperienced CEOs *think* they want loyalty. They *think* that what they want is a hardworking servant who's good at following cues. But don't kid yourself. When it comes to making critical decisions, loyalty can be a big handicap. What you need is someone who can stand up to your crazy ideas. This means a real two-way exchange; it also means that you'll frequently be the listener.

Understand, we're not talking about someone who will undermine your basic principles. We're talking tactics: how to move ahead, how to use resources to meet company goals. "You want somebody who can help you think things through," says Mike Shanker, formerly second-in-command at Broadway & Seymour Inc., a computer services company based in Charlotte, N.C. Often, that means somebody who can tell you you're wrong.

Find a style of communicating that works. CEOs, as a group, seem astoundingly undisciplined about the way they communicate with their number twos. They don't see such interaction as a big issue. Ironically, their seconds see it as their bosses' single biggest problem area. Many complain that their CEOs don't take the time to talk; others complain the communication is too random or informal which,

---

THE VIEW FROM #2:
Chico Lager

For two years, until January 1991, Lager was CEO of Ben & Jerry's Homemade Inc., Waterbury, Vt., the ice cream manufacturer whose 1993 net sales were $140 million. Because Jerry Greenfield had not played an active management role for several years, Lager shared operational duties with Ben Cohen and struggled to keep their respective leadership roles in balance.

"If you don't develop a relationship with the founder in which people perceive you as making decisions, as being a force to be reckoned with in the company, you'll have no credibility with the people who work for you. You go into meetings, and you're paralyzed: you get all this input, and instead of making a decision, you say, 'I'd better see what Ben thinks.' You can't operate that way. Or I'd go on record talking down this or that idea, but Ben would want to do it. Then I'd have no credibility when I had to go around saying, 'Hey, guess what, we're going to do this, and it's a great idea.' It became a very negative dynamic within our organization."

in their minds, indicates lack of respect for their position.

Communication is one of those areas you simply can't ignore. With good rapport and clearly spelled-out roles and responsibilities, catch-as-catch-can communication may work well. But don't count on it. Finding the approach that's best for the two of you may take effort and planning. Many number twos find that scheduled weekly or bimonthly meetings help them gain a clearer understanding of what the owner is thinking. Such meetings also offer a regular forum for presenting new ideas.

Talk more than you think you have to. Some CEOs and their deputies go a step further in the communication department. They set up special meetings just to talk about *how* things are going between them. Often, those meetings are held off-site, away from constant interruptions — over breakfast, perhaps. As explained by one deputy, an executive from Florida, these conversations are not just catch-up sessions but focus specifically on what's not working and how to fix it: "I'll use our sessions to say, 'Here's a situation we could have handled better. Next time, could you try to do it this way?' And my CEO does the same." A second-in-command from a company in New Jersey underscores the importance of meeting this need: "When you work as the number two, it's easy to get demoralized. It's a very lonely job, so you need to create a mechanism for feedback."

Don't lock horns in broad daylight. We said it before: Disagreements can be good. They can lead to smarter, better decisions. But be conscious of *where* you have them. Understand that if you and your number two voice your differences in front of other people, you'll lose control over how things are interpreted once a decision is made. No matter what the issue is, employees are going to look for a loser, and that "loser" will have a tough time implementing the decision once the dust has settled. "It can set off a really negative dynamic within the organization," says one right hand, who's had to eat his words more than once.

You can't anticipate every disagreement. But you should be able to flag the other person if potential differences emerge. One CEO explains how this works: "We can tell, when we're sitting in a meeting, if we're not on the same sheet of music. Usually, we table that part of the discussion and find a time to talk about it privately."

Go away often and don't call. Beware of communication overkill. Technology makes it much easier for CEOs to get away — and, at the same time, harder for them to actually leave. We heard about a CEO, for example, who would regularly use the car phone to call number two, just minutes after pulling out of the parking lot, sometimes just to ask, "What's happening?" To which came the reply, "Nothing's different from when you were here, except it's a little quieter."

If you want your deputy to make decisions independently, you have to let him or her do it. Of course, you can be sure there will be some choices you wouldn't have made or possibly won't like. Owners are forever agonizing over what to do about that. "In your heart, it's so hard to say, 'Here's a problem; now go and solve it,'" admits John Bourget, CEO of Beta One Inc., a market research company in Farmington, Conn. If you want the relationship to work, you have to learn to understand how the other person thinks and support that person's decisions.

If you feel the urge to check in all the time, you have a problem. Get rid of the car phone. Or maybe you need to rethink what you really want.

The cornerstone is trust. Sooner or later, practically every right hand we spoke with made it clear that trust was what mattered most in a relationship with the boss. More than anything else — more, even, than money. As many of them noted, trust is hard to define but not hard to recognize. Saying you trust your number two, as near-

THE VIEW FROM #2
P. J. Mayes

Mayes has played a variety of number two roles with four different companies, including the western U.S. distributor for Raleigh Industries, a large British bicycle retailer, and Sundance Spas, a manufacturer of portable spas. Her areas of responsibility have ranged from finance to customer service to human resources.

"The greatest weakness of all the entrepreneurs I've worked with is in managing people. When they got to the point where their companies were so large that they could no longer deal one-to-one with everyone, they had to have supervisors and managers; at that point, they were in trouble with their management skills, which was usually the reason they looked for a number two in the first place. Maybe they didn't place value on having people skills, or they didn't pay attention to it, or it was difficult for them. I don't know which, or why, but I found it to be a constant problem."

ly all CEOs say, is easy. But talk is cheap. Ask John Vinton, who, until he quit, was second-in-command at R. W. Frookies Inc., a cookie company in Englewood Cliffs, N.J.

"Owners don't realize it," says Vinton, "but they could say, 'By the way, I'm going to cut your paycheck by 10%, but I want you to run the company for me,' and it would still make number twos happier than if they said, 'I'll give you more, but I'll run the company.' When push comes to shove and somebody says, 'Go do that, do it your way, and I'm behind you,' that's what really turns people on. The absence of that drove me away." ■

WHAT'S ON THEIR MINDS?

Far and away, the main concerns of seconds-in-command focus on communication and roles and responsibilities. Next in line are the intangibles: personality and style. Here are the statistics from a recent survey of more than 150 companies by *Inc.* magazine.

FAILURE TO COMMUNICATE

62% of number twos say their boss communicates by catching up as-catch-can, but there is no formal way of communicating.

23% say their biggest problem with their number one is communication.

16% say their bosses never or only sometimes listen to them.

WHO'S IN CHARGE HERE?

64% of number twos said they aspire to be a number one.

46% of number twos who thought just one person should be in charge said they should be the one.

29% of number twos thought employees perceived them as running the company.

25% said they *do* run the company.

TIME FOR DALE CARNEGIE

42% of number twos said their boss needed to work on personality traits or people skills; only 13% of number twos said their own people skills needed work.

27% of number twos said their biggest problem with their number one consisted of differences in personality and style.

26% said their biggest area of disagreement with their boss concerned dealing with employees. ■

What Are the Five Cardinal Sins?

Sizing up the key threats to sound management

—

by Stanley Herz

In the business environment certain behavior patterns can damage relationships and inhibit the exchange of important information. Here are five hurdles to beware of — all of which involve communication with your team.

1. Being secretive

Knowledge is power. But knowledge withheld is also power, and that power can be destructive — even when the information withheld is itself innocuous. Consider the following case:

It is rumored that something drastic will shortly happen at the firm, a rapidly growing local business with 700-plus employees. Phone conversations are being increasingly preceded by slammed office doors. The mailroom is working overtime interchanging sealed envelopes officialized with the notation "confidential." The senior staff, normally a laid-back and informal group, are abruptly departing from their command posts in full dress regalia to attend unannounced meetings at unannounced locations. Who knows what is happening? Everyone! For whatever truths employees lack, they create. Erroneous information and paranoiac half-truths rush in to fill the void.

Stanley Herz is president of Stanley Herz & Co., in Somers, N.Y.

The company may be ready to announce a significant product line expansion, or it may be that the action is the official ritual preceding a reshuffling of responsibilities that will affect no one below the vice-presidential level. But for those who do not know, it can only mean a takeover, dissolution, and layoffs. That's human nature!

Secrecy at the top can start the rumor mill operating. But there's more — it also tends to sanction a kind of copycat secrecy as practiced by managers at lower levels.

To create the appearance of personal power, some managers operate behind a curtain of secrecy. It's an extension of childhood playacting: "I know something you don't know, and I'm not going to tell you." Such managers don't merely close their office door when doing routine work — they slam them with an attention-grabbing bang. If they take a phone call in a public area, they loudly announce, "This is too sensitive to discuss here; I'll take this call in my office." (Bang goes the door!) An upcoming meeting with their superior is publicly proclaimed as a confidential, tough decision-making session, even though the planned topic is coordination of the company picnic.

Secrecy erodes everyone's self-confidence. Subordinates perceive that trust and power go together. Because they are not trusted with company information, they feel impotent in their job. All too frequently, they also see themselves as about to be victimized by the information that is being withheld.

Confidentiality should be utilized only when it is absolutely essential.

2. Not communicating clearly

Here's an oft-repeated late-night movie scene. In a dark basement somewhere in war-torn Paris, members of the Resistance huddle around the short-wave radio. The disconnected words from the speaker intermittently rise above the constant static.

Advance the time to the present, replace the blacked-out basement with the fluorescence of a modern office, and still only parts of the message are getting through. This static, though, is not from atmospheric disturbances; it comes from three barriers to communication — modification, screening, or ambiguity — erected by either the sender or receiver of a message. Both situations result in the withholding of unpleasant but necessary information.

Modification: The sender of a message intentionally alters it in order to distort the impact on the receiver. The manager of a department, for example, may temper the criticism of a subordinate so as not to offend or not to create a confrontation. A subordinate may embellish a status report to circumvent the wrath of an angered manager.

Screening: The listener hears only that which he or she wants to hear. The motive behind screening is self-protection. Employees with low confidence or self-esteem are especially vulnerable to screening. They block out the part of the message that threatens their well-being. Who hasn't been invited to give an honest opinion and then found the questioner taking argumentative exception to that opinion?

Ambiguity: Vague generalizations are lent the respectability of factual data. When a manager does not go beyond the surface in identifying a problem and then transmits that superficiality to subordinates to act on, the result is ambiguity. It is a form of deception that produces only the semblance of progress. An executive's assertion that "we should computerize because it's good for business" is so indefinite that many computer installations never get past the conceptual stage. A manager's order to "do something about financial reporting" is so vague that it neither identifies the problem nor suggests the standards sought.

Both modification and screening can be eliminated if management creates an honest and empathic environment in which the dissemination of unpleasant news can be accepted as advancing both individual and company interests. Criticism, when used as a positive tool for furthering personal or professional growth, is rarely resented. A dismal status report, perceived by everyone as the first step in correcting a business problem, can be presented coherently, nonthreateningly, and without modification and will be received without damaging apprehension. The danger of ambiguity is eliminated when the atmosphere invites open discourse. If the message is buried in superficiality, subordinates' responses will quickly reveal the need for specificity or direction.

3. Socializing

Can friendship be bad in a business environment? A difficult question. But certainly it can be awkward and an impediment to achieving business objectives. Close social camaraderie constitutes the concrete support for a rewarding personal intimacy. But creating an unequal power relationship by mixing that relationship with management can crumble the support, collapsing both friendship and business effectiveness.

A common situation is one in which friends start out as peers and then one is appointed to a higher position. Large organizations often circumvent the potential difficulties by placing the promoted employee in a different division, where established congenialities will not hamper performance. But the frequent interactions and fast-paced informality of an entrepreneurial organization typically make such separation difficult if not impossible. Even though the friends' interactions are frequent and informal, objectivity, fairness, and sometimes toughness must take the place of habitual companionship and camaraderie.

Far more perilous to organizational synergism is a superior who uses camaraderie as a management tool. Instead of restraining personal relationships, he or she encourages weekend socializing with employees and spouses, organizes evening card games, and leads the staff from office to lounge for a few "friendly" drinks. For some managers, such practices can lead to problems instead of cohesion, rapport, and team building. Friendship becomes substituted for leadership. Such managers may see their subordinates as parents or siblings, from whom attention and respect can be obtained.

Whatever the cause, maintaining out-of-office social bonds with subordinates poses the following threats to good management.

- Staff members who are not so favored may be alienated by a value system that appears to recognize alliance above performance.
- Unfavored employees may be less candid or cooperative with peers tagged as the boss's buddies.
- Subordinates not receptive to social overtures will view them as onerous overtime business obligations.

- Favorites may inappropriately hold their tongues or feel secure as they slack off.
- Spouses' interactions with the boss and other personal considerations may prove distractions — affecting what should be nonrelated business decisions.

For the entrepreneurial firm, the issue of socializing must be managed with exceptional tact and good sense. The business media are filled with the histories of promising start-up enterprises that met their doom on the rocks of well-intentioned friendship.

4. Suppressing bad news

A certain legendary king beheaded any knave so foolish as to bring him ill tidings — a lesson not likely to have been wasted on his messenger service.

Considering the fear many managers feel in presenting adverse findings to their superiors, one would suspect that locked in dank subterranean record retention centers, along with old general ledgers and yellowing computer printouts, are overstuffed cartons of heads once worn by former colleagues guilty of issuing unfavorable reports.

Let's look at a typical — albeit fictional — case of an accounting manager, "Stephen Walden," who may have had that fear.

> Stephen's reports to senior management often emerged from an almost mystical metamorphic process that transformed the most dismal prognosis into glowing expectations. In addition, he repeatedly obligated himself to unrealistic completion dates, even when more time was available. His boss, the controller, was eager for overdue feedback on workloads and staff utilization, but Stephen was oblivious — he continued to accept all requests thrown his department's way without a whimper of protest. His staff was, of course, resentful of the impossible workload and demoralized because deadlines were missed.
>
> The most ruinous action, however, was one that prompted the controller to administer the coup de grâce: During a routine audit, it was discovered that to make things look rosy, Stephen had instructed his staff to build up significant deferred assets on the balance sheet so as to force the monthly actual profits to conform to earlier forecasted results.

The moral of Stephen's story? Achieving objectives often calls for the unpleasant tasks of (1) identifying and broadcasting problems whose very resolution depends on people knowing about them and (2) applying effective solutions.

5. Reproaching with praise

Praise — a sin? Yes, praise can be a backhanded demotivator.

Misguided managers specifically use oblique praise as a means to criticize without confrontation. A compliment to a subordinate for working extra hours is actually intended as condemnation of a nearby peer for devoting insufficient time to a task. Rather than being inspired, the third party takes the spurious praise for what it is — public insult.

An employee will be pleased and motivated by expressed approval from a superior whether or not coworkers are aware of it. If praise is offered publicly, as at a promotional celebration, care must be taken that others do not perceive the occasion as a slight to their own self-esteem. ■

The Vital Signs Assessment

How's it going? That's all Pat Lancaster needed to know. But getting useful answers to that question from his managers was anything but simple. How do you get your leaders to give you a report without your seeming overly intrusive? How do you get people to assess their energy level honestly, say what they're worried about, or discuss department morale without sounding like a snoop?

Lancaster tried the usual management tricks. Management-by-walking-around, for example, yielded sketchy data at best. "People responded based on their most recent conversation or the latest customer interaction they'd had," claims the founder of Lantech Inc., a $50-million stretch-wrapping machinery manufacturer in Louisville. Hunting for clues in financial reports proved equally disappointing: "Numbers are great, but they talk about the past," Lancaster says. "I needed current information reflecting human motivations and conflicts."

In 1986 Lancaster hit upon the solution: group-leader reports. Filled out weekly by his five top managers, the reports give "an aerial photo" of the entire company. Early on, though, Lancaster wasn't sure whether his new form was the best idea or the worst. Week after week the write-ups brought bad news about his then 14-year-old company. "There was infighting. Departments blaming other departments for botched deliveries and promises to the customer not kept," Lancaster says. In Lantech's decentralized structure, departments such as standard products, custom products, and research and development are separate profit centers, and each is headed by

Sending information down the line is a snap compared with pumping it upward. Lantech managers' weekly reports unclog communication and keep the company healthy.

one of Lancaster's top managers. The reports clearly showed that group leaders were spending far too much time protecting their profit centers and too little time attending to customer problems.

Armed with that feedback and more, Lancaster put his company through a complete overhaul by instituting team-building programs, companywide training, and regular customer-focus checks. The report results were not the only stimulus for the corporate makeover, but they provided key early warning signals.

Eight years later the reports are far less emotionally charged but no less helpful. "This form gives me comfort," Lancaster says. "I travel 50% of the time, and I get these faxed to me wherever I am. They're the first pages I read on my stack." He figures he's gained at least 20% more time thanks to the reports — time that used to be wasted either wading through garbled communications or refereeing conflicts between managers. "Meetings used to get bogged down by blurry communications." Now they're "snappy and to the point," he says.

"Anyone should be able to fill out this form in five minutes," Lancaster explains. That's why the entire exercise fits on two sides of a single page. Moreover, Lancaster veered away from a question-and-answer format, preferring to use a string of open statements that invite managers to respond. Rather than interrogating his people with a slew of accusatory questions, Lancaster hoped to initiate conversation and then allow each manager plenty of latitude.

But the 52-year-old CEO offers one cardinal rule: "Never use the information to play 'gotcha.' If you do, then you might as well not do it at all."

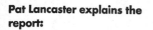

6 GOOD FORMS

Pat Lancaster explains the report:

1A It doesn't matter to me whether group leaders handwrite this or do it on the computer. It's short and shouldn't take more than five minutes to fill out.

1B I ask for it weekly — as fast as our organization is moving, we can get out of sync in only a week. I want it on Thursday because I meet with these five leaders every Monday. I want to be aware of any issues before then so I know what to keep my ears open for.

2A When personal energy is heading south, there's a good chance a leader isn't feeling good about his job, so this is a critical issue. I've tried to make my query uncharged and nonjudgmental. I'm asking about the leader's fuel gauge. It's rare that anyone checks low. Answers usually range from medium to high. Also, as I review the reports, I know to keep each individual in mind. Some people smile all the harder when things are tough.

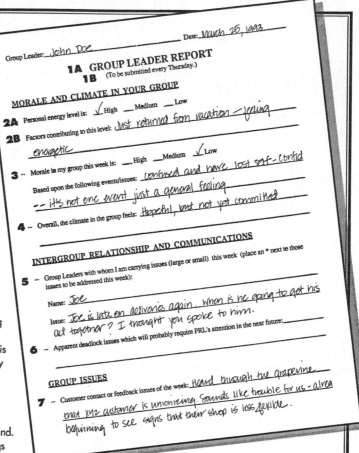

Group Leader: _John Doe_   Date: _March 25, 1993_

1A GROUP LEADER REPORT
1B (To be submitted every Thursday.)

MORALE AND CLIMATE IN YOUR GROUP

2A Personal energy level is: ✓ High __ Medium __ Low

2B Factors contributing to this level: _Just returned from vacation — feeling_
energetic.

3 — Morale in my group this week is: __ High __ Medium ✓ Low
Based upon the following events/issues: _confused and have lost self-confid_
— it's not one event just a general feeling.

4 — Overall, the climate in the group feels: _Hopeful, but not yet committed_

INTERGROUP RELATIONSHIP AND COMMUNICATIONS

5 — Group Leaders with whom I am carrying issues (large or small) this week (place an * next to those issues to be addressed this week):
Name: _Joe_
Issue: _Joe is late on deliveries again. When is he going to get his_
act together? I thought you spoke to him.

6 — Apparent deadlock issues which will probably require PRL's attention in the near future: _____

GROUP ISSUES

7 — Customer contact or feedback issues of the week: _Heard through the grapevine_
that XYZ customer is unionizing. Sounds like trouble for us — alrea
beginning to see signs that their shop is less flexible.

2B This fleshes it out — tells me what's sapping people's energy. Here, someone may be tired, or overcommitted, and it might help if the two of us review the schedule.

3 I match this answer against the personal-energy response. In this example, the manager's energy is high, but his group's is low. I can see that his people don't share his optimism. I'll keep a very close eye on this situation to see how they work together. Also, if group energy is low, it might indicate that the manager's energy is low despite his claims.

4 The answers here point to the future. Usually, I see a longer view — more upbeat. Frankly, if there weren't a more optimistic spin here, I'd really get worried.

5 When we first started using these reports, you'd see finger-pointing among departments with no hope of resolution. If I see someone laying blame or hear a one-sided story, I step in. But if I see people working together to resolve the problem, I stay out of it.

6 Some people have a hard time asking for help, and they invariably leave this blank. You have to have some knowledge of each individual, and if there's no direct request for help here, I can check other sections of the report for indirect appeals, say, for example, number 14.

7 Here's where I want the managers to tell me what their customers are doing and what's new with them. I want to know that managers are spending time with customers; otherwise, I start to worry that we're too internally focused.

8 This is what I call an alignment question. The leader attaches charts showing how the profit center is doing against such predetermined measures as on-time delivery, reduced start-up defects, and shortened lead time. These standards are set yearly and are similar from profit center to profit center.

9 Was anybody fired, given an award? I'm looking here for signs of leadership ability.

10 My managers use this as an opportunity to ask me for help with compensation questions as well as personnel-management problems. I try to respond to these quandaries within a day or two.

11 This item offers one of the most useful opportunities for those who use it. It's another non-pejorative way to get people to tell me things they might not otherwise mention. Lots of times the responses here underscore comments made elsewhere in the report. I'm a better coach when I know what's on someone's mind.

12 If something I've said has caused any confusion, here's where I find out about it. This manager heard me say two conflicting things and wants to know the score. Also, this query sends the message that I am a CEO who is willing to be told that things aren't always perfect, or even great.

13 Each one of these five leaders knows a lot, and I want them to pull away from their day-to-day duties to think for a moment about what's going on In the world around us that I might have missed.

14 I want to know as soon as there's any indication a deadline might be missed. Here's a tip-off that perhaps explains why there's anxiety in this report or in other reports. If one guy is not meeting deadlines, I often see the ripple effect in other reports.

15 Each leader has a set of personal objectives against which that leader is measured in the quarterly review. But rather than having the leaders glance at these measures only once a quarter, I want them to examine them weekly. The idea is to keep leaders intimately aware of expectations so they're not surprised at review time. It saves me from rude awakenings, too.

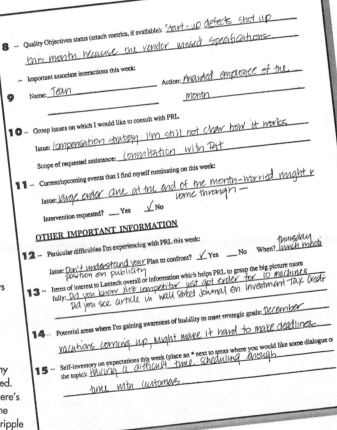

The Productivity-Boosting Gain-Sharing Report

Back in 1980 the future didn't look so good for Ed Rogan and the plastic-knob manufacturing business that had been Rogan Corp.'s bread and butter for decades. As sophisticated instrumentation moved from analog to digital displays and no longer needed old-style controls for calibration, company president Rogan feared that "technology was going to make us obsolete." So he invested more than $2 million to replace the molding machines, and he introduced new products.

Rogan knew the success of his strategy rested on ratcheting down expenses dramatically. Yet labor, which constituted a large chunk of costs, seemed untouchable. Rogan's shop-floor employees expected annual raises regardless of the company's performance. And to buck that, he feared, would set off "a big cultural battle." Rogan visited Mexico with an eye to relocating operations there but preferred to stay in Northbrook, Ill., where the company had been since it was founded, in 1934. Instead he cast about for a solution that would "satisfy our concern for our people who were loyal, as well as let us survive."

In 1983 Rogan's quest led him to consider a gain-sharing program that would encourage employees to increase their overall productivity. The technique pegs workers' bonuses to improvements in efficiency. Rogan and Tom McGrath, a consultant at Jackson Gainsharing Co. in Marion, Ind., worked for six months analyzing the company's financial statements to determine the historical cost of labor as a percentage of expenses. Using that information, they set a target for productivity. Once output efficiency surpassed that goal, employees would enjoy the rewards.

This carefully designed weekly gain-sharing report has produced savings in labor costs and a steady stream of good ideas and proposals for efficiency.

Rogan realized that success would require universal enthusiasm. He had to sell the program to the workers, who would need to understand both its details and its implications. He firmly believes "this is not something to try alone. Bring in a professional." As an outsider, McGrath was in a position to act on the shop floor as an ombudsman who could consider without prejudice the concerns of employees.

Rogan rolled out the program in 1986. "We wanted to start in an up cycle," Rogan says, "so we could have a modest payout." For the first four-week cycle, gain sharing paid out an extra $11,712, and for the next, $12,279. In the first year and a half, gain sharing rewarded employees with checks equal to 16.3% of their wages, in addition to their regular pay.

For a gain-sharing plan to succeed, employees must see the link between their performance and their pay. Accordingly, Rogan has institutionalized regular publication of the company's production and financial results. The company posts every day's shipping totals on the factory walls. The weekly gain-sharing report focuses everyone's attention on production improvements and efficiency. Every Friday Rogan or one of the four other members of his steering committee (they rotate on a five-week cycle) reviews the report with every department and shift.

It's not just a stand-up presentation. Questions are encouraged and receive clear, direct answers. Committee members know it's crucial that each of the 102 workers in the program understands his or her own potential to affect the bottom line.

And employees *have* learned — as evidenced by the variety of ways they've made improvements on the shop floor and contributed more than 300 ideas for increasing efficiency.

▽6 GOOD FORMS

Using March 1993 as an example, Ed Rogan explains how to read the gain-sharing report.

1 This is the report for the 85th four-week period since we started. At the time, we'd been doing this for six and a half years. The four-week cycle is tied to our production/shipping schedule.

2 A push in week #4 typically follows a bad week or two. With the economic uncertainty that surrounded the new president, we chose to work overtime regularly rather than hire new employees. Week #2's low overtime pay shows there were fewer hours worked that week.

Now I try to reconstruct exactly what happened in weeks #2 and #3. It could have been that one of two things was going on: On-time delivery was up for that week, so production might have been higher. Or, some department's work in process was low. That week, I learned, it was the latter. The important thing is that these numbers alert me to a shift in the work flow. To keep everyone's confidence and enthusiasm high, I have to be able to say, "Here's what is happening — and what we're doing about it."

3 From Gross Sales, the amount we bill, we subtract Returns, what our customers send back. One of the beautiful things about the program is that now we literally pass the returns around and say, "Hey, this $500 order was sent back by XYZ company. Why?" Until we started the gain-sharing program, we hadn't done anything to make our whole company aware of the problem of defective work. Last year, rework took $8,000 out of gain sharing. Employees can do something about that. So we post a chart that tracks rework and scrap and how much they cost. Our employees know that individually they can affect their paychecks.

GAIN-SHARING REPORT

1 PERIOD # 85

	WEEK #1 3-9-93	WEEK #2 3-16-93	WEEK #3 3-23-93	WEEK #4 3-30-93	TOTAL
2 WEEK ENDING					794,417
GROSS SALES	198,355	173,328	178,709	244,045	(6,464)
3 RETURNS	(1,132)	(1,269)	(3,125)	(938)	787,953
NET SALES	197,203	172,059	175,584	243,107	16,157
4 INVENTORY	(4289)	(19,001)	35,509	3938	804,110
VALUE PROD.	192,914	153,058	211,093	247,045	155,193
5 TARGET 19.3%	37,232	29,540	40,741	47680	90,428
REGULAR PAY	22,492	22,616	22,416	22,904	20,028
OVERTIME PAY	5,936	3464	5,479	5,149	4,216
VACATION PAY	1,054	1054	1054	1054	3,480
HOLIDAY PAY	870	870	870	870	772
PERSONAL PAY	193	193	193	193	9600
INSURANCE COST	2,400	2400	2400	2400	1248
OTHER	312	312	312	312	129,772
TOTAL LABOR	33,257	30,909	32,724	32,882	

GAINSHARING EARNED (LOST)

WEEK #1	WEEK #2	WEEK #3	WEEK #4	TOTAL
3,975	(1,369)	8,017	14,798	25,421 23.0%

4 We don't get credit for orders that are filled out of Inventory. We get credit for products when we build them. That's what those parentheses mean. In week #1, orders worth $4,289 came out of inventory. In week #3, a lot of orders came through, including $35,509 worth of new products that we put into inventory because they wouldn't ship for a week or two.

5 This percentage of the Value Produced [19.3%] is what we've determined is a fair return on the company's capital investment. It took more than five months to settle on this figure. In the previous 10 years direct labor had been costing us about 21% to 25% of production. We figured that if we could get a couple of percentage points' improvement, then the company would gladly give anything better than that — the difference between the 19.3% target and the Total Labor — to the employees as an efficiency gain.

6 The key number is Value Produced. This line represents the orders produced by our people in that period. They have no control over whether orders are on credit hold or whether the customer asks us to reschedule six or seven months down the road. Labor builds the product, and in this gain-sharing system, we award credit for work when it is done, whether the orders ship or go into inventory. Real orders. Real work.

7 We break pay into guaranteed Regular Pay and unguaranteed Gain-Sharing-Earned Pay. And when we see consistent improvement in our efficiency, we change the mix. In December 1991 people voted to add another personal day and holiday to benefits, and in November 1992 we raised regular pay by 5%, but the cost to the company remains the same. We were able to do those redistributions because our people earned them. If efficiencies don't go up, gain sharing doesn't work. In a successful plan, people get used to that extra paycheck. So, following a redistribution, our people dig in and get that unguaranteed Gain-Sharing-Earned portion back up again.

8 We're trying to make employees aware of all the direct costs of running this place. Everybody in the company is paid weekly. So we take Vacation Pay for the year and divide that cost among the 52 weeks. Same with the 10 paid Holidays and the Personal Days. "Other," which includes maternity leave, jury duty, worker's comp, and illness not covered by Insurance, can change. When our controller introduced a new health plan that saved us $900 a week, everyone was ecstatic.

9 When I flip the board around in presentations, people's eyes now go right to this figure [gainsharing earned or lost]. They know that their gain-sharing check is a portion of that number and is determined by multiplying the gain-sharing percentage—which is the 23% we derived by dividing total gain-sharing dollars into the total pay—by their regular and overtime pay for that period. Then they scan the other numbers to figure out what made the difference to that bottom line during the period.

What's the Law?

*As recent changes in the law turn
workplace litigation into a gold mine for lawyers,
even small companies may find themselves on the
sharp end of an employee lawsuit. Here's
what you can do to protect yourself.*

—

Age discrimination. Wrongful termination. Sexual harassment. Rights of the disabled. A business owner or manager who has been ensnared in today's bewildering web of jurisprudence is likely to turn deeply resentful of a system that critics say has gone haywire.

Employment litigation has exploded. According to the American Bar Association, the number of discrimination lawsuits has risen by more than 2,200% during the past two decades, now accounting for an estimated one-fifth of all civil suits filed in U.S. courts. Already an epidemic, employment litigation is sure to worsen as the workforce grows more diverse.

The ramifications of the explosion are creating havoc in thousands of companies. Legal defense costs can be staggering. Awards to plaintiffs can cripple small businesses. Moreover, litigation often takes several years, consuming huge amounts of management's time and energy. Even for employers who are ultimately vindicated, the process itself is punishing. And in the wake of even one of these fights, companies often undergo a sort of personality change, turning legalistic and strained as management moves to prevent exposure to claims from job applicants and employees.

"The whole country is much more litigious, but employees are phenomenally more litigious," says Miami lawyer Elizabeth du Fresne, who once represented plaintiffs and now defends management.

Few people would argue that antidiscrimination laws are uncalled-for. There are still racists. There's still discrimination against older people and people with handicaps. And there are still managers — of both sexes — who think putting their hands all over the help is one of the fringe benefits of being the boss.

Still, the impression one gains from interviews with numerous lawyers and employers is that a well-intentioned body of law has become tremendously burdensome and abused. *Berserk, warped, twisted, absurd:* those are the sort of terms employers use when describing their night-marish legal tangles with workers.

One small-company president, who spent $50,000 on legal fees fighting a wrongful termination charge, sums up his feelings this way: "We've been in business and owned by the same family for 80 years. We had a nice reputation in the community. The fact that this employee was able to drag us through the courts on an utterly worthless claim and cost us all this money and aggravation made it clear to me that the system is out of control."

Even attorneys are appalled at the abuses they see. Robert Fitzpatrick is a Washington, D.C., lawyer who has practiced employment law for 25 years, representing both management and employees. He is fervid about eradicating discrimination; he cut his teeth as a civil rights lawyer in Mississippi in the 1960s. Still, he is disturbed by what he now regards as "a legal war" in the workplace.

"There's always a small percentage of cases in which the person was blatantly and egregiously wronged, discriminated against on the basis of race, age, sex, disability, whatever," Fitzpatrick says. "Those are the cases that a judge and jury ought to hear. But that's not how the system works now. It's an outrage when you have to pay $100,000 to defend yourself against something that anybody can tell in two hours is bogus."

Judges, too, sometimes think things have gone too far. Consider a 1991 discrimination case in Los Angeles, in which the plaintiff, a 56-

year-old construction company executive, claimed he was forced to quit his job because of his age. After a 38-day jury trial, he was awarded $2.1 million in economic damages, $2 million for emotional distress, and $1.6 million in attorneys' fees and costs: a total of $5.7 million.

In reviewing the case last year, an appellate court judge upheld the verdict and award as legally valid. But then, in his decision, he took the highly unusual step of writing that this area of law "is quickly running out of control and the citizens of California will be the ultimate victims and losers. Commerce in California cannot flourish with such multimillion-dollar verdicts readily attainable."

Expanded Legislation

Starting in 1963 with the Equal Pay Act, Congress began a long legislative campaign to expand employees' rights. Part of the impetus was a big drop in labor-union memberships. For several decades before, unions had shielded roughly a third of the workforce from the whims and caprices of management. Their decline left a growing number of employees without recourse for perceived wrongs. Increased legislation essentially made the courts a de facto replacement for union grievance procedures.

Four federal laws have generated most of the ensuing litigation. They are Title VII of the Civil Rights Act of 1964, which prohibits discrimination on the basis of race, religion, sex, or national origin; the Age Discrimination in Employment Act of 1967 (ADEA), which protects workers who are at least 40 years old; the Americans with Disabilities Act of 1990 (ADA), which outlaws discrimination against people who are disabled, including the obese; and the Civil Rights Act of 1991, which has set off a gold rush by plaintiffs and their lawyers.

State lawmakers followed Washington's lead. As a rule, they incorporated the federal statutes into their states' legal codes. With a number of the laws providing for so-called concurrent jurisdiction, plaintiffs have the option of bringing charges in either federal or state court, whichever is more advantageous. In practice, most discrimination suits end up in the federal system.

Meanwhile, another major trend was sweeping over state judiciaries. Until the early 1980s most states recognized the common law doctrine known as employment at will. Once a cornerstone of free-enterprise philosophy, the at-will principle holds that an employer can fire someone for a good reason, a bad reason, or no reason at all, so long as the firing isn't discriminatory or doesn't violate a collective bargaining agreement.

By 1989, however, courts in 45 states had accepted several theories that eroded the at-will rule, giving rise to claims for wrongful termination. Among them was the implied contract exception, under which job rights may be inferred when no explicit contract exists. (Sometimes rights are construed from the language in employee handbooks.) Then there's the broadly defined public-policy exception. Under that one, employers cannot fire a person who, for instance, blows the whistle on a fraudulent or criminal activity involving the employer.

Perhaps the most far-reaching example, though, is the good-faith-and-fair-dealing exception. It implies that a dismissal must always be for cause.

In 1992 Rand Corp., a research organization based in Santa Monica, Calif., issued a landmark report on the impact of those new doctrines. It found that only five states still maintained a fire-at-will policy unencumbered by the new protections: Delaware, Florida, Georgia, Louisiana, and Mississippi. All three exceptions had been embraced by courts in eight states: Alaska, Arizona, California, Connecticut, Idaho, Massachusetts, Montana, and Nevada.

There is no federal wrongful termination law, so under those doctrines fired employees bring action in state courts, often adding on a discrimination claim. Multiple charges are, in fact, the norm. "It is very infrequent that people sue only for discrimination anymore," says du Fresne. "They also sue for battery, for intentional infliction of emotional distress, for negligent hiring, or negligent retention. All of these have unlimited compensatory and punitive damages. And suits can be brought against companies and individuals alike, so managers' personal assets are now on the line."

Understandably, employers feel besieged. "There are so many laws that they hardly know what to do," says Adrienne Fechter, a Tampa lawyer who once defended management but switched to the plaintiffs' side after the Civil Rights Act of 1991. "They're afraid that almost anything they do could be a violation."

It's not just the crazy quilt of laws that irks employers; it's also the laws' complexities. A single termination now can arguably violate dozens of statutes, which sometimes overlap and even contradict one another.

Observes Miami employment lawyer Michael Casey, "Nowadays it's rare that a fired employee will not have some basis for a claim to get into court. So the message from Congress to employers is, Before you fire minorities, women, or anyone over 40 or before you fail to hire or promote them, you'd better have your ducks lined up in a row 10 miles long, meaning, don't do it."

Even what many would consider scrupulous employment practices are no guarantee of protection. Indeed, says Pittsburgh employment lawyer Laura Candris, "There is nothing you can do to insulate yourself from all risk of being sued. Nothing can preclude all possibilities of having a claim brought."

More and more employers are learning that the hard way. The number of discrimination claims has jumped sharply in recent years. According to the U.S. Equal Employment Opportunity Commission (EEOC), some 270,000 allegations were filed in 1993 with it and its 82 state and local counterparts. Complainants numbered more than 150,000 — some had lodged more than one charge — up from 125,000 in 1992 and 110,000 in 1990.

Of the 52,400 cases fully investigated by the EEOC in 1992, only 10,500 of them — about 20% — were determined to have reasonable cause for action. But even when the EEOC renders a no-cause finding, the "wronged" employee may still file a lawsuit.

Leading the list of recent filings were claims based on race and sex discrimination, including sexual harassment. Next came age-related charges. But claims under the ADA are building fast. In 1993, the law's first full year of application, they hit nearly 25,000. The ADA issue is still new to the courts, but as case law surrounding it develops, the action is likely to heat up quickly.

"We are heavily into sex and age as the issues being litigated in courts right now," says du Fresne. "But two years from now, disability may be hotter than anything else." If so, the ADA could become a highly volatile and vexing problem for companies. Employers are not required to accommodate disabled employees under workers' compensation laws, for example, but they are required to do so under the ADA.

Lawyers, Juries, and Money

Nothing else has fueled the current onslaught of workplace litigation more than the Civil Rights Act of 1991. There are three big reasons for that: juries, money, and a giant surplus of lawyers.

Before 1991 a plaintiff in an employment discrimination case appeared before a judge, not a jury. Plaintiffs who prevailed in such a bench ruling were entitled to equitable relief: reinstatement with back pay and perhaps front pay, plus attorneys' fees and costs. It was basically a make-whole remedy.

With no legal provision for damages, the potential for recovering serious money was virtually nil. Thus, the odds of a plaintiff's bringing a lawsuit were diminished by the unavailability of lawyers willing to take the cases.

"If I'm a plaintiff's lawyer sitting in my office and you walk in and describe your case to me, the first thing on my mind is, 'Will I get a fee for it?'" says Martin Payson, a partner in a large employment-law firm in White Plains, N.Y. "Bear in mind that the individual is most likely out of work and probably can't afford my fee. Unless there is the possibility of a substantive recovery, it doesn't pay to take the case."

That changed dramatically when, under the 1991 act, plaintiffs in Title VII and ADA cases became entitled to compensatory and punitive damages, plus back pay and legal fees. In the political firefight that erupted over the legislation, business lobbyists extracted one break: the damage awards are capped under a sliding scale. For a company with more than 14 and fewer than 101 employees, the cap is $50,000. (It's worth noting that Title VII and the ADA do not apply to businesses with fewer than 15 people.) The awards top out at $300,000 for companies with more than 500 employees.

By piling on multiple tort claims, however, a plaintiff's lawyer can sidestep the caps. In a sexual harassment case against a Miami businessman in Florida, for example, Fort Lauderdale lawyer Karen Coolman Amlong won approximately $1.5 million for her client. In addition to sexual harassment and sex discrimination, Amlong charged the man with battery, invasion of privacy, and intentional infliction of emotional distress. Moreover, under the laws of some states, such as California and New Jersey, there are no caps on damages.

In any case, the caps could soon be gone. The Equal Remedies Bill, which would abolish them, is pending on Capitol Hill, and it has strong support. "The caps enable companies to budget for discrimination," argues Ellen Vargyas, senior staff counsel at the National Women's Law Center, in Washington, D.C. "For a highly profitable firm with under 100 employees, $50,000 is nothing — it's lunch money. We think plaintiffs should get whatever damages they can prove."

Besides damages, the 1991 act also gives plaintiffs the right to a trial by jury. That greatly raises the stakes for employers, because juries tend to empathize with plaintiffs. According to another study by Rand, plaintiffs win 70% of jury trials.

Plaintiffs' attorneys often object to the suggestion that juries might be biased against businesses. "If we don't trust juries, we don't trust democracy and we don't trust ourselves," insists New Jersey plaintiffs' lawyer Nancy Smith. "I have confidence in people's ability to do the right thing."

But not everyone is so sanguine about jurors' objectivity. Lynn Lloyd Laughlin is one skeptic. He practiced employment law for 20 years before founding Employment Dispute Resolution Inc. (EDR), an Atlanta firm that seeks to resolve claims through binding arbitration. One reason companies become EDR's clients is that employers have a near-visceral fear of juries, especially in discrimination suits.

"The question is whether an employer or a manager can get a jury of his or her peers," Laughlin says. "Rarely do managers — let alone company owners — end up on juries. It's really a jury of the employee's peers."

That is very clear in age discrimination cases, he adds. "Juries are notoriously sympathetic to age claimants. The average awards are running twice what they are for any other discrimination claim. The reason is that everyone on the jury either is in the protected class [40 or older] or hopes to be. And if the plaintiff looks like someone's mother, say, or grandfather, the plaintiff is halfway home."

Maybe juries do favor plaintiffs. Maybe they don't. But either way, they are unpredictable, and that throws a wild card into the equation for accused managers trying to decide if they should fight a case to the finish or settle and be done with it. There aren't many options.

The Cost of "Legalized Blackmail"

Unhappily for employers, the combination of jury trials and damage awards coincides with a third explosive ingredient: the overcrowded legal profession. There are about 740,000 lawyers in the United States, and by some estimates, as many as a third of them are unemployed or underemployed.

"Out here, big law firms in San Francisco and Los Angeles are laying off 10% to 20% of their workforces, so there are a lot of hungry lawyers around," says William Smith, a plaintiffs' lawyer in Fresno, Calif. "You have lawyers who, five years ago, would not have listened to someone talk about a sex harassment case. Now they do listen, because they need the business."

The National Employment Lawyers Association, a San Francisco bar group for plaintiffs' lawyers, has about 1,900 members and is growing by about 50 a month. In addition, personal injury lawyers, skilled at playing to juries, are pouring into the field in search of a big hit. Many accept cases on a contingency fee basis; if they win, they usually take 33% to 45% of the award.

"This is now much less a field that lawyers go into to do good and much more a field that people get into to make money," says du Fresne. Indeed, to thrive, lawyers representing discrimination claimants need not hit a punitive damages jackpot. The mere threat of a lawsuit — sometimes even just a letter on legal stationery — can be enough to persuade companies to settle.

And no wonder. In all out litigation, defense costs run anywhere from $20,000 to $200,000, depending on the length and complexity of the case. Fees like that can dwarf settlement costs.

"My rule of thumb is that the blackmail value of a Title VII case prior to the 1991 amendments was $2,000 to $5,000 for a quick settlement," says Laughlin. "Now it's more like $20,000. It can cost employers between $5,000 and $20,000 just to defend themselves through the charge-filing stage, when claims are brought before the EEOC or a state agency. That's before a formal lawsuit is filed. To hire a good defense lawyer, it will generally cost about $5,000 just to open a file."

Then there's the nuisance factor. Suppose you are a business owner who has been wrongly accused of discrimination. You are so angry and feel so betrayed that you decide to fight. Damn the costs; the principle of the thing is too important. You will quickly face a blizzard of legal paperwork in the form of discovery requests, interrogatories, and notices of deposition. All that takes time and money. Then your lawyers may create position statements, motions, pretrial statements, courtroom exhibits, jury instructions, and maybe a trial brief. You may have to hire an expert witness and pay that person, too.

"You incur a heavy expense and loss of productive use of your staff," says Candris. "Not only is your reputation damaged, but you're not there to run your business. That's why clients refer to these things as legalized blackmail. The cost of achieving justice is so high and burdensome that the rational thing to do is settle and move on."

Finally, even if you're willing to endure all that, you not may end up in court until months or years later, only to face a hostile jury. How's that for a bargain?

There are also macroeconomic consequences to the employee-rights revolution. The Rand study of the effects of wrongful termination liability found that after a state adopts the most liberal tort versions of the covenant of good faith and fair dealing, its aggregate employment drops by 2% to 5%. The horror stories in the headlines and the threat of suits, the authors said, are affecting companies' personnel practices in ways that boost the costs of doing business, make workers more expensive, and decrease the incentive to add people to the permanent payroll.

That squares with what employers told us. "People are not hiring as much," says Ron Cohen, president of Cohen & Co., an accounting firm in Cleveland, and president of National Small Business United. "They are using a lot of temporaries. They're working people overtime. These legal issues are so serious that employers are avoiding hiring employees. There is just too much baggage that comes with them."

Lawsuit-Proofing Your Company

While there's no ironclad way to protect your company against litigation, smart companies are implementing comprehensive preventive strategies. In addition to educating their people about legal pitfalls and enlisting the employee handbook to spell out termination policies, these companies insist on meticulous documentation in hiring, counseling, and termination procedures.

A good example is the Community Bank of Homestead, in the Hurricane Andrew–devastated area south of Miami. Twelve years ago the independent, then 75-employee bank brought in an experienced human resources professional, Marlene Porter, to set up its personnel department. Before that, the bank had few formal personnel policies. Porter designed a soup-to-nuts program that has successfully kept the bank out of court despite the fact that during her tenure, roughly 200 employees have been let go. Porter's tactics are both preventive and defensive:

• *Screening.* Porter's first step was to ensure that Community Bank was hiring the right people and then positioning them in the jobs most appropriate for their skills.

Under her new system, the first step for a prospective employee is filling out an application, which includes a release form giving the bank the right to check the individual's background and test for use of illegal drugs. If the bank is interested in the applicant, an appointment for an interview is set. Before any interviewing starts, however, the job hopeful completes a two-page "personality test" that measures such things as attention to detail, patience, and competitiveness. The point of such a rigorous screening, though there are no guarantees, is to spot — *before* they are hired — potential employees whose skills, temperament, or work style will be a bad fit.

• ***Interviewing.*** Porter has personally schooled all the bank's managers in discrimination laws, and she continues to conduct training for supervisors every month. During interviews, for instance, managers know exactly what can and cannot be asked. Illegal questions include, How old are you? Are you married? and even, Do you have a car? "The car question could be perceived as discrimination against low-income people," Porter says.

The trick, she adds, is to ask open-ended questions. "People love to talk about themselves," says credit manager Roberta Greaves. "You can learn a lot just by listening." All the interviewers fill out a work sheet, giving their impressions of the candidate and stating whether he or she should be hired. If each interviewer says yes, Porter herself conducts the final interview. By that stage, she has assembled all the data needed — credit checks, work histories, the psychological profile, drug tests — to reach an objective hiring decision, and it's all documented.

• ***Clarifying the ground rules.*** Once hired, a new bank employee receives a handbook. Among other things, it lists offenses that can lead to termination: reporting to work under the influence of alcohol or illegal drugs, use of profanity or abusive language, possession of firearms, insubordination, fighting or assault, theft, destruction, defacement, on-premises gambling, and falsifying or altering bank records. To make sure the handbook covers all the bases and implies no contracts with the employees that the company can't deliver on, Porter subscribes to a personnel policy service that, for a fee of several hundred dollars a year, supplies a thick volume of lawyers' explanations of all key personnel issues, as well as updates as required.

• ***Instituting a progressive system of evaluation, documentation, and action.*** Even with its intensive and extensive hiring procedures, the bank sometimes brings in people who don't perform as expected. It deals with them under a progressive system, handled by the supervisors.

"If an employee does something significant enough that it could result in termination, the manager documents it on what we call our employee-counseling form and meets with the individual," Porter says. "That's the beginning of a progressive system of evaluation and action. You talk with the employee, and the employee has an opportunity for rebuttal. But the system sets a time limit — usually 30 to 90 days — for the shortcoming to be corrected. If the situation is no better after that, you meet with the employee again. You warn that there will not be a third counseling session. We try to take the monkey off our back and put it on theirs, because generally they terminate themselves if they don't do what we're asking them to do."

Throughout the process, supervisors are required to put all actions down *in writing*. "You have to document everything, because if you don't, you don't have a leg to stand on," says Greaves. "I did have to terminate someone, and there was talk of legal action. But because we had full documentation, nothing came of it."

• ***Creating a good working environment.*** By installing legally sound and defensible policies, a company can reduce the likelihood of being sued, but perhaps the greatest defense against potential litigation is creating a well-managed, fair, and motivating organization. If all of your company's management practices stress fairness and openness, you're likely to be as lawsuit-proofed — and, by the way, productive — as you can be. "Our philosophy is that if we're good to our employees, they're going to be good to our customers," Porter says. "And we're very good to our employees." For the Community Bank of Homestead, that's good business. Its net profits were up 416% last year. "And," Porter continues, "though we have had to terminate people, we have never had a lawsuit."

Knock wood, Marlene. ■

Leading Your Team

Taking Charge
Means Letting Go

Jack Stack, CEO of Springfield Remanufacturing Corporation (SRC), believes that a good part of taking charge is letting go. To this chief executive, a strong advocate for sharing detailed financial data with employees, managing people means empowering them to manage themselves. It means sharing responsibility with your people and doing all you can to see that they are capable of accepting, handling, and — a point Stack stresses — enjoying that responsibility.

"If you are going to take care of other people, you have to take care of yourself first," he says. "That applies to the company. If our people don't feel good about themselves, they aren't going to be good at remanufacturing engines. It's that simple."

In word and action, Jack Stack appears to be the walking, breathing embodiment of the outlook and many of the strategies recommended in this guide. In October 1989, in a frank and open discussion, he talked about "being the boss" with *Inc.* magazine. In 1994, we caught up with Jack to see how things were going five years later with SRC, with him, and with what he refers to as the Great Game of Business. The update, on page 233, sums up the score in a game that just continues to get bigger. ■

Being the Boss

*As extraordinary as Jack Stack may be,
he is typical of a whole generation of managers.
After all, he didn't set out to be
chief executive officer of a $95-million
company with 800 employees.*

The Plot

Back in the 1980s, a middle manager at one of America's worst-run companies is sent on a mission to shut down an ailing plant in Springfield, Mo. The guy is barely 30 years old, a college dropout. When he shows up at the plant, he finds a workforce of 165 people who are so demoralized the only real question is whether the Teamsters or the United Auto Workers will win the upcoming union election. Somehow he is able to rally the workers, stave off the union, and save the plant. Four years later he buys the division with his fellow managers and builds it into the star of its industry, using an original — some would say revolutionary — approach to management.

Such is the unlikely saga of John P. Stack, a man who has fascinated *Inc.* ever since 1985, less than three years after he negotiated the leveraged buyout of Springfield Remanufacturing Corp. (SRC) from International Harvester Corp. At the time he was still in the process of inventing what came to be known as the Great Game of Business, SRC's unique management system.

The Game is based on the premise that business is essentially a game — one that is no more complicated than, say, baseball or football, probably less. Yet, as Stack explains, most people don't understand it because they've never been taught the rules. At SRC, he asserts, everyone learns the rules and plays the Game, from the receptionist at the front desk to the guy who cleans engine parts.

Inc.: Most company presidents get a certain charge out of occupying the top slot, despite all the aggravations. Do you like being the boss?

Stack: Well, no, not really. A boss is forced to set examples, and I'm not a good example setter. I really don't like living in a glass house. People pay a lot of attention to the guy who's in charge. What he says is always being compared with what he does. And that's the way it should be. If I'm going to say something, I'll do it, too. But I'd rather not be under that microscope, because I know one day I'm going to slip.

Are you worried that the company will turn on you?

Stack: I hope not. I've worked pretty hard to keep that from happening.

What do you mean?

Stack: Well, you can go back to the buyout. I don't own 100% of SRC. I own 19%. The rest is owned by the employee stock ownership plan and various employees. I could have had more, but that was plenty for me. Not wanting to be accused of being greedy probably had something to do with it. But more important, I didn't want to be alone. I was going to be leading the charge up the hill. I wanted to make sure that when I got to the top of the hill and turned around, there was a bunch of people coming with me.

A lot of company founders would say you're crazy. Do you really think you're safer as a minority stockholder than as the sole owner?

Stack: I've learned that there are certain higher laws in business. One of them is, "You get what you give." I don't know where I got those laws. I probably got them from supervising 2,000 or so people at International Harvester and then here.

It sounds as though you had already developed a lot of your ideas about business before you came to Springfield.

Stack: Absolutely. I learned a lot at Harvester.

Give us an example.

Stack: One of my first big lessons was in 1972 or '73. We had to ship out 800 tractors to the Soviet Union, and I was in charge of scheduling the parts. At the time there was a severe shortage of the parts we needed, but without those parts the tractors wouldn't go to Russia and our department would get killed. As I recall, we had until November 1, and this was October already. On paper it couldn't be done. So I put up a big sign saying, "OUR GOAL: 800 TRACTORS," and I explained to my guys exactly what was going on, what was at stake. That was unusual, because Harvester was a very quiet company. I'd go to meetings, and the understanding was always, OK, here's what we have to do, but don't tell anybody.

How did your people respond?

Stack: They were amazing. They went into the factory each night and crawled over those tractors and figured out what parts were needed and how many tractors were short those particular parts. Then they got the parts any way they could. On October 31, we hit 803. Boy, did we send up the balloons.

Why was that such an important lesson to you?

Stack: Because it showed me what people could do. I saw these guys get hungry. I saw them push and accomplish things they never thought were possible. I saw satisfaction on a daily basis. I mean, these guys didn't know they were working! I thought, My God, if I can get people pumped up, wanting to come to work every day, what an edge that is! That's what nobody else is doing. Suppose I could run the right numbers, so that even a sick guy wakes up in the morning and says, "Man, I feel terrible, but I really want to go in there and see what happened." That's the whole secret to increasing productivity.

In a way, that's the definition of a good boss, isn't it? Someone who creates an atmosphere where people want to come to work in the morning.

Stack: I guess. Anyway, it absolutely convinced me that secrecy is nonsense. From then on, I was going to give my people everything I've got, and eventually that grew into the whole idea of teaching people how to make money.

Wait a minute. You're getting ahead of us here. What do you mean, "teaching people how to make money"?

Stack: Well, think about it. Most people who work in companies don't understand business. They have all kinds of misconceptions. They think *profit* is a dirty word. They think the owners just slip it into their bank accounts at night. They have no idea that 46% of business profits goes to taxes. They've never heard of retained earnings. And there's a good reason for all this ignorance. No one teaches them how business works.

I worked at the Harvester plant in Melrose Park, Ill., for 10 years. Every Friday I went to a staff meeting where the plant manager said, "We gotta make more money; we gotta be more profitable." But he never taught me how to make more money. We got plenty of orders: deliver a crankcase to such-and-such line, make sure that workers are safe, get so-and-so's productivity up. I never knew anything about making money, and here I'd supervised hundreds and hundreds of people. Finally, it dawned on me that there was a better way.

Which is. . .

Stack: It's the way businesses have been run for a long, long time — with financial statements. If people know how to use them, that's really the simplest way to run a business.

Hold on. Take a 23-year-old guy with a high school education and an entry-level job at SRC. You're going to teach him to read financial statements?

Stack: That's right. When people come to work at SRC, we tell them that 70% of the job is disassembly or whatever and 30% of the job is learning. What they learn is how to make money, how to make a profit. They don't have to play the Game, but they do have to learn it. We teach them about after-tax profits, retained earnings, equity, cash flow, everything. We teach them how to read an income statement and a balance sheet. We say, "You make the decision whether you want to work here, but these are the ground rules we play by."

Every week our supervisors report on the updated income statement, showing how we're doing in relation to our annual goals. And of course, the quarterly bonuses are tied to those goals. So the numbers are just flying around. The more people understand, the more they want to see the results. They want to know how well they are doing and if they are contributing. There's internal competition and peer pressure, and they get caught up in it. It's a game — the Great Game of Business, as we call it. It's a mechanism for getting people to come in to work every morning and enjoy it.

Did you start out with this idea of teaching people how to make money?

Stack: No, I started out with the idea that I really didn't want to be in the position of having to lay people off.

What do you mean?

Stack: I just think you take on a big obligation when you hire somebody. That person is bringing home money, putting food on the table, taking care of children. You can't take that lightly. Of course, it's a two-way street, but — as much as possible — you should make it their choice whether they leave or not.

OK, but what does that have to do with your Game?

Stack: That's how the Game got started. After the buyout, we had an 89:1 debt-to-equity ratio. As a corporate entity, we were nearly comatose. We began with $1 million in working capital, but we owed $8 million, and all the assets were pledged. So I looked at this situation, and I realized there were two things we couldn't do. Number one, we couldn't run out of cash. Number two, we couldn't destroy ourselves from within. If either one of those happened, we'd lose the company, and 165 people would lose their jobs.

How might the company have destroyed itself from within?

Stack: Bad morale. The danger was we'd get into a situation where people would turn on each other. So how do you avoid that? It became obvious to me that we had to communicate with people through the financial statements. They had to know the company's situation at every point. We had to tell them where the cash was and then make sure they were involved in deciding what to do with that cash. That's how the Game evolved.

In a sense, you're saying this provides people with a kind of job security.

Stack: It provides them with the only kind of job security that means anything. Look at Harvester — a company that went back a hundred years, one of the 30 largest in the country, more than 100,000 employees. My dad retired from it. I worked there for 14 years altogether. I just assumed my job was secure, and I had no way of knowing it wasn't. Then Harvester went down the tubes. So that's one thing the Game does: It gives people a scorecard and a way to influence the score. It tells them how secure their jobs really are. It doesn't provide guarantees, but there aren't guarantees anymore.

At the same time, it reduces your responsibility for their job security, doesn't it? It gets you off the hook.

Stack: It delegates the responsibility, yes. Just like it delegates every action in the company. It doesn't put all the emphasis on one guy.

How does it delegate every action in the company?

Stack: By identifying each person's role. Our people know exactly where they show up on the income statement and how they contribute. So responsibilities are completely delegated. The Game provides a structure whereby the individuals support the body. It teaches people the fundamentals — what each one has to do to make the company successful If your fundamentals get out of whack, you find out right away, and you don't move until they're back in line.

Who makes sure that you don't move?

Stack: Usually, it's your peers.

If all these responsibilities are delegated, what does that mean for you as the boss?

Stack: My role is to make sure the Game is working. For example, we have two companywide goals every year. One is profitability, and the other changes from year to year, depending on the particular weakness we see in the company. This year we've targeted liquidity, measured as current assets divided by current liabilities.

Why liquidity?

Stack: It's something we don't have under control, and it's the only thing that can really hurt us. We have to control the money, the spending. Otherwise, if we grow too quickly, we're going to run out of cash. If we run out of cash, we're not going to have a company — or rather, the company is not going to be ours anymore. OK, so we completely missed our liquidity target in the first quarter. Now it's true that you often don't hit your targets right away if you've picked a really good goal. If you solve the problem too easily, it may not be a real weakness. But even so, you expect some progress in the first quarter. In this case, the progress was very disappointing.

Whose fault was that?

Stack: I think it's my responsibility to make sure those goals are met. I mean, we're talking about a major problem that affects the long-term security of the employees. If the problem isn't being solved, I need to do everything I possibly can to get the organization focused on it. So we put together a high-level task force to reduce inventory — I'm talking about really visible people in important positions around the company. We pulled them off their jobs to focus on this particular problem. At the same time, we straightened up accounting to make certain we're 100% on top of all our receivables. Of course, this sends a message. It creates an atmosphere in which everybody is working toward the same goal and doing his or her part to get the bonus.

It's interesting that your Game relies so heavily on incentive compensation systems, and yet what really inspires you is getting people to work for rewards other than money.

Stack: I'm not foolish enough to believe that money isn't a major motivator. It just isn't necessarily the only one. I guess what I'm really obsessed with is getting rid of the living dead. I can't stand going into factories and businesses and seeing all these faceless people around. They don't look healthy, and they don't act healthy, and they're a big problem for corporate America.

Faceless people?

Stack: The people who are there because it's a job, whose attitude is, "I have to be here, but I don't have to like it. I'll do it for my family, not for myself." You can't believe how I hate this. We should be able to tell this person, "It's your obligation to be happy. Find somewhere to be happy. Don't sit around me and be miserable." Then we wonder why we have a productivity problem. Well, you can't have high productivity with faceless people. I think the answer is a system where everybody can have fun, even the people who put washers on bolts. They can be playing something else at the same time. Statistics, rewards, and incentives are one way to do that — to make people aware, to stimulate them, to give them the opportunity to use their intelligence and achieve something.

Let us play devil's advocate. We often see incentive systems that have the opposite effect, that become a mechanism of control and that make work less fun, not more.

Stack: That happens if you have shortsighted or unquantifiable goals. You need goals with a larger meaning.

In what sense?

Stack: Our goals are always based on the security of the company, so the larger meaning is to create jobs and keep people working. If we fail to reach a goal, the company is at risk. Each goal is a must, not a want. I mean, we're trying to create a company that will last 30, 40, 50 years. More important, we're creating a system that makes everybody aware of the company's strengths and weaknesses and that forces the weaknesses to be addressed.

You say the larger meaning is to create jobs. Why isn't it to create top-quality products for customers?

Stack: There's another higher law, which is, "If you are going to take care of other people, you have to take care of yourself first." That applies to the company. If our people don't feel good about themselves, they aren't going to be good at remanufacturing engines. The more time they spend in training programs, education, and getting involved, the better the end product is going to be. They have to be in the right frame of mind, free of mental stress; they can't be worrying about their job security. Happy people are productive people, and productive people do all the little things required to be great at remanufacturing. That's what the Game is all about.

But can't you focus too much on making people feel good about themselves? Some companies get so involved with corporate culture and self-improvement they forget about their customers.

Stack: There's a big difference between what we do and what you're talking about. Those companies get caught up in a kind of emotionalism. We do the opposite. Our Game takes emotions out of the business. We go by the statistics, and the statistics don't lie. We train our people to see that success means making sure one plus one comes out to two. We're talking about income statements and balance sheets, not about cafeterias and parking spaces.

A lot of people would argue that businesses thrive on emotion, that companies don't do enough to motivate employees, that we need more pom-poms and inspiration, not less.

Stack: Don't get me wrong. I'm really big on pom-poms and celebrations and inspirational messages. I just don't think they should replace solid information about the condition of the company. People should understand why those pom-poms are there. They deserve to evaluate the situation for themselves. I don't want people to sit there and passively accept leadership. I want them to become active in leadership, and that means giving them a constructive path to follow.

OK, so you go by the numbers. But haven't you ever gotten into a situation where the numbers tell you to do one thing and your heart wants you to do something else?

Stack: Do I ever feel torn? Yes, of course. I felt incredibly torn after General Motors canceled those 5,000 engines in December 1986. I mean, the numbers said we had to cut 100 people from the payroll or risk the company. But that kind of layoff would have been a tremendous failure of management. You've got to take responsibility, even if there was no way you could have seen it coming.

That decision had to be painful.

Stack: It was awful. Because you're deciding whether to take somebody's job away. You could protect your own ass. But you'd sit there and stare at the ceiling and think about these people who were told they had a job. It should be their choice, not yours.

What did other people think?

Stack: There was a small group of senior employees who didn't want to take the chance. They weren't close to the new group, the ones who would be laid off. They said, "Hell, if it's between me and them, let it be them." And they had a very good point. In order to get by without a layoff, we would have to get a hundred new product lines up and running in three months. And if we failed, we would have had to do a much bigger layoff, get a new infusion of outside capital, and change the whole thinking of the company.

So what happened?

Stack: Eventually those senior people came around. That's probably what sold me more than anything else. The hard-core guys came back and said, "Geez, we've been thinking about it, and we can weather it. We'll have to train these kids, but we'll make it. We can do it."

Was that an emotional decision?

Stack: No, I think they'd figured it out statistically. We told them we thought it was an impossible task, but they could break down the elements of the job in more detail than we could. I guess they just realized they had 33% more left.

You must feel pride in the way you dealt with that situation.

Stack: I don't know. I think the system took care of itself. If I'd heard something else from the organization, I might have had to react differently. But when those guys said, "Let's try it," that was all I needed.

What was it like to introduce all those new lines?

Stack: It was pure hell. We told people that the pressures would be overwhelming, but I don't think we had any idea how overwhelming they were really going to be. It was like recovering from a stroke — very slow and very painful, and it hurt. It really hurt. I'm talking about long-term pain. I think we're only getting over it now.

But you made it without any layoffs?

Stack: Yeah. In fact, we added 100 people.

It's interesting that you feel so strongly about letting employees decide whether to stay or leave, about letting it be their choice. You must have a hell of a time firing people.

Stack: Well, I don't want to work around unhappy people, and if people aren't happy, I don't mind telling them that they're unhappy and they should go somewhere else. Of course, you have to understand, I really don't have to fire many people. This system does a lot of the work. The nonperformers take themselves out. Peer pressure takes them out. But, yes, anytime somebody leaves, you feel the loss.

Even the deadwood?

Stack: Deadwood is such a small percentage. It's the ones with talent who are really tough. But even losing deadwood is tough because you spend a lot of time and money training, teaching, and motivating them.

How do you deal with the talented ones?

Stack: That's probably the most stressful part of my job. I mean, when you know some of them have incredible talent but you just can't harness it, you can't focus it, you can't get it into the system — it kills you. And then, of course, you start questioning whether the problem is them or you. You start saying to yourself, "Maybe we just have a style conflict here. Maybe I'm being too possessive. Maybe I don't want to let go." Fortunately, the system serves as a reality check.

In what way?

Stack: A style conflict won't necessarily show up in the numbers. A performance problem becomes very clear very fast, and everybody knows about it. Then the pressure gets intense. You have to do something. I can't explain to 450 people why we didn't deal with a situation — not if it costs them their bonuses.

Is there anybody you can talk to about those kinds of issues?

Stack: I think I talk to everybody. We're all very, very close.

Are you saying that it really isn't so lonely at the top after all? What's the difference between being the number-one person and being number two, three, or four?

Stack: First, there isn't always a distinct number two, three, and four. In the past decade especially, people have become very coy about designating a chain of command. It gets in the way of building a team. You can say who does what when you're gone, but you can't go much beyond that without undermining team spirit. In that context, the number-one person has to be prepared to work exclusively on deviations and problems. If something is going right, you have to let it go right, no matter how good you may be at that aspect of the business. Otherwise, you can't function as number one, because your role as number one is to focus on what's going wrong. When the numbers show there's a problem, you've got to make sure it gets fixed.

So you're taking care of other people's problems. Who's taking care of your problems? The board?

Stack: There are definitely situations where I rely on the board. For example, the managers may not be able to reach a consensus, and I'll have to take sides, knowing that my decision is going to be detrimental to somebody. In those instances, it's good to have a board to help work through the problem. Having a board also helps me explain a decision to people in the company, especially with regard to wages and compensation. It's easier to say, "The board looked at the numbers and decided this wasn't a good time to give a raise." It depersonalizes some tough decisions.

Does the board set your salary?

Stack: No, not really. The board reviews it. But I don't have to go along.

It sounds as though you disagree.

Stack: Yeah, they think it should be higher. They're afraid that, if anything happened to me, they couldn't hire a new president for what I'm making.

What do you think?

Stack: I guess I'm superstitious. I think that if I took more out of the company, something bad would happen. It's an instinct, a gut feeling. I'd argue that I'm making enough right now. I'm certainly not hurting.

Do people know how much money you make?

Stack: No, it's part of an aggregate in the financial statement. I suppose someone could figure it out, plus or minus 20%. But we may take the company public someday, and then it would be printed in the prospectus.

Doesn't your salary put a ceiling on what you can offer other top people?

Stack: Yeah, but it hasn't hurt our ability to recruit. I mean, our compensation program is competitive, we have a good benefits package, and we offer a lot more than most companies. For one thing, there's the pot at the end of the rainbow if we take SRC public or sell it. For another, we give people a tremendous lesson in entrepreneurship. After you've spent a year or two here, you walk away with a lifetime of lessons in running a business — your *own* business.

Do you actually make that pitch when you recruit people?

Stack: Pretty much, and we deliver on it, too. We just lost an executive who says he learned more here in the past year than in his entire career up to that point. He went off to take the top spot at another company.

But let's say somebody comes in because of wanting this pot at the end of the rainbow. Doesn't that put tremendous pressure on you?

Stack: Not really. That's how the whole system is set up. Anyone who walks in here finds 500 people trying to do the exact same thing. The reaction then is, "Holy cow! I've never seen anything like this."

Another case of delegating responsibilities.

Stack: That's right.

If you delegate enough responsibilities, you could make yourself obsolete.

Stack: My job *is* to make myself obsolete, and I'm getting there. In many ways, I'm not the boss of SRC anymore. Our system is the boss.

Update on SRC

From a recent conversation with Jack Stack

First of all, SRC is thriving — more than thriving. In the first quarter of 1994 sales were at $27 million. CEO Jack Stack projects that sales for the year will reach $95 million to $100 million. The company objective of 15% growth internally, per year, is being achieved. Today, SRC employs 800 people. There have been no layoffs. Point of information: SRC did not go public; there was no need to, because sufficient working capital was generated internally.

Second, the Game is still played. In 1989, Jack said, "Give people the opportunity to use their intelligence to achieve something." Today, confronted by the evidence, his conviction is even stronger. "The Game is a powerful force," he says. "As you tap intellectual capacity, everyone gets smarter."

At SRC, the Game gained momentum. Here's what happened, in Jack's words: "Starting in 1989, we went on a diversification path. We now have 13 companies that were the result of ideas from our own people, and we're expecting to produce two more baby companies this year. We provided the working capital for these offspring. Generally, SRC owns 51% to 80% equity in them."

Jack's parent analogy is particularly apt. One sees this clearly as he describes feelings that have come with decentralizing: "You suffer when they [the new companies] lose: did you supply the right support? Did you step back too soon? You even suffer when they win — you're not really needed in the same way. And," he continues, "the hardest thing is letting go."

How are the "babies" doing? For the most part, just fine. For example, one of the first — started by a group of sales, marketing, and engineering people led by Eric Paulsen — started remanufacturing oil coolers. Sales were $250,000 in the first year; by year-end 1994 the number is expected to be $5.5 million.

The newest arrival — Jack gets a whole lot of satisfaction from this one — is called BizLit. As part of the Game, Denise Bredfledt, SRC's director of training, developed a manual to help SRC's hourly employees understand and interpret financial data. BizLit sells the manual and offers training programs to accompany it.

The 1994 target for the Game is return on assets, a goal closely tied to the welfare of the offspring. The objective is to determine a fair way to allocate capital back to the new ventures — to support needs, to reward success.

Before signing off, Jack had this to say: "We spend 62% of our lives at work. Those who become winners at the Game carry their enhanced self-esteem and confidence away with them. The implications of what they've learned affect the way they interact with and contribute to their families and communities. I think it's a difference that ultimately affects society." ■

The Experts

Susan Cejka
Cejka & Co.
222 South Central, Suite 400
St. Louis, MO 63105
(314) 726–1603
Fax: (314) 726–0026

Susan Cejka is founder and CEO of Cejka & Co., a health-care consulting firm in St. Louis. Ranked on the *Inc.* 500 list of fastest-growing privately held companies in America in 1986 and 1987, the firm specializes in physician and administrative recruitment and placement, compensation planning, medical staff development, strategic planning, and integrated systems development.

Stanley Herz
Stanley Herz & Co., Inc.
100 Mill Pond Office Complex, Suite 103
Rte. 100
Somers, NY 10589
(914) 277–7500
Fax: (914) 277–7749

With over 20 years of experience in recruitment, career advancement, and corporate management, Stanley Herz, founder and president of Stanley Herz & Co., in Somers, N.Y., has published many articles and lectures frequently on those subjects. An executive and consultant for some of the nation's leading corporations, he has also counseled emerging business ventures on management and long-term growth.

Gary B. Kushner
Kushner & Co.
141 E. Michigan St., Suite 400
Kalamazoo, MI 49007
(616) 342–1700
Fax: (616) 342–1606

A recognized expert on benefit plans for small and midsize employers, Gary B. Kushner is founder and president of Kushner & Co., in Kalamazoo. He has advised three U.S. presidents on health care and has testified before the U.S. Senate Finance Committee, House Ways and Means Committee, and House Small Business Committee. Kushner is a member of the Small Business Association of Michigan and a past Chair of its board of directors.

Ruth G. Newman
RGN Communications
8A Still St.
Brookline, MA 02146
(617) 734-3586

Ruth G. Newman founded RGN Communications in 1985, to perform employee communication studies, design communication training programs, and handle major editorial projects. Prior to starting her own business, she managed communications at three Boston-area consulting firms and lectured at the Harvard University Graduate School of Business Administration. Newman is the author of *Communicating in Business Today* (D.C. Heath, 1987) and of articles published in leading business periodicals.

Joan B. Pinck
Juran Institute, Inc.
26 Dwight St.
Boston, MA 02118
(617) 482-2922
Fax: (617) 482-6770

Joan B. Pinck, vice president of Juran Institute, headquartered in Wilton, Conn., consults on quality management. Previously, she was director of research administration and policy at Beth Israel Hospital, in Boston. Pinck served as assistant dean and lecturer at the Harvard University Graduate School of Business Administration and assistant secretary for higher education of the Commonwealth of Massachusetts.

Richard C. Rose
Dataflex Corp.
3920 Park Ave.
Edison, NJ 08820
(908) 321-1100
Fax: (908) 321-6590

Richard C. Rose is chairman and CEO of Dataflex Corp., a specialist in network integration and leader in the computer resale industry with sales of more than $70 million. His article on p. 49 is excerpted from *How to Make a Buck and Still Be a Decent Human Being: A Week with Rick Rose at Dataflex,* by Richard C. Rose and Echo Montgomery Garrett. Copyright © 1992, by Richard C. Rose and Echo Montgomery Garrett. Reprinted by permission of HarperCollins Publishers.

DeAnne Rosenberg, C.S.P.
DeAnne Rosenberg, Inc.
28 Fifer Ln.
Lexington, MA 02173
(617) 862–6117
Fax: (617) 863–8613
DeAnne Rosenberg specializes in management education and supervisory development. The first woman to speak under the auspices of the American Management Association, she has been a professional presenter at meetings and conferences for more than 20 years. Her articles on performance management and motivation appear regularly in the business press in the United States and abroad.

Eddie C. Smith
Management Compensation Services
8687 E. Via DeVentura, Suite 113
Scottsdale, AZ 85258
(602) 994–1373
Fax: (602) 951–3206
Eddie C. Smith is a principal in Hewitt Associates LLC and president of Management Compensation Services (MCS), a division of Hewitt Associates. Before joining MCS, he was Hewitt's direct compensation practice leader for North America. Prior to entering the consulting field, he was vice president of human resources at a large industrial manufacturing company. Author of numerous articles on compensation, Smith has addressed the topic at numerous national conferences for *Inc.* and the American Compensation Association.

The Contributors

Portions of this guide were written by the following members of *Inc.* magazine's editorial staff: **senior writers** — John Case (The Secrets of Success, The Realities of Team-Based Management); Jay Finegan (What's the Law?); Martha E. Mangelsdorf (Dual-Purpose Sales Supervisor's Checklist, Ground-Zero Training); **associate editor** — Leslie Brokaw (The Annual One-Page Company Game Plan); **staff writers** — Elizabeth Conlin (Vital Signs Assessment); Michael P. Cronin (Screening: What You Can and Can't Do, The Eye-Opening Employee-Benefits Worksheet); Tom Ehrenfeld (Do It by the Book — The Handbook, That Is; Productivity-Boosting Gain-Sharing Report); Susan Greco (The Interactive Employee Review); Teri Lammers Prior (What It Takes to Build a Team, How to Read Between the Lines, The Foolproof Interviewer's Guide); **reporter** — Phaedra Hise (Motivational Employee-Satisfaction Questionnaire, Double-Duty Sales Script); **editor-at-large** — Bo Burlingham (Being the Boss). ■

A

B

C

Notes

Notes

Other business books from Inc. *Magazine*

How to *Really* Create a Successful Business Plan
• By David E. Gumpert

How to *Really* Start Your Own Business
• By David E. Gumpert

How to *Really* Create a Successful Marketing Plan
• By David E. Gumpert

Anatomy of a Start-Up
Why Some New Businesses Succeed and Others Fail:
27 Real-life Case Studies
• Edited by Elizabeth K. Longsworth

**301 Great Management Ideas from
America's Most Innovative Small Companies**
• Introduction by Tom Peters
• Edited by Sara P. Noble

**Managing People: 101 Proven Ideas for Making
You and Your People More Productive**
From America's Smartest Small Companies
• Edited by Sara P. Noble

How to *Really* Deliver Superior Customer Service
• Edited by John Halbrooks

To receive a complete listing of *Inc.* Business Books and Videos, please call 1–800–468–0800, ext. 5007. Or write to *Inc.* Business Resources, P.O. Box 1365, Dept. 5007, Wilkes-Barre, PA 18703-1365.